Heroic Tropes

HEROIC TROPES

Gender and Intertext

PIERRETTE DALY

 Wayne State University Press   Detroit

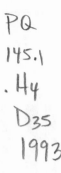

PQ
145.1
.H4
D35
1993

Library of Congress Cataloging-in-Publication Data

Daly, Pierrette.
  Heroic tropes : gender and intertext / Pierrette Daly.
    p.   cm.
  Includes index.
  ISBN 0-8143-2427-4 (alk. paper)
    1. Epic literature, French—History and criticism.   2. Heroes in
literature.   3. Archetype (Psychology) in literature.
4. Authorship—Sex differences.   5. Sex role in literature.
6. Heroines in literature.   7. Quests in literature.
8. Intertextuality.   I. Title.
PQ145.1.H4D35   1993
809'.89287—dc20   92-32623
                                                           CIP

Designer: Mary Krzewinski

To
Dennis

CONTENTS

7

ACKNOWLEDGMENTS

I am grateful to the Faculty Grants Committee of the University of Missouri–St. Louis for a leave from teaching and to the American Council of Learned Societies for a grant to travel to France.

I am also indebted to several members of Women in French in St. Louis who patiently listened to various stages of this book, and who discussed the issues and the critical problems it raised. I particularly acknowledge Harriet Stone for her editing and comments, Susan Rava for her sustained encouragement, and Colette Winn for her interest in reading the manuscript. I also thank my dissertation director, Michel Rybalka, for my background in French literary criticism.

Some material in this book was originally presented and discussed at conferences and published in different form in Paris at Albin Michel and S.D.E.S.–C.D.U., and in the United States in *George Sand Studies*.

INTRODUCTION

Centuries ago Penelope's son claimed that speaking was men's business and sent her to her rooms, where readers still find her silently unravelling her woven work. Through the ages, like Telemachus, literary communities have validated men's stories—the text of Ulysses—while they have neglected women's—the *texte* of Penelope.[1] Recently, however, a considerable number of critics have addressed this problem and pointed out how, as a consequence of the failure to canonize women's works, scholars have assumed that their heroic tropes were simply a *revers* of men's. In fact, they have a specificity of their own.[2]

The symmetry and permanence of canonized critical discourse and the object of its study (men's stories) constantly enlighten our understanding of their writings. When we investigate genres featuring heroic tropes, we notice that generic definitions parallel narratives of the genre itself. Canons define heroism by naming outstanding men who write and by situating them in territories and time.[3] Definitions of the earliest epic poems, for example, include the bard's name, Homer, his country, Greece, and the time span of the genre, 1,000–400 B.C. Correspondingly, *The Odyssey* names its protagonist, Ulysses, in narratives of his extraordinary deeds in time periods and in territories named according to his journeys.[4] When we turn to other genres, other nations, and other centuries—when we read the autobiographical *Lettre à un ami* of the French philosopher Abelard and Rousseau's *Les Confessions,* for example, and notice that the monk and the *philosophe* narrate their stories by naming and situating themselves in spatio-temporal terms—we conclude that their narratives take root in ancient stories of extraordinary men, and we are certain that our conclusion is well-founded.

There is such certainty in these canons that we hesitate to modify them. For instance, guided by these canonic definitions of heroism, we observe that George Sand's *Histoire de ma vie* follows a practice which is almost contrary to that of Abelard and Rousseau in their autobiographies, and

11

we conclude that she does not define herself as a heroic woman.[5] Sand denies her paternal and conjugal claim to history in the very first chapters of her life story, stating that she is neither the wife of Marquis Dudevant nor the legitimate descendant of the Dupins who trace their ancestry to kings in France and Poland. Then she states that the ties to the maternal side of her family are more binding because they were formed through her mother's womb. Indeed, Sand claims to be the daughter of common people, that is, of those who have no written proof of birth. As we see, if we apply canonized theories to women's works, we notice that they resist them, and we are tempted to conclude that their heroism is a mere reverse of men's. To theorize otherwise would be to modify canons. To observe that Sand's bonding to a maternal body is not a canonized trope and that canons do not open avenues of understanding to women's writings is a risky enterprise. This can be attempted, however, if we assertively formulate a theoretical framework that bases itself on a close examination of the specificity of their stories.[6] I undertake such a formulation in the present study.

This research, addressing the sexual identity of authors, brings me face to face with conundrums of post-modern criticism on the esthetic of gender. The controversy centers on two major problems.[7] First, how can I speak of the sexual identity of authors when structuralism has chased them out of the text? Second, how can I consider the "reality" of experience when proponents of modernity claim that the text cannot refer to anything but itself? To bring authors (men and women) and contexts (the referential reality) back into the text, I selected genres which feature protagonists whose existence is proven extra-textually through documents.[8] The corpus of this study is thus composed of memoirs, confessions, correspondence, and autobiographical works of fiction.

My investigation of heroism directed me to the earliest stories of the Western world. The first chapter synthesizes the results of reading the narratives which constitute ancient Greek mythological archetypes.[9] I located three mythic couples whose interplays feature gender-specific human fears and weaknesses: Echo and Narcissus, Amazons and Greek heroes, and Medusa and Hermes. I then interpreted these paired myths twice, in scenes where they act individually and in scenes where they interact. This double analysis adds new meaning to the specificity of each.

For example, I first explain how Narcissus's self-obsession represents a fear of alienation characteristic of the quest for autonomy.[10] I then demonstrate how Echo, doomed to repeat others' words and never speak for herself, personifies two weaknesses: one, the lack of autonomy which critics now call women's docile *heroism*, and two, the propensity for hearing and understanding others to the detriment of the self.[11] Finally, I consider Echo

12

and Narcissus in scenes where they interact. Echo falls in love with Narcissus, but, as she is unable to speak in her own words, she cannot tell him she loves him. He, obsessed with contemplating his own image, fails to see her. In combination, their faults illustrate complementary fears of separation and union. Narcissus personifies exaggerated states of autonomy, and Echo extreme self-abnegation: the first self-love, and the second lack of self-interest. Together they dramatize a lack of communication between men and women.

I turn next to stories of Amazons and Greek heroes, which are antipodal to those of Echo and Narcissus. While the latter never touch, the Amazon and the Greek hero do, but only in scenes of violence. When the wandering Amazon enters a territory named by the hero as his nation, he engages her in combat, then kills and rapes her. The narratives of these meetings convey a pervasive sense of defeat and guilt.

A third, and lesser known, scene in which mythological archetypes intermix features Medusa and Hermes. This one is particularly significant to the present inquiry, for it highlights the way that original stories of the invention of language are related to sexual identity. According to an early version of the myth, Medusa first invented the alphabet.[12] Yet Hermes is the most commonly recognized mythological representative of language. A scene where the two interact suggests an explanation of this transference. Medusa once lent the consonants to Hermes and sent him on an errand, but she kept the vowels. Since Hermes was a liar and a thief, why not create our own variation of the myth and conclude that he stole the vowels from Medusa because he needed them to speak?

In sum, my analyses in the first half of this preliminary chapter demonstrate how, because of their polyvalence, myths, stories, novels—in fact, all writings—lend themselves to a variety of interpretations. Above all, my readings signal that the sexual identity of fictional characters is an important factor in the invention of narratives and that the esthetic of storytelling has been guided by sexual biases since the dawn of Western civilization.[13]

Pursuing my inspection of prototypical heroic characters, I also read two ancient texts: *Ahura's Tale,* the autobiography of an Egyptian princess inscribed on fragments of papyrus, and Homer's poem, *The Odyssey.* Ahura's story, although told in the first person by three different scribes, is the first recorded instance of a woman's autobiography. While it has no immediately discernible kinship to the French women studied in later chapters, it introduces an allegorical motif which will recur in their works: a double quest for love and knowledge. After Ahura conquers a husband, she undertakes a risky adventure—a search for the book of the gods, a metaphor for reading and writing. This second quest ends tragically when Ahura is punished by the gods for having stolen their power. During her life, she loses her child and her husband; after her death, she is buried apart from them and her body is split from her soul. (Evidently, a second scribe writes this part of the story.) Her autobiography does not end here, for in a later century a third scribe continues to write about her in the first person, reporting that her spirit spoke to him and asked him to move her tomb. This is another metaphor for reading and writing. What he means is that he read the book of her story written by a scribe from a previous century. Historians have testified to Ahura's existence, to the fragments dating from different centuries, and to the fact that her tomb was moved to the site of her husband's. The Egyptian princess used a book (although since she "wrote" that she could not write, she presumably dictated her story), and this text served to reunite her with her family. Here I demonstrate how two quests, the first specific to women writers, *heroinism* —the quest for love—and the second universal, heroism—the quest for knowledge—are interdependent. Subsequently I refer back to this seminal text in my study of heroism in women's writings, as I refer back to the canonized Homeric text, *The Odyssey,* in men's writings.

My reading of the stories of Ulysses opens on traditional interpretations and then shifts to more radical ones. Unlike Ahura's story, which was only lately discovered by scholars, *The Odyssey* has long been the most widely recognized prototype of narratives of heroic quests. This text, standing at the juncture of oral and written storytelling, informs us about two processes of separation: of narrator from protagonist and of protagonist from home. Initially, Ulysses told stories of his adventures in the *first* person to entertain his hosts, and these are the stories Homer penned in the *third* person to separate "I" the narrator from "he" the protagonist. Second, the quest took Ulysses away from his family.

We find a sharp contrast in narrative strategy and in story content between Ahura's and Homer's texts. Her story is narrated by a universal "I" (three scribes writing in the first person), while his is narrated in the third person. Furthermore, the Egyptian princess reunites her family through language, while Ulysses does so through application of justice, reestablishing order in his territory by slaying the disorderly pretenders to Penelope's hand. While Ahura may be associated with Medusa, Ulysses belongs to a group of Greek heroes who fight for their territory. The conjoint analyses of archetypical heroism in this preliminary chapter illustrate my approach to the works of several French writers who constitute the principal focus of my study.

A medieval manuscript written in the first person feminine and masculine—the correspondence of Heloïse and Abelard—is the subject of the next chapter. Through various discursive categories, Abelard defines himself as an extraordinary man: he exhibits his guilt and repentance through the liturgical formulae of the confessional, his steadfastness through quotations from sacred biblical writings, and his verbal superiority through the tropes of knightly heroism of the *chansons de gestes.* To distance himself from his

14

wife, he suggests that she name herself *Heloïm,* and he quotes cogent biblical parables, calling on God to intervene between them. While Abelard's dialectical arguments propose that inseparable contradictions sustain the ideal of their love in a superior category, Heloise's ideology, independent of such antithetical thought, recognizes no divisions. She subverts his discourse by defining herself in carnal relation to him. To show that she is outside recognized categories, she calls herself marginal, a courtesan. My analyses illustrate how the tension created in the correspondence is metonymic of the tension which existed when the correspondents transgressed their individual roles in the separate religious communities to which they belonged, at first as tutor and student, then later as monk and abbess. Like the Greek hero and the Amazon, the two meet in conflict, and the outcome is defeat and guilt.

In the third chapter, I juxtapose the memoirs of Antoinette Bourignon and Jeanne Guyon to the letters of Mme de Sévigné. The two memorialists, writing for their confessors and steeped in the doctrines of Jansenism, echo the liturgical discourse of Abelard. The *épistolière,* on the other hand, educated at the court of Louis XIV and writing for her daughter, operates within the discourse of women's private conversations. I find important divergences in their references to the female body, not only because these women's lifestyles are so dissimilar, but also because their implied readers— in the first case a confessor and in the second a daughter—deeply affect their choice of rhetoric. In the century of the litote, the two memorialists sublimate the body in tropes of mortification, while Sévigné secularizes it in the coded anecdotes of a group of superior women.

In the fourth chapter, my attention shifts from the intertextualities of women to those of men. I first show how the protagonists' discourse in Rousseau's autobiographical novel, *La Nouvelle Héloïse,* is modeled on that of the medieval correspondent of the other sex. The letters of Julie echo Abelard's moralistic admonitions, and those of St. Preux praise Heloise's passionate and hedonistic commitment to love. I then prove that in his *Les Confessions* Rousseau exploits Homeric tropes of heroism transmitted through the French romance. I detail the development of a quest which, unlike his predecessors', is neither purposeful nor linear. Rousseau's is a promenade in "maternal" nature which disengages him from the competitive world of men. Ultimately, I show how he gives birth to the noncompetitive Romantic hero by feminizing his male protagonist.

In the following two chapters, I apply the previously developed framework to four major writings by George Sand. First I point out how Aurore Dupin, alias George Sand, disguises herself as the omniscient nineteenth-century narrator to manipulate sexual logic. Studying the interplay between her narrator and the protagonist of her first novel, *Indiana,* we come to understand that Sand's struggle with novelistic traditions provides us with a fertile terrain for the investigation of the *revers* effect. She herself emphasizes how writing about a woman from a man's point of view distorts the ethic of the protagonist. Narratives of Indiana's actions belie the stereotypical platitudes about women which the author makes the narrator deliver in direct addresses to readers.

Next I show how Sand, participating in the revolutionary acts of the Romantic generation, composes an experimental novel. In *Lélia*, her most controversial work, she dismisses the omniscient narrator of previous novels and lets all her protagonists speak in the first person. My reading clearly demonstrates how Sand finds her own voice and, speaking in the first person feminine through both Lélia the artist and Pulchérie the courtesan, narrates problems of the double quest for love and knowledge. The metaphor of prostitution in *Lélia* represents both sexual impotence and artistic failure. This finding supports my reading of *Ahura's Tale:* that there exists a trope specific to women's heroism in the interdependence of the quests for love (sexual) and for autonomy (artistic production). [14]

Problems inherent in women's artistic creation are the subject of my study of two more of Sand's works. In a discussion of the *Künstlerroman, Consuelo,* my analyses of the interior quest for self-knowledge highlight the import of the Romantics' penchant for transformation to the development of women artists. In evaluating the *Histoire de ma vie,* I point out that when Sand reflects on her craft, she touches on problems of writing and gender, particularly on the two facets of the male persona she invented by wearing a waistcoat and adopting a pseudonym. Finally, in my analyses of the central chapters of her autobiography, I demonstrate how my own theories of the risk inherent in the quest for knowledge—first formulated from my reading of *Ahura's Tale*—are validated by Sand herself.

An examination of Hélène Cixous's *La Venue à l'écriture* and Julia Kristeva's "My Memory Hyperbole" summarizes and concludes my work. In readings of these brief autobiographical essays, I apply the theories developed in previous chapters to highlight the challenge to gender identity, a trope common to two writers whose iconoclastic approaches to *écriture* vary greatly. Outlined by unusual configurations, Cixous's circular and Kristeva's multi-leveled, the stories of their journeys both describe quests unlike that of the Homeric hero. Speaking through "I," "you," "we," and even "she," Cixous transforms principles of identity to encode the *jouissance* of the female body into a multitude of subjects. Kristeva, who proposes that intellectuals think the speaking subject in new ways, speaks through two voices, "I" and "we," to narrate the story of herself as an individual within a number of groups. The language of both women subverts traditional narratives of autobiography, Cixous by speaking the inventive discourse of mad-

16

ness and Kristeva by combining the intellectual discourses of philosophy, psychoanalysis, and literary criticism.[15]

As it addresses heroic narratives of the self in the works of men and women, my study promises to enrich the theoretical framework in which we read. In both traditional and revisionist readings of autobiographical works, through a process of comparison which considers similarities as well as contrasts, I delineate the gender bases and biases from which the esthetics and ethics of critical discourse originate.

Archetypes: The *Quest à Deux* and the Hero's Journal

In his psychoanalytical definition of narcissism, Freud attributes the trait of obsession with one's physical appearance to women. In his autobiographical confession of an Echo effect in his speech, Abelard ascribes the characteristic of insubstantiality to a man, himself. Yet when we read ancient narratives of the two archetypes in anthologies, we notice that Narcissus is *he*, a young man, and that Echo is *she*, a young maiden who became a wind spirit. More importantly, we become aware that there exist narratives where these two archetypes interact. What has happened, we may ask, to make Freud construct narcissism as a woman's weakness and to cause Abelard to construe hollow words as a man's fault? How have both of these archetypes been subjected to such major modifications—especially gender-crossing—and why has their interplay been ignored?[1]

To Freud, narcissism represents an obsession—exaggerated concern of women with their appearance causing them to fail to develop a realistic, mature image of themselves. In ancient Greek mythology, Narcissus is a handsome young man who falls in love with his image in a fountain. Obsessed with his own beauty, he constantly reaches into the water to embrace himself. The archetype we have seen in most pictorial representations, that of a young man sitting by a pond, does not capture the original meaning of its narrative. The ancient version tells us that each time Narcissus embraces himself, he disturbs his image. This adds significance to the myth. Narcissus's disturbing of the smooth surface of his reflection prevents him from catching a true image of himself.[2] Furthermore, the ancient story does not end there: the myth increases its meaning in a scene where he espies Echo.

Mythological Archetypes I: Narcissus and Echo

In the ancient Greek version, Echo is punished because of her preoccupation with other people's affairs. She loves to start arguments and to have the last word. One day, as Juno's husband is amusing himself among the muses, Echo contrives to detain the goddess so that she cannot see what he is doing. Juno discovers Echo's complicity and condemns her never to speak first *and* always to have the last word. Since she can only respond to what she hears, Echo is unable to initiate a conversation. In time, as the archetype grows, her action, echoing, comes to signify the repetition by any individual—man or woman—of others' ideas. As a result, the myth of Echo is now incorporated into all aphorisms about speech devoid of meaning.

In versions now forgotten, ancient myths describe scenes of interaction between Echo and Narcissus. Let us see how their interactions enrich the significance of both archetypes. In one of these scenes, Echo sees the handsome Narcissus and falls in love with him, but she cannot call him. Similarly, Narcissus, obsessed with embracing his own image, cannot see her. She waits for him to speak, and when he does, she keeps repeating his words to get his attention. He hears her but cannot see her, since she is a ghost. Then one day she comes so close to him that he catches a glimpse of this wind spirit; but he is frightened and recoils at the sight. Echo dies because of this rejection, and, for having refused her, Narcissus is condemned by the gods to fall in love with his own image—as well as with many other beautiful maidens who keep seeking him out. The two archetypes are antithetic in that they represent opposite states of exaggerated autonomy and dependency. Narcissus, reproducing his image by looking into the water, is both the one and the other, subject and object of his thoughts, a paradigm of autonomy. The nymph Echo, repeating others' words, is never the subject of her own discourse. Incomplete without others' voices, she is the paradigm of dependency.

Both Echo and Narcissus misrepresent; Narcissus, performing his gesture, and Echo, speaking her words mechanically, empty human behavior of its meaning. Narcissus incessantly blurs his image in the water as he embraces himself, and Echo repeatedly loses her words, her substance, in the air. In the illusory realms of mirrors and echoes, outside human reality, the characteristics which would identify them as man and woman are perpetually lost. Neither the image of Narcissus blurred in the water nor the voice of Echo imitating the entire range of the vocal register can be distinctly attributed to a man or a woman. As the following chapters will demonstrate, narratives constituting these archetypes often cross the borders of sexual identity, men associating themselves with Echo and women with Narcissus. The exaggerations and illusions which dominate these stories illustrate a failure to participate in a superior human endeavor: verbal communication.

20

Mythological narratives featuring the interaction of these two archetypes relate the same anamorphosis as the critical discourse of commentators who interact with the subjects of their study as if they had no sexual identity. These critics claim that sexual identity is not a valid factor in the formulation of theoretical frameworks.

Let us look briefly at some variations of the Narcissus archetype which demonstrate how it came to be linked to women in Freudian psychoanalysis. We may retrace the idea of narcissism as a female characteristic back to the Ovidian Eternal Feminine, to the poetic ideal which inspired the Romantics, and, eventually, to Freud. Before psychoanalysis, the Romantics wrote much about the muse who inspired them and gave "it" a female identity. They called it the Eternal Feminine (after Ovid). Later, this muse—a mirror image within the poet's inner depth—was transformed by Freud into the Narcissus archetype. For him, the Eternal Feminine no longer stood for a female spiritual inspiration, but for the vanity of women. Thus the Eternal Feminine, obsessed with herself, took on the role of the Narcissus archetype. "He" no longer represented the exaggerated self-concentration of a man to the exclusion of others (exaggerated autonomy), but the obsession of a woman with her physical appearance. The archetype not only crossed genders, it also lost its inner spiritual properties. Then Freud invented a new narrative for the now female Narcissus archetype and linked it to his penis envy construct.

When he coined the term *penis envy,* Freud proposed that his female patients' problems were due to their lack of what visibly identified men. Women, claimed Freud, were vain, self-centered, and child-like creatures who had to decorate themselves to compensate for their horrifying void. They could, however, complete themselves by bearing sons. Pursuing this theory to its moral consequences, Freud proposed that since women were not integral (whole), they lacked integrity. Having a poor sense of justice, they had to depend on men for moral leadership. These ideas reflect the order of society in his time, and they continue to influence intellectual thought. The success of his thinking in the modern age reflects the extent to which the distribution of sexual roles and power remains constant. The import of this Freudian theoretical construction to today's critics lies in its clear association with sexual politics.[3]

After Freud, in a roundabout way, his disciples changed the gender of Narcissus (as narrated in the ancient Greek version) back to the masculine. Following his lead, some of them developed ethical systems based on degrees of men's need for autonomy (which in its exaggerated state is narcissism) and canonized it as normative. For example, men are believed to reach a stage of adulthood—a strong sense of ethics—only after a secure

21

sense of sexual identity has been established by separating from the mother. Here, in fact, these theorists speak of separation from *all* women, as to be a man is to be "different" from the other, not only the mother. This is an exaggeration, a rejection of half of humanity. It is narcissism. When men have reached this last degree of independence, and only then, is intimacy with a woman possible. This is a valid theory of ethical evolution in cases of male individuation and the development of a sense of ethic, but it is narcissistic to apply it to women. Its validity for the development of female ethics is questionable and, in fact, it has now been challenged by scholars. It is not normative. Critics who favor psychological and psychoanalytical literary approaches have often written about Freud's theories.[4] It is understood that the mother-child dyad must be severed to reach autonomy, but this separation is not always an extraordinary act. It does not constitute heroism in women's stories. Granted, it is significant in men's stories where, as some critics suggest, it is an oxymoron: desiring the mother's body while rejecting its maternal function.[5] But this trope is almost absent in women's stories.

In ancient versions of the myth, Narcissus's obsession with his own image is the cause of his alienation from all humans, not merely of his separation from a maternal figure. Theoretical discourses positing that individuation is a process of personality development based on assertions of maleness which call for separation from the un-identical other—the mother—are not variants but mutants of the myth. In its most primitive meaning, the narcissistic error is an obsession with the self (autonomy) which excludes the individual from *all* humanity, not only the mother.

Paradoxically, in *L'Enigme de la femme,* as Sarah Kofman points out, Freud's allusion to Narcissus calls attention to his own obsession with the autonomous dream of separation from the mother. Departing from the male body as a norm (his own image), he viewed his female patient as different, not in her specificity, but in her departure from his normative standard.[6] She is an incomplete man. Because he was preoccupied with the mirror image of man, Freud failed to hear the true meaning of his female patients' discourse and denied their *author*ity as speakers. His discovery of the subject's alterity in relation to and with language was important, but the most well-known proponent of that thought, Lacan—inspired by this original statement—posited that women were that alterity, and, like Freud, he denied them authority.

The theories examined above lead us far from the original versions of the myth. Lately, Kristeva's views of narcissism takes us even farther. She proposes that it is an archaic drive which precedes and surpasses any identity sign (sexual or other). This proposal adds broad implications to the concept.[7] My own work in this book will take us another step beyond. It will constitute another narrative, yet another variant of the myth of Narcissus—one which will consider its interplay with the myth of Echo. By interpreting these myths in conjunction with each other, I hope to enhance their richness and open avenues to the understanding of narratives of the self in the works of both men and women.

Mythological Archetypes II: Amazons and Greek Heroes

Juxtaposing narratives of these archetypes to those of Narcissus and Echo allows us to view a configuration of the spectrum within which interactions between men and women occur. The narratives either dramatize or neutralize their differences. Ultimately, this helps us to explore the limits of the very conventions through which we perceive male and female identity, and, once we are aware of them, to surpass them. Our analysis of characters becomes more distinct and our assumptions of heroism change. Men and women seem more heroic, more exceptional.

The features of the Amazon archetype which have subsisted through the centuries, prowess and independence, are not its only characteristics. They have been preserved because they are recognized by men and are the ones that are valued in the male hero. A hero's prowess and independence show he excels in endeavors linked to sexual identity. Demonstrations of strength and independence show his autonomy, his success at differentiating from women. Heroically representing his group (men) and performing those skills valued by them, the Greek hero stands *above* and therefore *apart* from them, superior, God-like as an individual. Such is men's specificity of heroism. But women's heroism, as we will see in the narratives of Amazons, has a specificity of its own.

Although ancient versions endow Amazons with outstanding attributes not endemic to male heroism, oral traditions have preserved few of these narratives. One has to research obscure documents to discover them. First, according to Heredotus, Amazons were engaged in four activities: they worshipped a goddess, hunted, raised grazing cattle, and lived from plunder. With the exception of the last, these activities are no longer associated with Amazons. Second, proofs that the myth may have authentic origins—claims that tombs attesting to tribes of women have been located—are not being investigated. Third, and most important, those ancient versions tell of the Amazons as hunters, nurturers, and loyal members of a group of women who were non-competitive among themselves. We must notice that the nurturing and non-competitive aspects of the women's interaction, the most important, have been the most neglected. Furthermore, history continues to attribute less and less credibility to any possible proof of the existence of Amazons.[8]

The authenticity of documents which prove that such a tribe of strong, independent women existed is constantly challenged, while oral stories which tell of their subjugation in conflicts with Greek heroes are accepted. Reference is always made in history and anthologies to a group of strong, autonomous women, but their individual feats are unrecorded. If ancient Greek male heroism is defined in deeds associated with a specific name, ancient Greek female heroism is defined in anonymity and defeat. The name of a single Amazon is given only in conjunction with that of a hero who vanquishes her, so that "Amazon" usually signifies an anonymous group of female warriors, a few of whom were defeated by Greek heroes. The only names which have survived for posterity are those of Amazons who were killed and raped. Thus we know of Penthesilea and Hyppolyta, nocturnal figures who were overcome in battle with Theseus, Achilles, and Bellerophon, solar heroes.

Such are the stories which have persisted throughout the ages. Relief sculptures, statuary decors, and mosaics of major monuments of the archaic Classical or Hellenic periods depict Amazons exclusively engaged in military activities. Gladys Amad remarks: "Ni scènes de sacrifices à Artémis, ni scènes de chasse où les amazones s'attaquent aux fauves ne se retrouvent dans l'art classique grec."[9] (Neither scenes of sacrifices to Artemis, nor hunting scenes where the Amazons attack wild beasts are found in classical Greek art.) Amad also concludes that the Amazon, as one of the major themes of this art, personified the barbaric enemy of civilization and was rarely represented without the presence of a heroic warrior. In other words, she was portrayed as an enemy of the hero's nation.[10]

Subsequent interpretations in French history, literature, and psychoanalysis continued to picture Amazons succumbing to the attack of an eminent hero and to focus on pathetic representations of their defeat in combat. Their myth was often revived in times of conflict; during wars of religion in the Middle Ages, for example, the archetype flourished again, this time as a witch. Joan of Arc was accused of witchery and burned at the stake, and it was her suffering rather than her valor as a warrior which caught the public's imagination. Then posterity sanctified her as a martyr. Later, the image of the strong woman was further devalorized. Whereas artists of ancient and Classical Greece had represented Amazons as beautiful maidens, French revolutionaries said of the women who participated in combat: "Encore si ses dames étaient jolies, mais ce ne sont que des têtes de Méduses dont l'aspect pétrifie."[11] (If only these ladies were pretty, but they all have Medusa's heads whose look is petrifying.) For eighteenth- and nineteenth-century writers, the image of the strong, independent woman was bifurcated by a division between the muse and the Medusa. She personified both sides of an inner conflict between man's creative spirit and his suicidal instinct. Prévost's *Manon Lescaut* and Mérimée's *Carmen*, two temptresses who first inspire and then ruin the lives of their lovers, exemplify this new double image of the Amazon.

While mythology locates the scenes of the Narcissus-Echo archetypes in the diffuse elements of air and water, it situates the drama between the Amazon and the Greek hero on the surface of the earth. Land masses divided and demarcated by the hero's group are called nations, and, when the nomadic Amazon travels in areas claimed by men, they construe her presence as an act of aggression and one of their group engages her in combat. Convention dictates that the men are on the side of justice.

Mythological Archetypes III: Medusa and Hermes

Psychoanalytical thought continues to misrepresent the muse and the Medusa—archetypical strong women—by shrouding them in the mysterious cloak of dream interpretation. In Jungian theories, a man's anima, his benevolent feminine part, inspires him to be creative. The anima is an obvious derivative of the Romantic muse, the seductress who inspires men but threatens to sap them of their life force. As Jung postulates, if a man's anima becomes too dominant, "she" weakens his intellect. Where male characteristics are normative, female traits are necessary antitheses. Therefore, a woman's animus is simply the complement of a man's anima, a masculine part of herself. As a man's anima should not dominate, neither should a woman's animus. Jung's disciples advised a female patient whose animus ruled that she was acting in an Amazonian way and told her how to act in a socially acceptable manner:

> Or, les Amazones sont symboliquement caractérisées comme 'femmes-tueuses d'hommes': elles veulent se substituer à l'homme, rivaliser avec lui en le combattant au lieu de le compléter . . . la femme rivalisant d'une manière malsaine (hystérique) avec la qualité essentielle qui seule intéresse le mythe: l'élan spirituel. . . . Cette rivalité épuise la force essentielle propre à la femme, la qualité d'amante et de mère, la chaleur d'âme.[12]

> So, the Amazons are symbolically characterized as 'women-killers of men': they want to substitute themselves for men, to rival by fighting instead of completing him . . . the woman who rivals in such an unhealthy (hysterical) way with the essential and only quality which concerns the myth: the spiritual *elan*. . . . This rivalry exhausts the essential strength of women, the outstanding quality of lover and mother, the warmth of the soul.

As we can see, for their female patients Jung and his disciples posited a "*revers*" of theories based on observations of conflicts specific to male patients. Today, however, linguistically oriented psychoanalysts stage a more openly confrontational scene. First, Lacan chased women out of the symbolic order, stating that the formation of symbols and their expression in language was gender-linked to the father:

> C'est dans le *nom du père* qu'il nous faut reconnaître le support de la fonction symbolique qui depuis l'orée des temps historiques identifie sa personne à la figure de la loi.[13]

> It is in the *name of the father* that we must recognize the support of the symbolic function which since the dawn of historic times has identified him as the figure of the law.

For Lacan, as for the Greek hero who contemplates the dead Amazon lying at his feet, woman is a sort of inanimate object, the "female body" which the "male subject" ponders. She is the hysterical body of his hysterical text. Lacan's position vis-à-vis women and language is more radical than Freud's. While the father of psychoanalysis gave woman a voice (his), Lacan refuses her any role in language:

> There is no woman except she who is excluded by the nature of things which is the nature of words, and it must be said that if there is something about which women themselves complain enough for the moment, it's certainly about that—simply, they [women] don't know what they're saying, that's the whole difference between them and me.[14]

We are reminded of the intriguing narratives of the creation of language featuring Medusa and Hermes. The search for the inventor of the alphabet is a most fundamental quest, and one which is obviously linked to sexual identity. Whoever first invented it was extraordinary, that is, heroic. Thus narratives of heroic quests provide a proper field for the study of a quarrel worthy of investigation. As we have already stated, a hero, as determined from such ancient texts as the Homeric epic, is someone who displays qualities of strength and storytelling peculiar to men who, by special inspiration, have the ability to transcend the limitations of sense (some were blind) and to secure the past from oblivion.[15] Thus extraordinary individuals are not only the men who perform extraordinary deeds, but also those who preserve them by narrating their stories: writers. Men are the protagonists and narrators of these stories, and they are extraordinary because of their membership in a group defined by sexual identity. It follows that since women do not belong to that sexually-identified group, they are excluded from the scene of heroism and of its narratives. Women are not excluded because they do not tell stories, but because they are women. To define their heroism, must critics depart from canonized definitions and search for qualities admired by a group of women? Would not such a search reveal a simple *revers* of man's heroism? Indeed it would not, for the task is multi-faceted. We must locate seminal texts of women who tell their stories and compare them to each other to discover commonalities. Then we must compare them to similar stories by men to locate areas of similarities and divergences. For instance, we are informed by canons that heroes possess to the highest degree the qualities admired by men as a group, that is, because they are superior to other men; yet women do not necessarily perceive themselves as heroic because they are superior to a group of women.[16] In sum, the search for the specificity of female heroism should consider the interplay of both women's and men's works.

Ahura's Tale: Stealing the Book of the Gods

Let us examine a recently discovered autobiography of an extraordinary woman, a princess from ancient Egypt named Ahura. We owe the discovery of this seminal text to the recent flurry of inquiry into the genre. George Misch, a researcher investigating the earliest manifestations of the genre, unearthed this story about the life of a woman who died about 1324 B.C.[17] This text, as it comes to the reader in translation, offers many challenges. First, it is in three unsigned fragments of papyrus inscribed at different times and consequently, as scholars surmise, written by three scribes. Second, because women did not have access to the profession of scribe, these scribes were probably male, yet the story is narrated by "I"—a woman in the first person. Third, although translators have been unable to pinpoint the generation or dynasty of the origin of each fragment, the existence of the princess is documented.[18] She was the sister of Na.nefer.ka.ptah, a son of Ramses II. Fourth, a mixture of fact and invention complicates the task of historians trying to decipher historical events from fantastic happenings, such as speaking with spirits. A fifth problem is even more perplexing: the narrator (presumably Ahura) telling the story of her life writes that she cannot write. This makes the reader pause and question the authenticity of the tale. According to all definitions of autobiography, the voice speaking in the first person, "I," is traditionally attributed to the person whose name appears in the title of the story or book and who is, we assume, writing it; that is, "I" should refer extra-textually to Ahura, the daughter of an Egyptian pharoah.[19] Yet she whose "real" life is narrated in the first person wrote that she could not write. Information about the reliability of this statement on the part of the narrator is not available to us, so we are forced to take it literally and to conclude that she dictated her story to a scribe. The other two scribes were either writers of fiction or historians.

These divergences from traditional literary conventions certainly contributed to scholars' neglect of the work. Now, however, critics may enter into a discourse with Ahura's story and bring it across the barriers of time. It becomes accessible when we place it in the "monumental" time of living women's condition. We understand that the story of the "I" encompasses and surpasses the dimensions of the history of Western civilization, which measures time in terms of men's outstanding events and space according to their conquests of territories. Ahura's story, told in a universal "I," fulfills Kristeva's definition of feminism as "an aesthetic practice which brings out the singularity of each person, and the multiplicity of every person's possible identifications" (with atoms, from family to stars).[20]

Ahura's story begins with her wish to marry her brother, Na.nefer.ka.ptah, in spite of her parents' refusal. Her father tells her that it is not customary for a brother and sister to marry if there are only two children in the family. But Ahura persists and continues to appeal to him, apparently with great humor, for eventually he laughs at some amusing remarks she makes and allows the marriage. The couple marries, has a child, and is very happy. The husband, who wants to become a scribe, goes to Memphis, where he spends his days reading inscriptions on catacombs and monuments. One day, as he is studying in the chapel of the gods, a priest derides him for reading worthless writings and then advises him to read a book written by the god Thoth himself, as it will give him magic powers. The theme of voyage as search for knowledge is invoked as Ahura then travels with her husband and child. She accompanies her husband until the last three days, which she spends by herself waiting in a trance; she stares into space without moving while he brings the book up from the bed of a river. He reads the book and, as the priest predicted, after the first page he understands the language of birds and fishes and has the power to enchant them. After the second page he sees the light and all the gods appear to him. Ahura also reads the book and gains the same powers. Concerned with the preservation of knowledge, she asks her brother to copy it. It is at this point in the story that the writer says she/he cannot write: "As I could not write, I asked Na.nefer.ka.ptah to copy the book" (101). He inscribes the story on papyrus, then dips it in beer and drinks the liquor, which now contains the ink of his writing. These actions anger the gods, who condemn the family to die. All three are drowned, but on separate occasions, so that the bodies of the mother and child are buried far from the husband's. Ahura's *Ka* (or spirit) leaves her body and travels to the site of her husband's tomb. The two remain there with the book between them until years or even centuries later, when a scribe named Setna arrives. He asks Ahura's *Ka* for the book and she agrees to let him have it in exchange for a favor. He must have her remains and the child's brought to the tomb of her husband to join her *Ka*.

An unusual exercise in plurality and singularity in Ahura's auto-biography—the three voices narrating in a way that implies one author—defies our understanding of the social and sexual functions of identity. The authors were unidentified, probably because of the Egyptians' understanding of writing and reading as sacred activities forbidden by the gods and because of their belief that to own a story was sacrilegious. The absence of the storytellers' signatures either on the cover or at the bottom of the text, together with the lack of pronouns to separate them from the protagonist, presents us with a unique homophonic text that brings out both the multiplicity of the three scribes (men) and the singularity of the "I" (a woman).

This autobiography also challenges principles of heroism. The events related do not conform to those of traditional single quests. Here we find an early manifestation of a trope specific to women's stories, the double quest.[21] The tale first focuses on a conventional female quest and then shifts to an irregular one: from finding a husband to reading and transcribing a book. It should be noted that the second, the search for the book of knowledge, transgresses cultural taboos. Ahura's fragmentation (the separation of her body from her spirit) results not only from her having had the book copied, but also from her individual accomplishment in a culture that favored a global vision of the self. Ancient Egyptians conceptualized time as a tunnel leading back to the commonality of one's ancestors. As a result of her temerity, Ahura was trapped in that tunnel. She was unable to unite herself with her family and her ancestors until she asked the scribe to free her spirit. The third scribe, Setna, writes that the book was left between the two spouses at the burial site and that she offered it to him. He claims that "I" gave him the book in exchange for having "me" freed from the tunnel of time. From the perspective of today's critic, the second quest *à deux* is a singular heroic trope.

This autobiography also compels us to review the conventions of identity. The Egyptian Thoth and his Greek and Roman equivalents, Hermes and Mercury, personify the gift of communication. According to Egyptian lore, Thoth invented hieroglyphics and created the world by the force of his word, and it is evident that the power of creation through words contained in his magic book is central to *Ahura's Tale*. Ahura triumphs in the end because she has acquired the god's skill: communication. The priest's prediction that all who read Thoth's book would have the power to regain after death the shape they had on earth explains Ahura's power to speak from her tomb through the three scribes. This first-person story was passed on from generation to generation. *Ahura's Tale* is an extraordinary text, not only because Ahura was a woman of high social standing who was clever enough with the spoken word to marry the man she loved, but also because she was initiated as a special individual into the highest achievements of her culture: reading and, another activity forbidden to her sex, writing. Over and above all of these unusual aspects, the text is special because of its singular practice of monophony. Ahura's monophonic voice gives us a new perspective on the role of sexual identity in tropes of heroism.

Homer's *The Odyssey:* The Differentiated Hero's Journey

The unusual field of vision which we have observed in the ancient Egyptian text coexists with a contrasting perspective that can also be traced back to another ancient text. In *Ahura's Tale,* the three narrators are comparable to stage actors speaking *for* the protagonist. In Homer's *The Odyssey,* one narrator features himself as separating *from* the protagonist. Whereas the Egyptian text belongs to a tradition of anonymity, Homer's belongs to one of nomenclature. Here the voice speaks as a distinct entity through third-person narrative. Comparing Ahura's and Homer's texts, we become aware of the origin of the distinction between narrators and principal characters. Homer describes how Ulysses spends evenings reciting orally the events of his voyage, and these are the very events he is narrating in the written poem.

That Homer is the author, not Ulysses, is the first degree of distance recognized by critics; that the narrator is not the author (Homer) but a fictive character is a second degree; and that the author is an "implied presence" invented by the reader, as proposed by Booth, is a third degree.[22] Today, now that the concept of referential author has been invalidated, now that no referential reality is attributable to "him" or "her," what remains to be studied are categories of writing: a voice rather than a person. Consequently, the search for the sexual identity of authors must first address itself to categories of writing which denote this, and we shall hereafter call it "narrative voice." Examining this voice in Ahura's story, we find that it varies from the voice in Homer's tale. Whether this constitutes a significant gender difference needs to be substantiated by a study of voice as it participates in men's and women's heroic tropes.

This attention to gender difference, this "resisting" reader's awareness, allows the critic to notice striking variances in the opening passages of *Ahura's Tale* and *The Odyssey.*[23] In the Egyptian story, the first plot is a woman's marriage: Ahura's wish to create a home by marrying her brother. In the Homeric tale, the tension is first created by a move away from home. In this narrative, Telemachus, like his father, undertakes the quest for autonomy. In Ahura's case, however, the quest *à deux*—for knowledge and book reading—is undertaken after she is bound in a close relationship with her brother-husband. Ulysses' story begins in the second part of the quest, when he is already separated from his wife. Although his stated intention before leaving was to return home directly from the war, the twenty-year time lapse between his departure from the battlefield and his arrival home makes his resolution suspect. His story of the twenty years spent away from home is interwoven with geography, as he names places according to the time of his events. His trajectory traces an imaginary line from one island to another when he names them. As Michel Serres observes, the journey of Ulysses is a journal—the words share the same root.[24] *The Odyssey* is a chapter in the linear *history* of Western civilization, our cultural memory, which is structured through the records of the deeds of men. By contrast, Ahura's story resists our attempts to fix it in spatio-temporal measures.

The three unidentified voices and the quest *à deux* in the Egyptian tale neutralize differences, while in Ulysses' story the third-person narrative dramatizes them. Penelope's time, like Ahura's, is unmeasurable; she cyclically unravels the threads of her cloth while Ulysses tells the story of his adventures. Homer's poem delineates a linear mobility—the events of a voyage—which is opposed to the cyclical stillness of a woman, Penelope. The hero's existentialist (ontic) enterprise ends at the essentialist (static) presence of Penelope. Thus, comparing spatio-temporal representations in these narratives, we begin to articulate the specificity of men's and women's heroic tropes.

The plot of *The Odyssey* begins to move forward when Athena, disguised as a man, visits young Telemachus to relate his father's adventures and to instruct him to leave his mother. We are immediately struck by this gender-crossing. Why does she dress as a man and why does she lower her voice? Is it to illustrate that women have no authority over men and that Telemachus would only obey a man? If so, why not send Hermes, the god of communication? We come to the conclusion that Athena personifies both sexes to represent the boy's antithetical wish for fusion and separation. He stands at the threshold of union and differentiation. Telemachus must leave, but first he must free himself of maternal influence. The scene of separation occurs, significantly, after his voice has changed to a man's register. When he speaks in public, addressing the pretenders who have been waiting for Penelope's hand during his father's twenty-year absence, everyone is astonished to hear the authority in his voice. The initial scene makes it clear that Penelope has had no voice (no power) in public and therefore could not have settled the conflicts in the great halls downstairs. Her authority had been confined to her rooms upstairs, and her son reminds her of this when he expresses his budding male maturity: "Go to your rooms, and see about your own business, loom and distaff, and keep the servants to their work; talking is always the man's part, and mine in particular, for the man rules the house."[25] After he asserts himself in this manner, clearly defining spaces either male (public) or female (private), the narration starts. Telemachus leaves in search of his father and of his own maleness. The first peripetea of his quest, his departure, is thus an affirmation of male authority accomplished through the suppression of female authority.

31

The narrative of the quest for autonomy in *The Odyssey* moves against Penelope as it departs from her space and inaugurates a strategy of oppositions which symbolically abolish her influence over son and father. She personifies "essence," and the tension of the voyage is created by the hero's wish to return to this essential point of departure after the existential quest. In short, the voyages of the men move against and toward her silent, still presence. Male voices claim exclusive rights to tell the unfolding of historical events which depend on those they exclude, women. Ulysses' journey is generated by an indispensable *revers,* Penelope. Does her celebrated "unweaving," her daily pictorializing nightly erased, represent how she must remain silent (and unknown) while the hero nightly tells his story after dinner to repay his hosts for their hospitality? Is the mysterious tapestry a synecdoche for the guilt of writing books, of taking language away from the Medusa, and is this guilt linked to the maternal?

These gender-linked functions of narrative and anti-narrative are dichotomized in four major episodes where obstacles erected in women's zones delay the husband's voyage home. The ongoing narrative is threatened, and sometimes even stops, when Ulysses enters spaces occupied by seductive women. In the first of these, sirens menace him and his crew; in the second, Scylla and Charybdis endanger the ship; in the third and fourth, Calypso and Circe keep him prisoner on their islands. All of these women impede Ulysses' movement, for when he enters their spheres his voyage-narrative halts, and he has no story to tell. He loses his voice, and Hermes, God of communication, has to intercede for the action—the narration of the journey—to be renewed.[26]

Of all these passages which describe Ulysses' encounters with women, the episode of the singing sirens most obviously dramatizes how women's voices threaten the ongoing narration of his actions.[27] His success in this test of heroism depends on his ability to hear the sirens without being seduced by their song. Individually unnamed but collectively identified as female, they call men to the ocean, an indivisible, unsafe element which eludes mastery. In psychoanalysis, as in mythology, the ocean represents a dangerous attraction. Jung designates it the archetypical unconscious experience of beatifically losing oneself in the multitude. In *The Odyssey* the ocean is gender-linked to women. Falling into their territory, into the ocean's liquidity, is comparable to returning to the womb, that is, to a state pre-dating the sexual identity being preserved by the voyage. Ulysses prepares for his passage through the sirens' zone with an intensity that tells of his fear. After instructing his men to tie him up before sailing ahead, he blocks their ears with wax. The ship enters the zone of the sirens and Ulysses safely listens to their voices. The risk seems to lie in listening to women.

Ulysses tells of three more major trials in women's sphere where he perseveres in his cause as representative of men: the episode in which Calypso and Circe keep him prisoner and the one in which he safely navigates between Scylla and Charybdis. The storytelling of these obstacles he overcomes to affirm his autonomy is as adventurous as the adventure itself, and his prestige grows with each narration. But what happens when there are no more adventures to tell? A double-bind sustains the tension of the voyage; when the ephemeral, existential journey ends, so does the storytelling which asserts differentiation. Ulysses has promised to return to the sacred place of a different temporality, that of the bedroom of fixed rituals where Penelope laments and weaves. In the bedroom, her locus, the poem reaches its climax and the narrative of *his*tory ends.

While Ulysses had been absent from his site of sacred union and reproduction, competitive men from other territories had penetrated its great hall downstairs.[28] As time passed, they had threatened to move upstairs and take over the bedroom (marry Penelope). In the eyes of the countrymen who shared his cultural values of the sacred, Ulysses was justified in brutally butchering the pretenders when he returned home. His sacred site of peace and permanence had been threatened with chaos. When he reestablished order, when he purified his home and became reunited with Penelope, his story reached its climax. In Ulysses' story, home represents the sacred place of eternal return in pre-historic societies where familial rituals (washing of the feet, for instance) erase the weight of memory. The duration of the ephemeral journey's profane linear time is suspended in sacred rituals.[29] So end oral stories. But Homer stole this one. He wrote Ulysses' narratives and inserted them into the profane. He inscribed them, thereby disallowing the ritual of oral storytelling and forgetting. As we saw in *Ahura's Tale,* writing secularizes stories.

Of interest to the present gender-specific study are the two opposed temporalities and sites which maintain the tension of the narrative. The hero organizes his story of exploration during the linear voyage on a time line measurable by individual events rather than by light and dark. His narrative halts in the different temporality of women's zones and finally dies out in the cyclical time and fixed place of rituals, the conjugal bed preserved by Penelope. The stillness of Ulysses' wife safeguards him against the risk of alienation inherent in the narcissistic quest for differentiation. A final scene of recognition between the spouses reveals its importance. After twenty years of separation, Penelope says that she is not sure whether the stranger facing her is her husband, as he claims to be. She asks the servants to take out her bed and put it in the hall so that he may sleep on it the first night. Her suggestion contains a riddle which Ulysses instantly recognizes, and he interrupts her, exclaiming that it is not possible to move the bed because he himself has carved the bedpost into a tree. Penelope realizes that he is her husband and acknowledges his authority. She then echoes his orders, reasserting the bedroom as her zone of silent stillness. There the narrative of travel, adventure, and final revenge finds its resolution.

Conjoined readings of *Ahura's Tale* and *The Odyssey* illustrate how representations of heroism in the texts of men and women do more than merely complement each other. They highlight similarities, contrasts, and specificities. We find parallels in the role of the spouses in both stories, as the male character in Ahura's story complements hers and the female character in Ulysses' story complements his. Ahura's brother is a foil for her display of cleverness; she is superior to him in that while he makes the priest laugh by reading silly wall engravings, she makes her father laugh with clever words. Similarly, Penelope's silent passivity enhances Ulysses' verbal activity.

Comparing the two female characters, we find a contrast. Ahura is subject to transformation and evolution, but Penelope is not the agent of her fate. Her son even chases her from the great hall, and she never changes or moves from the women's rooms. Ahura, however, undertakes a quest for knowledge of the world. While Penelope has no authority, while she laments, pleads and echoes, Ahura demonstrates her authority in various modalities of voice, commanding, requesting, cajoling, and humoring.

We also find contrasts when we compare the risk of the quest in the story of the heroic man with that of the woman's. Situations which are considered risky and actions which are taken by the protagonists to solve difficulties vary. Ahura's first quest, the union with a man, poses no problems. She makes her father laugh, he allows the marriage between brother and sister, and the two live happily. But her second quest, the one for the book, is risky. Ahura's making her father laugh is an acceptable show of female non-competitive superiority and leads to marriage (*heroinism*), but her learning the language of the gods is not. We see an opposite pattern in the story of Ulysses. His extraordinary skills in language and battle are acceptable and pose no risk to the ongoing story; in fact, they *are,* on a deeper level, the ongoing story. For him, the danger lies in states of dependency. Ulysses is not himself when he spends time in the company of women. They put him in strange moods, relaxing him with ointments and even drugging him. With them he is not conscious, therefore not responsible. The solution each finds to obstacles placed in the path of the quest for knowledge differs. We see contrasts which highlight the specificity of each in the way Ahura and Ulysses deal with problems. Ahura triumphs in the end by using the book to trade with Setna and have her *Ka* and her family reunited with her body. Ulysses reestablishes his rule through violent actions and claims to justice.

The above readings of ancient texts lead to the conclusion that men's and women's texts do not always merely complement each other. Critics who would search for Penelope in Ahura's text, for instance, may conclude that the Egyptian princess is also a docile heroine in search of a husband. But in so doing they would remain blind to her talent for negotiation and to an even more important achievement: the quest for the book. Similarly, critics trained to recognize Homeric paradigms of heroism would conclude, after reading her story, that her brother is the one instigating the quest for the book and that she merely goes along. This time they would be blind to the specificity of her story. The book, narrated in three voices speaking as ''I,'' is the story of her life. Centuries later, when Setna reads it, he continues to write it in the first person ''I.'' He does not write of himself as ''he,'' because the story is not about him. A critical inquiry oriented to difference and favoring mastery would also conclude from the first-person narrative of Ahura's story that, since her brother is the only stated ''writer,'' she has no voice. A revisionist one, however, would conclude that she has a powerful voice, that of a goddess who speaks for all.

On the other hand, critics first trained to recognize Homeric paradigms and who later become resisting readers would find in *The Odyssey* a new specificity, for in this text lies the explanation of gender associations which exclude the writings of women from canons. Heroism in Homer's work is a rhetorical device, a clever way of telling a story of a clever man. In a harmonious esthetic of content and form, the heroic quest for autonomy spatially separates the hero from his family and the third-person narrative chronologically separates the narrator from the protagonist. The present study demonstrates how the most outstanding aspects of Ulysses' heroism are his distancing from, and his exclusion of, women.

As we see, the comparative study of texts (which will hereafter be noted under the term ''intertextuality'') opens a multitude of avenues leading to the gender specificity of heroism. The present study will pursue this promising line of investigation into the writings of men and women in French literature from the Middle Ages to the twentieth century.

Profane Love and the Discourse of Liturgy

The correspondence of Heloïse and Abelard has captivated literary imaginations since its translation from Latin to French by Jean de Meung. A number of other translations, some less faithful to the original, were published in English, Spanish, Italian, and Portuguese. The exchange of letters between the lovers was particularly popular in France, where it inspired novels, plays, poems, and parodies. Even in the Almanach they were cited as examples, in a maxim about the dangers of passion: "Gémissons sur leur tombe / Et n'aimons pas comme eux" (Let us grieve on their tomb / And let us not love as they did).[1]

The manuscript of the letters has generated numerous works in academic circles. The authorship of each letter became and remains the most often raised question. There is yet no definitive answer to this problem. The authenticity of the letters written by Heloïse has yet to be certified.[2] Because Abelard alone transcribed both his and his wife's letters, some researchers have implied that he may have revised hers. Given the lapse of two centuries between the original manuscript and the publication of its first translation, this problem will probably never be solved. In addition to the question of time, matters of style also make it impossible for scholars to solve this mystery. One problem is the formulaic style used in early monastic texts; another relates to the possibility that, as Heloïse was Abelard's student, she could conceivably have imitated his style. How could anyone then tease apart passages attributable to her from those possibly revised or added by her husband? Charlotte Charrier, who analyzes the style of the letters in an extensive study of the manuscript, *Héloïse dans l'histoire et dans la légende*, suggests that some of the biblical quotations in Heloïse's letters belong to Abelard and that one segment on the inferiority of women is so distasteful and objectionable it could not possibly be acknowledged as hers. Finally, there is now a consensus among scholars which overrides these conundrums of authenticity: whoever signed the letter is accepted as its author.[3]

Whatever we may conjecture about authenticity, the import of these letters lies in their subversive nature, particularly in Heloïse's use of Latin, the language of sacred liturgy and religious communities, to disclose profane love. One may wonder why the manuscript was preserved and why it did not suffer the same fate as the profane love poems Abelard is purported to have composed for Heloïse (the correspondence refers to them but no written versions have been found). The answer may be that the manuscript was preserved in spite of its sacrilegious nature (Heloïse's masochistic treatment of sexuality and Abelard's sadistic tales of castration) because it is somewhat imitative of St. Augustine's *Confessions* and, consequently, within the time-honored tradition of the exemplum.

All the ramifications of the marriage of Heloïse and Abelard in its societal context were and still are only vaguely perceived. These mysterious characteristics have never ceased to attract readers and writers. Each century has enriched Heloïse's licentious narratives emanating from a medieval monastery. The *précieuses* of the seventeenth century found in them the ideal of platonic love they espoused and practiced. Writers of the Age of Enlightenment who favored outspoken licentiousness found in them the opposite ideal; they were attracted to Heloïse's frank disclosures of sexuality. Later, the Romantics saw in her yet a new and different image. She was their muse. She inspired them because of her immense capacity to lose herself in love. Today our own interpretations are also colored by the ideology of our time, and we find in her text a fertile terrain for the exploration of gender differences. Feminists now search Heloïse's letters for signs of writing that is specific to women.[4] For the present study, the letters provide a unique opportunity to pursue the investigation of exchanges between men and women.

The first four letters contain passionate discourses of defiance as the lovers, reevaluating their tumultuous relationship, narrate the episodes which affected their lives. Readers learn the events which contributed to their tragedy. Abelard seduced his pupil and then married her to satisfy her guardian, but he did not live with her and form a family as social mores demanded; instead, he placed the child born of their illicit love with his sister and, after coercing Heloïse into taking the veil, left her in his abbey and returned to his celibate lifestyle in Paris. Because this was an insult to Heloïse's family, the uncle who was her guardian had Abelard castrated. The couple continued to live separately. Abelard was chased from one abbey to another, while Heloïse remained secluded in the one he had built for himself and lived as a nun against her will. The correspondence, which originated thirteen years after the events, caught up with the present when Heloïse's defiance was exhausted. The last letters, dealing with the present time of writing, contain her mundane reports on convent life and his directives for the management of the convent.

The early letters, however, participate in the arguments of the church and the aristocracy, two groups whose struggle for power centered on matters of marriage. Both had a stake in controlling reproduction, since inheritances were parceled out through family ties, but their edicts of conduct in matters of marriage differed sharply. The illicit romance of Heloïse and Abelard and the birth of their illegitimate child disturbed the order of both groups. The elder aristocrats, who ruled a society that rested on households, each with its own property, had a stake in the survival of the household. Occupying the dominant position as partners in a marriage, they imposed sanctions on wives. They forbade free love, as births resulting from adultery could deprive those related by blood of their inheritances. For their part, the heads of the church were not threatened by such births, since the foundation of their institutions rested on celibacy. This preserved the property of the church from being passed on to the laity. Consequently, legitimate or illegitimate births did not concern them. They did, however, fear the loss of their position as supreme rulers, and they attempted to control the powerful heads of households by showing more indulgence for extra-marital sexuality than for marital sexuality. They were even bold enough to regulate sexuality by condemning its enjoyment within marriage. The sexual act was intended solely to be performed for the purpose of reproduction. More egregiously, they asserted the equality of the sexual partners. Taking a stand against the elders, the church categorically stated its position on marriage: "A man who loves his wife passionately is guilty of adultery."[5] The tragic fate of Heloïse and Abelard is a consequence of these conflicts between the rules of the elders, which guided Heloïse's family, and those of the church, which ultimately governed Abelard.

He challenged the elders' supremacy in words and in deed by behaving as defiantly as the younger members of aristocratic families who were destined never to rule because of their position in the family line. He imitated those roaming bachelor knights whose reputation for meandering and sexual laxity was spread through the romance and the poetry of *courtois* love. Abelard not only seduced Heloïse, he composed poems about his amorous adventures.[6]

This societal context explains why Abelard, a theologian guided by the church's code of morality rather than the rules of the aristocrats, seemed inept at solving social conflicts. When Heloïse's uncle Fulbert confronted him with his responsibility for the child born out of wedlock, Abelard married his niece, acting in strict accordance with the letter of the law. But when the monk insisted on keeping the marriage secret, that is, when he did

38

not affirm to the elders that she was his spouse, he did not obey the intent of their law. He broke the pact which demanded that a man form a household by living with and protecting the woman he received from another man.

Abelard ridiculed her family, and society supported Heloïse's uncle when he had him mutilated. We should note that the death penalty for such behavior as Abelard's was not unusual. Perhaps Fulbert spared the monk's life only to castigate him more severely; one may notice the irony of his choice of punishment, since eunuchs were often hired to serve women in convents. Did he intend to imply that the role of Abelard, the great philosopher, master of his niece, should now be that of her servant? It is plausible that Abelard was aware of the irony of his punishment, as, in his correspondence, he himself refers to the custom of using eunuchs in convents.

Abelard's actions, guided by the rules of the church rather than by those of society, are also better understood in the context of the financial reasons underpinning their separate rules. The church did not operate in a mode of capitalist exchange as much as in a mode of spiritual rights. When, as in a modern marriage, Abelard left Heloïse in the abbey at Argenteuil and returned to his bachelor lifestyle at St. Denis, he broke a social taboo which did not concern him; whereas the social code of conduct called for a man to protect his wife, his called for the direction of her conscience. When he, a theologian, read Heloïse's letters and corresponded with her, he provided spiritual guidance and, consequently, acted in accordance with the church's pronouncements on the duties of ecclesiasts.

For Heloïse, guided by a personal ethic of love, marriage was not essential. She had lived in close contact with Abelard as his pupil before the marriage, and she would have preferred to keep this union based on learning and loving. But ultimately their passionate intellectual exchanges turned to carnal encounters. The solution they chose, taking legitimate vows of marriage without intending to live as a family, displeased all groups. Thirteen years later, the correspondence records their mutual discourse of defiance against the rulers and against each other.

Abelard's *Lettre à un ami,* in the tradition of the exemplum established by St. Augustine, retraces his misfortunes to show an anonymous reader that his trials are nothing in comparison to his own and to teach how repentance (confession) saves even the worst sinner. His tone, however, is argumentative rather than repentant. Through the folkloric imagery of the wolf and the lamb, he confesses and expresses remorse for having deliberately introduced himself as tutor into the household of a brilliant young woman with the intention of seducing her. He then admits that his castration was a proper punishment for his actions—he was struck where he had sinned—but he protests the timing: after the marriage. With rare exceptions of sincere confession and regret, his autobiographical letter follows this pattern. A paradiegesis rather than a confession, this contentious letter generates the mode, confessionary, and the style, argumentative and polemical, of the lovers' correspondence.

Heloïse's Letters: The Ethic of a Courtesan

The first of Heloïse's letters is a reply to the brief autobiographical letter of Abelard, which somehow reaches her in the convent where he has installed her as abbess. All of the bold stories of aberrations confessed in his letter pale in comparison with her audacious disclosures of desire.[7] Well tutored by him in the discourse of polemics, she expresses her vibrant sexuality and her disagreements with the church, with society, and with him, using his own rhetoric. She speaks from his locus and through his language. The function of her epistolary text is twofold: it is both an act of communication with a correspondent and an autobiography. (We may justifiably call it autobiography, since letters were openly read by members of monastic orders.) In the act of communication, she addresses Abelard and defies his definitions of her character and his directives on matters of conscience; in the act of autobiography, she works out her inner struggles.

From Paraclete, which was to have been Abelard's silent retreat, she sings her own praise as a hero, one who, although enclosed in his abbey, preserves her integrity. She recounts the tragedies of her life and affirms her ability to conquer them. She writes of a triply tragic fate. Intellectually superior—her reputation as an outstandingly intelligent pupil is mentioned by Abelard in his autobiographical letter—she no longer has access to the writings of the philosophers she had previously enjoyed as his pupil. Socially perceptive—she had grasped the ramifications of their legal union and warned Abelard that marriage would not assuage her uncle's anger—she is shut away from spaces where communication occurs on a wider scale. Finally, sexually intact, unlike Abelard, she has desires which are unsatisfied.

Heloïse first commiserates with her husband's tale of sorrows, then asserts a wife's right to more positive and current news. Abelard, however, refuses to respond to her present needs, for his orientation is to judgment day and the eternity of Christian time rather than to the living present. He denies Heloïse the rights of a woman of flesh, a wife, and bestows on her instead those of an abbess. At the end of this first letter, he indirectly acknowledges her claim to his flesh by giving her directions for the burial of his corpse.

Since acquiescing to his demands would be false to her own ethic in both her vocation and her marriage, and since she was his student, Heloïse finds her way within and through the ethical frontiers of Abelard's ecclesiastical discourse. She not only uses his own rhetoric, she practices his own method of argument. Although, as Linda S. Kauffman concludes, Heloïse does break "through the tyranny of forms," she does not describe herself as being "utterly and irrevocably in Abelard's power," and her "thralldom" was not so great "that she would willingly have embraced annihilation had Abelard commanded."[8] In the second letter, for instance, Heloïse criticizes Abelard's praise of her as a saintly abbess and as a lamb and states that she is a willing lover. She repeatedly portrays herself as a profane sexual being, not as a virtuous, self-sacrificing heroine. She challenges the very symbolism of the ecclesiastical robe he has made her wear: "C'est un mot de vous qui m'a fait prendre l'habit monastique, mais non la vocation divine."[9] (It is a word from you which has made me take the monastic habit.) She points out that it does not represent (or symbolize) anything for her.

The inherent conflict between his orders and her beliefs surfaces in violent imagery. Enclosed in his sacred abbey, she calls herself chained to God. She particularly protests against the socially acceptable solutions he has imposed on her. Although convent life filled the basic needs of women, and many deliberately embraced seclusion, she was not a free agent in the decision to spend her life in confinement.[10] Her letters well document the condition of wives and nuns, but hers, in fact, is worse. Abelard's abbess is a victim of the institutions which bind her body and soul. Her body legally belongs to her husband, who confines her, and her soul to Jesus, who, according to monks and priests—and Abelard is one—dictates that his daughters swear to devote their intellectual pursuits to his teachings.

In Heloïse's letters repudiating Abelard's affirmations and asserting her own dissensions, we find patterns of nondifferentiation specific to women's heroism. For instance, the status of separate identity, which is essential to Abelard's autobiographical narrative, is challenged in both the address and the text of her letters to him. Preserving her integrity and the necessary bond to him through a system of relations, favoring continuity and contiguity rather than division, her self-representations *contain* differences; dependent yet free, she preserves her individual ethic. Although she recognizes herself to be a prisoner within his marriage, his abbey, and his discourse, her persistence in naming herself in her own way rather than echoing him informs him that, within these confines, she adheres to her own principles. While he addresses her as an abbess, she, in an Amazonian show of determination, stands her ground and rejects that title. Neither her address nor her text accords with his nomenclature of her. Her first letter immediately challenges his authority and asserts her mastery of relationships:

A son maître, ou plutôt à son père; à son époux, ou plutôt à son frère;
sa servante, ou plutôt sa fille; son épouse, ou plutôt sa soeur; à
Abélard, Héloïse. (Address to First Letter)

To her master, or rather to her father; to her husband, or rather her brother; his servant, or rather his daughter; his wife, or rather his sister; to Abelard, Heloïse.

Wavering between ties that are familial and societal, the identification finally comes to rest on two individual yet linked names: Abelard and Heloïse. Whereas his letter praises her as abbess of his convent, hers omits any reference to her position in a social hierarchy. This address foreshadows the text of the letter, which also functions to destabilize the relations maintaining order. The body of the letter is even more subversive, for it rejects all legal and sacred titles and replaces them with a different relation:

> Bien que le nom d'épouse paraisse et plus sacré et plus fort, un autre a toujours été plus doux à mon coeur, celui de votre maîtresse, ou même, laissez-moi le dire, celui de votre concubine et de votre fille de joie. (First Letter, IV, 84)

> Although the name of spouse seems more sacred and strong [*fort*], another has always been more sweet [*doux*] to my heart, that of mistress, or even, may I tell you, that of your concubine and *fille de joie*.

Here, as elsewhere, the banal language of lovers reveals a willingness to risk loss of autonomy in love: "Je ne me suis rien réservé de moi-même, rien que le droit de me faire toute à vous" (First Letter, VI, 89). (I have reserved nothing of myself, nothing but the right to make myself totally yours.) Yet, in this declaration, the repetition of "nothing" associated with "self" is an indication of Heloïse's awareness of the risk inherent in the search for approval by one man, the loss of self-determination that occurs in heroic self-immolation.

Addressing the question of separate identity, the first letter narrates both a heroine and a hero, a woman without fear of disapproval who situates herself within the bond of lovers, outside the limits of society and church. But these Amazonian phrases affirming her participation in the sexual act are followed by contradictory admissions of masochistic self-flagellation. Although this conduct was acceptable in medieval convents, today we see in it symptoms of the extreme conflicts suffered by Heloïse.

The second letter is named the letter of her lament, but a close reading shows it to be an elaboration of the first letter of protest. Whereas in the first she blamed Abelard for seducing her and then subjecting her to the austerities of the monastic profession, in the second she takes responsibility for her own sexuality and for violating herself. She admits that when her sexual appetites surface in dreams, when the "needles of the flesh" assault her while she sleeps, she awakes and, becoming conscious, mortifies herself. We might ask, however, if the confession of sin (the dream) and atonement (the flagellation) constitute a pretext to narrate, through the conventional sexual imagery of the Middle Ages, a female hero, a nocturnal double of the diurnal, obedient nun Abelard praises. This interpretation seems to be supported by passages where Heloise answers negatively to Abelard's exhortations to prayer. He counsels her to exchange the sins of Eve for the saintdom of Mary in accordance with the new dialectics.[11] But her heterodox reply is that she desires him more than God: "C'est à vous bien plus qu'à lui-même que j'ai le désir de plaire" (Third Letter, V, 114). (It is you much more than him that I have the desire to please.) This idolatry both reasserts her sexuality and rejects the Christian ethic by which he invites her to sublimate desire into the spiritual, and therefore platonic, love of God.

Heloïse also contradicts Abelard when, in his autobiographical letter, he assumes all the blame for their sins. She insists on her participation: "J'ai eu le courage, sur un mot, de me perdre moi-même" (First Letter, IV, 83). (I had the courage, in a word, to lose myself.) Originating from within the boundaries of Abelard's sacred abbey and within the legitimacy of matrimony, both letters place Heloïse outside the sacrament of marriage and the hierarchy of feudal relations. Naming herself a courtesan rather than a wife, she indicates her independence and her wish to live without society's blessing. Through a variety of associations with Abelard, she disconnects the divisions which create social hierarchies and then reconnects herself through her body. Bold acknowledgments of unruly sexual impulses call attention to the dishonesty of Abelard's definition of her as a saintly nun and insert a woman's *jouissance* into the language of liturgy.

Abelard's Letters: The Chivalric Code of Ethics

In Abelard's confessions we recognize tropes from numerous genres: Homeric poems, *chansons de gestes, courtois* poetry, French romance, and exemplum. Let us first consider a text dating from Abelard's own century, Chrétien de Troyes's somewhat atypical romance, *Perceval,* or the quest for the Holy Grail. This poem opens on two simultaneous events: as Perceval is leaving home for his quest, his mother collapses at the gate; she falls, and he leaves in such a hurry that he does not notice. He never turns back to look and remains unaware of her death until the last episodes. Perceval's failure, in the first lines of the poem, to notice his mother's death is a strange occurrence which merits our attention. This incident also highlights the persistence of Homer's heroic tropes. Perceval and Ulysses travel away from and back to a maternal locus.

Not only does the story of Perceval's quest for knowledge of the world ignore the mother's death at the start, it ridicules her until the last

43

chapters. The young hero encounters trouble in the world of men whenever he acts according to her advice. For example, she advised him to seek God and visit holy places, but he is so naive that he mistakes knights for spirits and tents for churches. Yet if at first it seems that his mother's words fail to represent reality—if they are ridiculous and insignificant—the more aware, the less ignorant, and the more reflective he becomes, the more significance they acquire. While the early passages of knightly ventures where her counsels backfire are particularly amusing, later passages are somber in tone. Eventually the text transcends the misrepresentations of parody and affirms the appropriateness of his mother's emphasis on the spiritual. At the outset, Perceval was taught by knights to laugh at his mother's advice, but in the concluding scenes he realizes that she had not misrepresented the purpose of the quest. If at first his search for knowledge was directed to things of the world, if he mistook a knight for a god and a tent for a church, in the end he learns to be introspective and perceives that the inner quest (for knowledge of the sacred) is the one which has significance.

Perceval's quest for the Holy Grail and Abelard's search for knowledge, like Ulysses' voyage, reach their denouement when the hero enters a female locus. Perceval's adventures end shortly after the discovery of the Holy Grail, Abelard's manuscript concludes with a letter instructing Heloïse to care for his corpse, and Ulysses' journey is completed shortly after his return to Penelope's room. This trope is more obscure in the unfinished romance, but it is there. The mysterious Grail, a fantastic container from which Perceval receives nourishment, has distinct maternal connotations. It is carried by a maiden and contains a nurturing substance for the hero's body and spirit. The object in the maiden's hands escapes description. Its sacred meaning is only alluded to by preterition, as is Penelope's weaving, for it is not signifiable in language.

Although the heroic voyager seeks to leave behind the maternal, he inevitably returns to it. Shortly after the episode of the Grail, near the end of the unfinished romance, Perceval is reminded by a holy hermit that he must return home to pay homage to his deceased mother. It is here that the tone of the poem shifts from the parodic (misrepresentative) to the serious (representative or iconographic). The maternal, both dreaded and desired, is a mystical, sacred presence of beginnings and endings from which the protagonist withdraws in the quest for autonomy and to which he returns never to speak again. Thus language spoken and written by men and representing women as unrepresentable is a heroic trope. It is the paradox which creates the tension fundamental to the central narration of the quest motif.

Such associations are tautologies, propositions which only remain true by virtue of their form. The narrative of the heroic quest follows the Lacanian formula that man speaks because the phallus, the symbol of his sex, has made him a man. This formula, originating in a mind overdependent on sexual determination, collapses on itself. Its provides a strikingly workable framework for the analysis of Abelard's search for truth in language.

The medieval lovers' disagreements regarding their relationship appear in the very address of their letters. In the tradition of the exemplum, women—Abelard's wife and his mother—are not part of the hierarchy within which he constitutes himself as heroic. His first address distances Heloïse from himself by placing Jesus as intermediary between them: "A Héloïse sa très chère soeur en Jésus-Christ / Abélard son frère en Jésus-Christ" (91). (To Heloïse his very dear sister in Jesus-Christ, Abelard her brother in Jesus-Christ.) And the second one reads: "A l'épouse de Jésus-Christ, le serviteur du même Jésus-Christ" (117). (To the spouse of Jesus-Christ, the servant of the same Jesus-Christ.) Also, his mother's name surfaces only once in the long autobiographical letter, and this in a singular reference which leaves her and himself outside the familial context of closeness. Abelard writes that his tender mother, Lucy, presses him to return to Brittany for a forthcoming ceremony which will join her to a religious order. His inclusion of the maternal presence in this discourse seems justified by the religious context. He is motivated to run to her side to attend a religious ceremony.

In the first passage of the autobiographical letter, Abelard distinctly claims allegiance to a paternal territory conquered, named, and ruled by men: "Je suis originaire d'un bourg situé à l'entrée de la Bretagne, à huit milles environ de Nantes, vers l'est, et appelé le Palais" (*Lettre à un ami*, 15). (I come from a burg located on the border of Brittany, approximately eight miles from Nantes, towards the east, and called the Palais.) There follow the names and professions of men, the father (a soldier), the master who took the father's place (a tutor), and, finally, Abelard himself (a philosopher). This divisive method of introduction contrasts with Heloïse's inclusive address. Abelard names places and people to create a hierarchy of differences, while she, in a less definite and more indiscrete manner, names herself in the complexity of the roles which bind her. In the tradition of the Homeric formula, Abelard initially identifies through distinctions, first associating himself with his village by naming it, thereby distinguishing it and himself from other names of places. He then gives his profession, placing his name at the top of the hierarchy of categories from soldier to tutor to philosopher. But Heloïse refuses to situate herself in relation to her institution or its hierarchy. She never calls herself by her title, abbess.

As was the case for St. Augustine in his *Confessions*, the most important developmental step, the acquisition of knowledge, removes Abelard from the maternal sphere and inserts him into the paternal world. The father first guides this gender-based quest, and his bond to his son—to be severed later—is formed through studies. Abelard writes: "Plus je lui étais cher, plus il s'occupa de mon instruction'' (*Lettre à un ami*, 16). Here the term "cher" has a double meaning, dear and worthy. Intellectual pursuits initiate the son into the competitive patriarchal system of religious orders, and he strives for success within that milieu: "De mon côté, plus j'avançais avec rapidité dans l'étude, plus je m'y attachais avec ardeur" (*Lettre à un ami*, 16). (For my part, the more quickly I advanced in my studies, the more ardently I became attached to them.) He is quick to grasp the importance of words in the universe of theology, and this propels him into the manly domain of verbal debates. His love of discussion and his passion for scholastic competition are acknowledged by scholars, who have contributed to his reputation as a heroic (and tragic) figure in the history of philosophy.

With slight variations, Abelard's definition of heroism follows the code of manhood and chivalry of the medieval exemplum and the *chansons de geste*, two genres which, in turn, are modeled on the Homeric quest. Abelard encodes his superior intellectual agility in debating metaphysical questions in the language of the soldier's physical prowess in combat, stating that he has traded "the triumphs of battle" for the "assaults of discussion." (*Lettre à un ami*, 16). He conquers in the name of God and religion as knights do in the name of king and country.

Yet a woman, a *pre*-text, waits in a spatio-temporal dimension other than the measurable space and time of the narrative-quest. Pre-dating its very beginning, she will be disclosed when it ends. Heloïse represents, as did the *dame*, the Virgin Mary who mysteriously gave birth to Christ and who reclaimed his corpse.[12] A presence signified by its absence, woman *is* a place of origins which the hero vacates in the search for identity in the paternal order, where, by means of fantastic deeds, he emphasizes his maleness. A comparison of spatial imagery in Abelard's text reveals obvious similarities to Homer's text. Women are configured as major threats to the quest. Charybdis, Minerva, and Delilah are among the legendary female characters whom Abelard uses as personifications of the obstacles to his career.

This medieval philosopher is preoccupied with the symbolic rather than human reality. As Lief Grane remarks in his study of Abelard's philosophy, "the dialectician is not concerned with the *things* of the world but with the words by which we indicate these things. Logic is therefore the science of words; that is to say, linguistic logic."[13] Abelard reversed the arguments of Hegelian dialectics before its time. His practice of formal logic led him to argue that mind ruled over matter, for his traumatic castration could only be dealt with through repression. Consequently he writes of his castration: "Les atteintes portées à ma renommée étaient pour moi une torture plus grande que la mutilation de mon corps" (*Lettre à un ami*, 67). (The damage to my renown was for me a greater torture than the mutilation of my body.) This vision accords with the Lacanian pronouncement relating sex to language. Abelard, having lost what literally represents his maleness and symbolically his claim to the verb, comes to doubt the substance of his utterances. His concern about sexual identity is often quite transparent, as in the following passage from the autobiographical letter:

> Cependant, tandis que j'étais, de corps, caché en ce lieu, ma renommée parcourait le monde et le remplissait de ma parole, comme ce personnage de la fable appelé Echo, sans doute parce qu'il est doué d'un organe puissant, bien qu'il n'y ait rien dessous. (*Lettre à un ami*, 60)

> However, while my body was hidden in this place [Paraclete] my reputation spread throughout the entire world and filled it with my words, as did this character from the fable called Echo, doubtless because he was endowed with a powerful organ, although there was nothing beneath.

The synecdoche of the organ for the man is better interpreted in linguistic terms. Abelard views language, "ma parole" or the symbolic, as the signifier of a signified, "un organe puissant" or the phallus, whose referent is absent in Echo. Indeed, there is no substance to Echo's language, since she simply repeats other people's words. In Abelard's interpretation, Echo's voice is empty of meaning because it lacks the authority of the phallus. Echo, in a word, is a female archetype. It is easily understood that Abelard's view of himself as a speaker is diminished because his voice—no doubt slightly higher and feminine due to the castration—has lost the proof of his masculinity. Of course, his concern with regard to his maleness is understandable. Given the extraordinary circumstances which brought him to the situations described in the letter, he is naturally disturbed about the coherence of his masculine body image. It is also understood that his insecure sense of sexual identity may well exacerbate his tendency to control and to maintain an absolute separateness between men and women.

What concerns the critic is how Abelard projects this "reality" into the symbolic. He claims above all to have been persecuted for his philosophical views, yet much of his polemical activities center on his sexual attraction to Heloïse. His letter to a friend discloses how sexuality underlies the very choice of the topics he debates. He tells how, early in his career, his use of the new method of dialectic to question the canons of the church meets with fierce resistance in conservative circles. Later, he states that his betrayal of Heloïse's family entices his detractors to even more violent reactions. He is driven from one church, one school, or one abbey to another. When he preaches, his enemies question his right to speak in church and evict him. When he writes on the almightiness of God, he is forced to burn his book with his own hands. Significantly, all of these maledictions result from his seduction of Heloïse. His philosophical opinions, without his sins, would be mere verbal debates. Ecclesiasts react to his iconoclastic pronouncements on God's ability to engender himself by chastising him. For a castrated monk, his is an astonishingly controversial topic, and one for which he was understandably much ridiculed. One can imagine why his detractors attacked the passage which shifted concern for physical impotence into metaphysical cogitations.

Abelard's preoccupation with the symbolic and his concordant neglect of physical needs, his repression and projection, resurface in competitive games with language which complicate an already difficult position. A new conflict arises when he projects his need for comfort into the name of his abbey. He calls it Paraclete, the Latin word for consolation, and for the third member of the Trinity, the Holy Spirit. This is the weakest member of the Trinity; it is often suggested that he represents a feminine spirit. Abelard's persecutors object to this name, claiming that the church only permits a religious place to be named after the entire Trinity, or after God alone, never after the Holy Spirit alone. Abelard writes in the heroic mode when describing other conflicts with authority—having to burn his book, for instance—but he discloses his emotional needs in a defensive mode. His asking for consolation is a feminine trait, a weakness which needs to be justified. In order to appear less weak, he quotes authoritative sources: St. Jerome and St. Paul stated that great men from Solomon to Christ had many women as companions.[14]

His cerebral nature leads Abelard to delve into his cultural heritage for rhetorical figures. To describe the scene of his seduction, he conjures up strong animalistic imagery from the *fabliaux* and oxymorons from romance poetry. He is the wolf and she the lamb, and his blows are more tender than balm. To support his own behavior with Heloïse, he also draws on the rhetoric of Christianity and the autobiographical narratives of St. Augustine. There he finds examples of male dominance and female submission. The life story of the saint, a renowned example of Christianity's disintegrated view of self as a two-part being, flesh and spirit, associates the genesis of weaknesses of the flesh with women and strength of the spirit—intellectual achievements—with men. St. Augustine first narrates how he was conceived and nourished in sin by his mother, then how he was freed from base carnal instincts after her death. In a desperate attempt to chase away any remnants of a maternal legacy, St. Augustine claims to have taught himself to speak.[15] As Telemachus told Penelope, language is man's business.

Abelard has to maintain his reputation as dominant hero. When he likens himself to St. Augustine, the repentant sinner of great renown, he elevates himself. When he publishes passages of Heloïse's letters which derogate him, he aggrandizes himself as a stoic. Even when he leaves intact passages where she chastises him, he preserves his reputation as a hero. For example, he transcribes passages where she rebuffs him for his reluctance to relate to her in any dimension but the spiritual:

> C'est la concupiscence plutot que la tendresse qui vous a attaché à moi, c'est l'ardeur des sens plutôt que l'amour; et voilà pourquoi, vos désirs une fois éteints, toutes les démonstrations qu'ils inspiraient se sont évanouies avec eux. (First Letter, 83)

> It is concupiscence rather than tenderness which attached you to me, the ardor of senses rather than love, and that is why, once your desires where extinct, all the demonstrations which they inspired expired with them.

Yet these statements against himself do not tarnish his reputation, just as a lack of affection, rather than diminishing the prestige of a hero, elevates it. Often presented through someone else's deeds or words, the need for tenderness is nonetheless problematic. There exist no discourses for Abelard to emulate when writing to Heloïse other than the one he has learned. It strictly provides him with the vocabulary to praise her for controlling her sexual urges and for obediently performing her duties as a nun.

According to his transcription of the correspondence, she is the one who states the anti-feminist position of the fathers of the church on women's need for guidance. Several quotations from liturgy inserted in her letters jar with the general tone of her own phrases; one may speculate that he added these quotations when he copied the correspondence into the manuscript, for they echo the propositions contained in his autobiographical letter on the place of women by men's side.[16] Such is the quotation from St. Jerome, reporting that Socrates, during a quarrel with Xantippe, was showered by her with a "liquide impure" (*Lettre à un ami*, 27). The excessive number of these quotations indicates a defensive posture. They include references from Proverbs, the Nazarenes, Delilah, David, Job, Seneca, the Old Testament, Ely and Elissa, St. Jerome, the Pharisees, the Saudi Arabians, the Essenes, St. Augustine, and Socrates. The list even includes a woman philosopher, Aspasy, who, during marital therapy, advised Zenophon and his wife not to ensure their marriage through physical attraction but through mutual admiration of the soul's purity. Writing Heloïse's letters, ignoring her ethic of love and elaborating his own (mutual admiration of the soul's purity), Abelard, like Narcissus, gazes at this image of himself and, reading it, hears the echo of his own ethic.

Nonetheless, on three occasions Abelard's desire for women did motivate his choice of a discourse improper for a monk: when he composed and sang love poems (there is a brief mention of these in the autobiographical letter); when he transcribed the profane letters of Heloïse into a manuscript; and when he left instructions to have his corpse secretly transported to the abbey at Paraclete. The noncompetitive aspect of maternal language temporarily delivered him from the polemics of patriarchal discourse. Abelard sought repose in female presence but, as it threatened his reputation—and possibly his faith—in a paternalistic religion, he had to keep it secret. The poems were not transcribed, Heloïse's letters were manipulated, and the last letter was placed in the manuscript by someone else.

Abelard's search for consolation on earth casts doubts on his faith. It belies his belief that a peaceful eternity would be found in God's powerful, paternal presence. Otherwise why would he leave this "secret" document instructing Heloïse to preserve his remains in his personally consecrated place, the controversial Paraclete, where his corpse would be joined to hers in death. His instructions that they be physically reunited contravene the words in his letters which call for her to join him in the purity of the soul. What excuse was there for a philosopher to have a woman by his side? This was indeed *"impropre."*[17]

Exchanging Words for Things

The correspondence testifies to what happens in communications between men and women. It demonstrates women's problematic relation to language and writing. As we have seen in the first chapters of this study, ancient myths conveyed through an oral tradition are less exclusive of women than those communicated through written narratives. When they were oral they were unstable, still subject to a multitude of interpretations. We must remember that the most fundamental stories which captured the common imagination pre-dated Homeric and Judeo-Christian polarizations of the sacred and the profane. Writing was a prerogative of the gods, as Ahura's story reminds us. When men began to write, when they appropriated this prerogative for themselves, their polarizing tendencies caused them to exclude women from this activity. Similarly, monks, who were the first to codify French literature, expunged women's own language from texts—just as they cleansed abbeys after their visits.

It has been a generally accepted precept that, as Terence Hawkes states, language acts as a great conservative force.[18] One must agree, for one sees proof of this principle in the way present deconstructing theorists continue to obsess about woman being the opposite, excluded because of her otherness. But we may ask why, as Catherine Belsley does.[19] When we interrogate the letters of Heloïse, we begin to locate the origins of women's alterity (Heloïse's) in men's (Abelard's) narratives. In his letters Abelard calls her an abbess to separate himself from her. He has to give her an identity other than lover, for to do otherwise would implicate him in a relation with the impure, where differences are abolished. But in *her* letter she insists on naming herself his courtesan. In so doing she points to the cause of his exclusion of her: the impropriety of women's sexuality (her difference) in the language of a monk.

Although posterity has cherished the image of Heloïse as the docile, loving wife, a new image, that of a rebel, emerges in her language. When Abelard writes that God predestined her to heaven by giving her the name of Heloïse, a derivation of *Heloïm* (God), she refutes this definition and, embracing other ideals, unnames and renames herself according to a variety of relations and experiences based on maternal and sisterly female specificity. She affirms her ability to recount and conquer the tragedies of her life. And later, when Abelard, neglecting to acknowledge her as a woman superior in her capacity to assert her love and to disagree with him, asks her to exchange the sins of Eve for the sanctity of Mary, she refuses.[20] In these letters Heloïse is Amazonian. She stands apart, her conduct guided by her own ethic rather than that of Christianity. If she responds obediently to Abelard's coercive restrictions and agrees to take the vows, and if she submits to his regulation of her physical activities in the abbey, she does not accept his control of her consciousness. That is, she claims for herself the right to transmit her own tale, to narrate in her own words, the story of her desire. Heloïse replies angrily to statements which becloud her definition of herself as a woman of flesh, informing Abelard in the straightforward language of women troubadours that she would rather be a courtesan than a saint.[21] These assertions of a desiring, sexual woman subvert Abelard's symbolic order and desecrate the sacred abbey from which they emanate.

Like the Greek hero who views the Amazon in his territory as a combatant, Abelard views Heloïse's love and her letters as threats and seeks to subjugate her. He incarcerates her and then violates her text by revising it to insert echoes of his own words. Ironically, his polemical approach to texts tricks him, for he leaves enough of Heloïse's dissent for the reader to know her.

Posthumously, the first four letters of the manuscript radicalize the lovers' relationship, and the last letters neutralize it. Both correspondents clearly acknowledge the power of texts to guide events, alter the course of their lives within the monastic communities to which they belonged, and, after their deaths, give dignity to these unusual lives. Their common text is radical when Heloïse refers to the arrival of Abelard's letters as blows and when, commenting on his love poems, he declares that the pen is hardier than the mouth: "La plume est plus hardie que la bouche" (*Lettre à un ami*, 27). It is also radical when Heloïse rejects his definition of her as a saintly nun and renames herself not only a woman of flesh, but one outside the margin of

51

society, a courtesan. But it is neutral when, at his insistence, she writes of mundane matters—consultations and directions concerning the disciplines of monastic life—in the last letters. Heloïse confronted Abelard, but he dodged and moved the interaction to a religious communication. When she accepted the injunction to pray for him in return for his advice on the comfort and well-being of the nun's daily life, she capitulated and provided a noncompetitive way to dialogue. When the narratives of desire that polarized the lovers into female and male writers were abolished in the last letters, when the erotic discourse vanished, Heloïse and Abelard were no longer heroic; she was merely stoic and he mildly despotic. In the calm of Paraclete, the eye of the storm had finally come to rest.

The two discourses, side by side in the manuscript, offer a unique opportunity to interrogate the similarities, differences, and specificities in the writings of women and men about themselves, and to see what happens in the exchange between them. We notice that these stories of heroism are paradigmatic of ancient Homeric narratives. Abelard's abbey contained Heloïse within a space delineated by him and ruled by his time. The rhythm of life at the abbey was dictated by him. As in the Homeric poem, when the storyteller returns to his sacred female space, the narrative ends. Abelard has also built what Gilbert Durand calls a mythological space to "recreate the womb which he does not possess," and he returns to it in the end.[22] A striking feature of Abelard's story is that, unlike Homer's text, which never tells the content of Penelope's weaving, Abelard's includes a transcription of the woman's text. Nevertheless, we notice that, although Abelard's inclusion of a woman's words in a manuscript gives Heloïse worth as a writer, his manipulation of her text to insert his own quotations ultimately represents her as his Echo.

If we juxtapose Heloïse's narratives with those of the ancient Egyptian princess, we note that like Ahura, she seeks knowledge with her life companion. In the end, the quest for love and the quest for knowledge complement each other. Heloïse, like Ahura, uses her superior communicative skills to reunite herself with her loved one.

Heloïse's request to exchange words for things most accurately predicts the medieval lovers' legacy. Hers is a thing, a sign: the single tombstone which concretely signals the union of their remnants underneath. Readers who visit Père Lachaise cemetery in Paris see in the tombs a sign attesting to an extra-textual reality; the lovers are joined in the sepulcher because of the requests she left in her last letters. Those who read the correspondence see how Abelard completed his share of the pact, incorporating her letters, her words, into a manuscript which lives on as the prototype of written exchanges between women and men, autobiographical or fictive, from the seventeenth-century memorialists to Rousseau's *La Nouvelle Héloïse*.

52

What Susan Rubin Suleiman says about Monique Wittig and the "violence" she does to "mythical and historical memory" could be said of Heloïse. Her writing is also "necessary and salutary, in the face of centuries of [similar] violence directed against women's words, language, and memory by patriarchal institutions and patriarchal writing."[23] Wittig belongs to a tradition of subversion which dates back to Heloïse and the Middle Ages. The present analysis demonstrates how Heloïse's unabashed expressions of profane love in the dark, masochistic ages of Christianity spoke loudly against men's downgrading through elevation—that is, their symbolical placement of women's bodies in some impossible elsewhere, in a sacred ineffability, outside language. Heloïse's bold discourse of profane love subverted these images of women she had read about in canonized texts. We may venture to say that she used the profane words she learned from the confessions of sin and, encoding them in a text, configured the constantly erased weaving of Penelope's story. In effect, both texts constitute disclosures of profane, vibrant, and sexually alive women's bodies.

Mystical Quests and Gynocentric Discourse

First person narratives which refer to individuals whose existence is recorded historically—memoirs and letters, for instance—optimize the scope of critical inquiries into the degree to which the sexual identities of writers and readers guide the esthetic of rhetoric. When Guyon and Bourignon, seventeenth-century memorialists, directly address their directors of conscience, they imply their confessors' double role: guiding their conduct in "real" life as well as shaping their choice of rhetoric. Taking into consideration both the external influence and the literary tropes by which they create heroic characters adds breadth to a gender-specific study of ethics and esthetics.

Whether these memorialists intended to have their life stories read by the general public is but one of several questions which cannot be ascertained. Since they were aware that their readers shared information about the private and public events which they mentioned, they did not supply any details. This, together with the fact that the works of women authors are not included in most scholars' literary backgrounds, resulted in their being neglected. So little is known about these women and their writings that all we can certify is that we read books bearing their names, written for their confessors, and referring to events of their times. To fill this gap in our cultural heritage, the present chapter will include summaries of key passages and provide contextual background.

A Male Implied Reader: The Confessor in the Memoirs of Antoinette Bourignon and Jeanne Guyon

Let us first contemplate the role of the director of conscience in the lives of seventeenth-century women of the French aristocracy. He was a major influence, and the memorialists were aware of this. He was selected by the rulers of families to serve as confessor and spiritual guide, and devout women of the highest nobility could call him to their sides for consultation any time of day or night. While his official assignment was to guide their spiritual life, he was also often consulted for advice on major decisions not related to religion. He was, in fact, a sort of private psychoanalyst and counselor who exercised enormous influence in all matters. Although his official duties were to promote women's spiritual well-being, he might intercede for them in cases of conflict with the rulers and, siding with them, jeopardize his career. On the other hand, he could also collude with the family and act against the well-being of his charges—confessors occasionally sacrificed the women's interests when pressured to do so. Hence, at the side of a woman of such high standing as Guyon, this man sometimes tipped the balance of power between the aristocrats and the clergy, and he could be manipulated to do so by what she wrote in her memoirs.

It is no accident that Bourignon and Guyon gave their confessors' advice priority over their family's. Life events which show that their mothers turned away from them are, in fact, the subject of the opening chapters of their memoirs. These narratives demonstrate the absence of gynocentric tropes in their discourse. Misfits in their families and unhappy in the roles society imposed on them, Bourignon and Guyon turned to religion for solace and embraced the invitation to mysticism tendered by the Christian ethic of their time. Bourignon, a hermit within her own home, writes that she locks herself in her room to avoid parental tyranny and there, in solitude, kneeling at her prie-dieu night and day, conjures up blissful visions of the eternal life of the soul. Likewise, Guyon first writes that she is neglected in her youth by her parents, that she is then mismatched in marriage, and that she encounters even more difficulties with her husband's abusive mother, who incites the domestics against her. Such familial problems explain the women's turning away from their kinsmen. As a means of expressing her dissatisfaction, Guyon chooses solitude and spends the greater part of her day in silent prayer.

In the absence of maternal mentors, both women lament their missing womanhood by addressing themselves directly to the Judeo-Christian God in the discourse of their confessors. But obviously neither expects her writings to be made public. The Virgin Mary never speaks in public. They state in their prefaces that they are writing in answer to requests by their confessors and under their direction. Each supports this statement in the text itself by addressing him directly. The memoirs reproduce the *examen de conscience*, a preparatory step in the ritual of Roman Catholic auricular confession of sins. This process, not unlike the rituals of archaic cultures, erases the guilt of past events. Confession purifies the sinner from guilt in the present and assures a place in the eternal time of the soul's life. While the periodic ceremonies (usually a cathartic dance) of archaic societies were initiated to erase the past (history), the Christian ritual of the confession is purported to be registered in a great book, preserving a record of the past for eternity. The penance assigned at the confession compensates for the sins, and it is recorded, along with the sins, in an imaginary balance sheet for judgment day. Medieval Christian autobiographies (the first one is St. Augustine's *Confessions*) reproduce these ritualized accounts of suffering to prove to the greatest mediator, God, that the writers' repentance entitles them to eternal paradise. It follows that the principal characters of narratives of repentance are heroic above all in their ability to sin and do penance, with an emphasis on the latter. Their confessions testify to the extraordinary stoicism of Jansenism. The memorialists forego pleasures of the flesh and even extend their Jansenist inclinations to the point of deliberately seeking painful experiences.

Bourignon's and Guyon's stories of heroism participate in this spiritual tradition centering on misfortune. To emphasize their trials for the directors of conscience, both relate events of their lives dating back to their birth. (The first quote is from Bourignon and the second from Guyon.)

> Lorsque je vins au monde, j'estois si defigurée que ma mère pensoit d'avoir enfanté un monstre: a cause que j'avois des cheveux noirs jusques aux yeux lesquels couvroient tout mon front; & ma lévre d'enhaut estoit attachée a mon nez, & par ainsi la bouche ouverte: en sorte qu'on me cacha quelques six sémaines: mais aprés ce temps les cheveux tomberent d'eux-mémes, & ma levre fut détachée de mon nez par un chirurgien.[1]

> I was born so disfigured that my mother thought she had given birth to a monster. My upper lip was attached to my nose, so that my mouth was open. I was hidden for a few weeks, during which my hair fell off and my lip was detached by a surgeon.

> I was born, then, not at the full time, for my mother had such a terrible fright that she brought me into the world in the eighth month. . . . I no sooner received life than I was on the point of losing it. As soon as I was baptized, they . . . saw I had at the bottom of the back a tumor of prodigious size. Incisions were made in it, and the wound was so great the surgeon could introduce his entire hand.[2]

Both memoirs are written within a familial milieu, a social context, and an intellectual climate which the literary critic must consider. When we question why the women turn to men for guidance at an age when young women are usually guided by mothers who either teach how to adapt to societal demands or support them if they rebel, we see that this most vital formative bond is lacking. Both texts begin with tales of neglect by mothers who are repulsed by infants born imperfect, and both turn the deleterious lack of contact with the maternal figure into a heroic trope. They exaggerate the traits which have caused them to be rejected. Bourignon first states that her mother had an early dislike for her because she was born deformed and that she could not love her "comme elle faisoit les autres enfans, qui estoient tous blons & agreables" (143) (as she loved the other children who were all blond and nice). Abused by her mother and her older sister during her childhood, she tells of playing with her doll alone in her room. There she begins to imagine a divided self: "J'etois combattuë interieurement" (148). (I was in interior combat against myself.) She relates bouts with anorexia and catatonia in her youth and describes how she later overcomes these tendencies and even enjoys men telling her she is beautiful. She claims that her father prefers her to all his other children. Nevertheless, when he promises her in marriage to someone she dislikes, she silently retreats to her room. Alone at night, she secretly fashions a hermit's robe and hides it in her hope chest, along with a man's hat and a pair of old shoes. When the time is propitious for her, she disguises herself and escapes.

Guyon narrates similar episodes of neglect and negligence: "My mother, who did not much love girls, neglected me a little, and abandoned me too much to the care of women who neglected me also" (*Autobiography,* 9). During the arranged marriage, her mother-in-law and her servants also humiliate her. Finally she reports a cycle of mistrust which comes full circle when her own daughter spies on her.

Both women subscribe to the Christian doctrine which divides human experience into profane and sacred categories of body and soul and, correspondingly, segregates the text of the self into separate temporal categories, with the lower order consisting of the present moment on earth and the higher one equivalent to eternity in paradise. Events related to the body occurring in the profane time of the community are trivialized in favor of spiritual ones in the eternity of heaven. This disdain for the material body, matched by a fanatical search for solitude, attests to a complex reality; these morbid, extraordinary acts, these oddities, are the stuff of their brand of anti-heroism.

The lack of acceptance and guidance from the one who is the same, the mother, leaves these women unprepared for sexual awakening, and when it happens they refuse to accept it. Bourignon runs away from home rather than marry, and Guyon, who marries the man chosen for her and bears children, denies any physical sensation during the sexual act. The spirit of God always being with her disappoints and even infuriates her spouse: "He often said to me, 'One clearly sees you never lose the presence of God' " (*Autobiography,* 91).

Guyon intends to reach the pure state of quietism by killing the senses, for, once they are dead, there is "no longer need for mortification" (*Autobiography,* 82). She trains herself to have no "self-love" and, through lacerations, prepares her body to be the indwelling—a sort of Abelardian Paraclete—where she will live the life of the soul. No display of material concern must be seen on the exterior of a body which contains a sacred space. Struggling with the temptations of vanity, constantly surveying and abnegating the body, she takes extreme measures, such as having perfectly healthy teeth removed and willfully exposing herself to smallpox to scar her face. She takes pride in blazing oddities which proclaim her determination.

Guyon and Bourignon suppress any susceptibility to physical pleasures even before it arises. Judged ugly and unacceptable by the first potential female mentor, each grows more and more divided against herself. Undesirable to the one who is the same, they revolt against their own sex and turn, first to fathers, then to husbands, and finally to confessors, who promote sexual abstinence. At which level of political consciousness these memorialists understood that laws concerning marriage were the result of men's wish to control their sexuality cannot be determined, since no explicit statements to this effect exist in the texts, but self-control over their flesh was interpreted by the elders as an assertion of free will which threatened the very foundation of their hegemony. Neither Bourignon nor Guyon escaped the consequences of their abstinence. Fathers expressed in public, verbal orders their wish to limit their daughters' field of action until a proper marriage could be arranged. The confessors' efforts, on the other hand, were covert and more insidious, for it was their thought processes which they controlled. The first concern of the religious mentors to whom the memorialists turned for guidance was not to lead them to a satisfactory acceptance of their femaleness. To monks, who traditionally viewed women's sexuality as an aberration, narratives of self-inflicted pain were perhaps welcome (although penitents were advised not to harm themselves physically). The mentors' recommendations of a pious life held the promise of salvation from fathers and husbands who objected to their sexual abstinence and encouraged them to marry and reproduce.

Writing for the director of conscience takes the memorialist away from the concrete language of social interchanges between men and women. His influence may be observed in passages where the woman states that her formation as a writer begins with the *examen de conscience,* which is equivalent to the language one uses on the psychoanalytical couch. The memorialist's expressing herself in a dramatic, asyndetic discourse serves a double purpose. It causes her to be accepted by someone who encourages the emotional discourse of the confession, and it allows her to refute the docile expressions of heroinism.

58

As if in a privileged position vis-à-vis her deity, Guyon uses terms of the supernatural to speak of herself outside the domestic realm of married women. Her stories of apparitions, although strange to today's readers, were well within a tradition of previous centuries. Readers have deeply respected French thinkers' claims to the supernatural: Pascal, his hallucinations; Descartes, the nightmare which led to his *Cogito;* and Rousseau, his moment of illumination. But why do their contemporaries judge Bourignon's and Guyon's writings illogical and accuse them of heresy? If we examine the societal context of this judgment we understand that it is inspired by a long-standing custom of speciously associating female biology with weakness of intellect. Women's insurmountable inferiority arose from the idea that they were weak vessels subject to foreign insertions, an idea reinforced during the memorialists' time by the discovery, through studies of the human body, of the penetration of spermatozoa into the ovarian egg. In fact, after scientists observed that the uterus was subject to invasion, accusations of hysteria, of being possessed by a foreign presence, became common. The connotation of hysteria to the uterus—the Greek origin of the term—clung to the word. In the seventeenth century women were even more likely to be condemned for witchcraft than in the previous one, and denunciations multiplied. With regard to the charges leveled against Bourignon, Françoise Mallet-Joris points out that women were viewed as vessels carrying diseases:

> La sorcière est la femme pauvre, opprimée socialement; les épidémies de sorcellerie correspondent en général avec les zones géographiques où ont eu lieu des épidémies. . . . La "possédée" est souvent la religieuse sans vocation, la femme parfois cultivée, parfois même de grande famille, mais opprimée affectivement.[3]

> The witch is the poor woman, socially oppressed; epidemics of sorcery usually corresponded with geographical zones where epidemics occurred. . . . The "possessed" is often a religious woman without vocation, sometimes cultivated, even from a great family, but in fact oppressed.

In an intellectual climate wherein the church's view of the female sex as a lower species was at its peak, the memorialists embrace the trope of weakness and transform it into a form of saintliness. They strive to convince their readers of their urgent wish not to live the dependent life of domesticity, but to follow their independent spirit. Initially these narratives work in their favor, but eventually they turn against them. When they acquire followers, accusations of witchcraft are heaped on them.[4] The mystical quest liberates the women from traditional female social obligations, and they achieve a form of independence in the intellectual exchange with a spiritual man, who, considering their sex impure, accepts their withdrawal from physical sensations even though it leads to extreme states of mysticism. In their life stories, both Bourignon and Guyon reject consciousness of the everyday to live the superior eternal life of the soul.

Refuge in religion is not unusual at the time; it was encouraged, even in young children, who were often dedicated at a tender age to the Virgin Mary or to God by their parents. Religion is particularly omnipresent in Guyon's family. They place her in a convent at the age of three. The education she receives there for the sake of learning holy history later becomes a means to acquire other knowledge and, eventually, to achieve independence from marital oppression. It dictates a line of conduct which excuses her passive defiance of her tormentors at home. When her husband will not allow her to speak, she turns again to the orations from holy books she had recited in her convent years, and there finds freedom from oppression.

Masochistic tendencies inspired by scriptures bring her to tell stories derogatory to herself, stories which tell us that she deals with her anger as she does with her body, in punitive, passive-aggressive ways. It is evident to the reader that her excessive spirit of sacrifice often disturbs her household. When she reports that she turns the other cheek to those who insult her, she inadvertently reveals that her actions exacerbate rather than settle domestic problems. For instance, when her servants offend her, she is grateful to them, for they give her a cross to bear. She rewards them with gifts. She writes of her chosen state of mind: "True ravishment and perfect ecstasy are operated by total annihilation . . . death to all things created" (*Autobiography*, 72).

Her refusal to deal with everyday life in the name of spirituality certainly adds to the turmoil of the Guyon household. Her insolent humility at home is matched by an equal insouciance for customs in public. Her donation to the church of the enormous fortune she inherits from her husband causes greed and quarrels between priests. Her nomadic lifestyle—giving up her domicile, going here and there, wherever she is invited—disturbs the social order. As Mallet-Joris observes, her total availability was provocative: "Il y avait une forme de provocation à laquelle on ne pouvait pas ne pas répondre, d'une façon ou d'une autre" (Mallet-Joris, 235). (There was a form of provocation to which one could not not respond one way or another.)

Religion is supreme for Bourignon, for whom it also becomes the avenue to a nomadic lifestyle. Like Guyon, she narrates heroic deeds, such as leaving the paternal domicile at dawn disguised as a monk to run away from an arranged marriage. A fiercely independent young girl, she refuses her father's protection and undertakes solitary travels, disrupting entire communities: "Je partis donc le jour de Pâques de ladite année 1636, à cinq heures du matin. . . . Je cheminois joyeuse. . . . Avec l'intention de vivre pauvre . . ." (151–52). (I then left on Easter day of the year 1636, at five o'clock in the morning. . . . I happily went my way being happy. . . . With the intention of living, poor. . . .) Her arrival by herself in a village is indeed aberrant. It causes confusion. Peasants have to run to her rescue and save her from rape when the commandant of a detachment of soldiers (who has the right to demand anything from the villagers) wants to take her along with him. A priest offers the final protection by hiding her in his armoire until the soldiers leave. This event marks the beginning of Bourignon's relation to the men of the church who subsequently intervene for her and assist her.

Both memorialists speak of resisting familial demands that concern domestic life at home. Guyon, who was known for not speaking a word for weeks at a time, writes of an overwhelming urge to cut out her tongue with a knife so she will not have to speak to her mother-in-law or her husband. Bourignon, speaking the language of mysticism, tells her family about her resolve to join the silent Carmelites: " . . . et m'informois d'un chacun, Où etoit le païs ou demeuroient les chrestiens?. . . Mais personne n'entendoit ce langage . . . & fus contrainte de me taire & ne plus parler de cela" (144) (. . . and I asked everyone, In what country do Christians live? . . . But no one understood that language . . . and I was coerced to be silent and to no longer speak of this).

For them, heroism consists in refusing to conform to social customs. Both narrate this through preterition. When they reach the age of marriage and are called on to accentuate the beauty of female youth's complexion, hair, and breasts, they flagellate themselves to extract bits of their flesh, remove or cover their hair, and conceal their breasts under coarse clothing. Silently, through disguises, they communicate on a primitive level their rebellion against an oppressive social environment. These are *gestures* of preterition; they signal a presence through its concealment. Both also narrate themselves in accordance with the mythological archetype of the Virgin Mary, whose virginal conception is a denial of an affirmative: no sexual act impregnated Mary.[5]

To contrast societal demands to those of the soul, to underline her ultimate contempt for material things of the lower order, Bourignon divides the text of her life into two books, one for the higher order, entitled "La Vie intérieure," and one for the lower order, "La Vie extérieure." The first purports to tell the story of her soul, but it tells the same story as the second, only less introspectively and with more realistic details. To neglect societal conventions is easy for Guyon, who lived in the last half of the century when all social classes, even the court of the Sun King, were affected by the dark mood of Jansenism. Although she does not wholeheartedly subscribe to its philosophy, she emphasizes her determination to be indifferent to daily activities performed by the body. Such is spiritual heroism.

Religion provides a way to a more independent lifestyle and becomes an avenue to the world of the soul, where the women find acceptable words—they claim to be inspired by the voices of holy men—to validate their neglect of daily chores. Bourignon reports that a male voice guides her. As Joan was counseled to leave for the battlefield by St. Michael, the most popular saint of her time, so Bourignon is advised to leave her family in a vision of St. Augustine, the saint of her century:

> Un autre jour estant retirée en ma chambre . . . Je repetois souvent; Seigneur, que voulez-vous que je fasse? . . . Je vis tout à l'instant le Ciel s'ouvrir, comme un fort éclair, d'où sortit un personnage sur une petite nüe. . . . Je fremissois, neanmoins je disois, "Qui 'estiez-vous?" Il me repondit: "*Je suis Augustin.*" (7–8)

> Another day, having retired to my room . . . I often repeated; Lord, what do you want me to do? . . . I immediately saw the sky open, as a strong lightning [*sic*] from which a person on a small cloud [*sic*]. . . . I trembled, nevertheless I said, "Who are you?" He answered "*I am Augustine.*"

She continues with elaborate descriptions of miraculous vines growing in her room, which the saint asks her to cultivate. Guyon also reports a rich life of the imagination. Going against familial expectations, she claims that she hears a voice telling her that she has a mission. This justifies her leaving home in quest of the New Christians. In the tradition of saints who believe they have been blessed with extraordinary understanding, the women do not hesitate to act against fathers and husbands. With blind faith in their male inner voices, unshakable dedication to their cause—as well as a naive disregard for the risk of the enterprise—they take matters into their own hands and leave home: Guyon in the direction of Siam, and Bourignon in search of a desert, a place far from the world, where no one but true Christians live and which she believes is located in Italy. Neither, however, reaches her destination.

While the *précieuse,* the liberated woman of their time, conforming to the rules of those who live under the paternal roof, invites men into her salon and speaks to them as equals, Guyon and Bourignon, acting rashly in agreement with the ethics they adopted, follow their doctrine to more radical consequences. They stay away from social intercourse. The *précieuses*'s texts are a form of art for art's sake, but the memorialists' are the works of artisans. These women spend no time refining the text to make of it a work of art, for they do not consider themselves worthy of literature. One understands that the major function of their memoirs is—intentionally or not—political. They persuade men of the church to help them in their cause. Each succeeds in convincing the director of conscience of her mission. Twice Père La Combe has hospitals built for Guyon, and two priests use their position to have a convent built for Bourignon's orphans. Guyon spends years caring for the sick, and Bourignon realizes her dream. She prepares young girls for a trade, teaches them to write for personal growth, and reports that these children of the lower class become well educated and wise.

Orations and prayers dominate these life stories. We have to patiently scan their evocations of God to learn the events of what these women call their exterior lives. When we do, we realize how, when Guyon and Bourignon leave their fathers' domiciles to create spaces of their own and turn to priests, they usurp paternal authority and polarize the rulers of the aristocracy and the church. We also see how they become subjects of controversy, as factions for or against them are formed within both of these groups. We also understand how Guyon chose to spend her life writing. It is difficult to judge whether Père La Combe, the confessor, was acting on his own political exigencies or on her emotional needs when he asked her to tell him the most minute of her thoughts. Whatever his intent may have been, we owe some details from Guyon's life to his request. She reveals that, although at first she is unable to write about herself, with the guidance of a voice she calls her inner director she acquires a taste for autobiography and writes copiously.

These details tell us about the relation of reader to writer. We notice a lack of respect on the readers' part for the wishes expressed in both women's memoirs (which are, in fact, long letters to the confessors). For instance, a priest in Paris, after asking Guyon to write her private thoughts, repeats word for word in public what she has written in private. We also learn that Bossuet, the great orator of Meaux, asks her to write of real events (gossip from the court), and when she refuses, he tells the world—even warns the Pope—that she is a heretic. Whether she writes of her private or public self, Guyon is ridiculed and persecuted. Thus writing, an activity which she first finds pleasant, becomes another cross to bear.

When we read of these "real" events we learn of the courage of the memorialists in acting against the dictates of society. Both are unchallenged when their actions agree with traditionally female roles. They are assisted in erecting hospitals and convents, as these are institutions which promote occupations using traditional female skills, but they are challenged when their achievements are made public (when their confessors repeat from the pulpit what they wrote in private). As a consequence of their notoriety, they gather a number of followers and detractors.

Bourignon's productive years as leader of her convent end when accusations against her incite the orphans under her care to revolt. They claim to be possessed and celebrate black masses. This sacrilege furnishes her enemies with the proof they need, and they accuse her and her charges of witchcraft. Consequently, she loses the support of the church, and eventually, when the rebellion reaches the stage of mass hysteria, she is discharged. In her memoirs, she complains that her contribution to the upbringing of these orphans has not been weighed against their delinquency.

Such events inform us of the gender-specific political ramifications of witch hunts. Bourignon's own claim, that she hears the voice of God, is turned against her as her opponents accuse her of listening to the voice of the devil. The modern reader is compelled to compare Bourignon's case with Joan of Arc's and observe how, in the eyes of the accusing public, the identity of the presence possessing the witch varies to suit political purposes. To the French who gained by her actions, Joan must have been possessed by a holy presence, but to the English who lost the battle to her troops, it was evil. One can thus infer that the voice inspiring *La Pucelle* was identified as God's by the French because, when she enthroned Charles VII, she reinstated the patriarchy. It would likewise be logical to suggest that the same patriarchal hegemony found that Bourignon's charges were guided by an evil spirit because she promoted a feminist cause, women's education. Comparing the two, we are struck by the fact that, while Joan of Arc's ignorance was used to prove God's presence within her, Bourignon's was invoked to prove that of the devil. He accusers claimed that she was too ignorant to know the things she knew. They reasoned that, since she was too unlearned to make any intelligent statements, she must have been possessed by an intelligent devil.

Events from Guyon's life parallel those of Bourignon's. Her social standing calls for more respect than Bourignon's, and she is never accused of witchcraft. As a member of the upper nobility, she occupies a more enviable position and even takes a *noblesse oblige* stand vis-à-vis her social standing. Also, having become a wealthy widow at an early age, she enjoys greater freedom (in fact, the position of widow was so favorable to women of the seventeenth century that Bossuet warned against it). But while Guyon is never accused of witchcraft, she is not spared from calumny. Her correspondence with La Combe and Fénelon brings her accusations of heresy, and she is jailed—unjustly, as she explains in numerous passages.

Since the charges of witchcraft against Bourignon stemmed from her sex—the void in her body which made her subject to invasion—so did the charges of heresy against Guyon. Innuendos found in her correspondence with La Combe and Fénelon legitimized an investigation of a more scandalous nature: the possibility that she had sexual intercourse with her correspondents. Biographical information with regard to this investigation shows how her persecutors, like Abelard's, engaged in a flurry of public polemics. She also became the eye of a storm. Père La Combe was incarcerated for the rest of his life and died insane as a result of his association with her. When the church leaders had him imprisoned for supporting her heresy but found no evidence of it, they looked for something else to substantiate their suspicions.

64

They freely interpreted obscure passages from La Combe's correspondence with her and, calling them erotic, coerced him to write her a letter of confession. All he could bring himself to write to satisfy them is:

> C'est devant Dieu, Madame, que je reconnais sincèrement qu'il y a eu de l'illusion, de l'erreur et du péché dans certaines choses qui sont arrivées avec trop de liberté entre nous. (Mallet-Joris, 418)
>
> It is in front of God, Madam, that I sincerely acknowledge that there was illusion, error, and sin in certain things which happened between us with too much liberty.

Whatever these "certain things" may have been and whether he was the author of the letter are accusations which have never been substantiated. To authenticate the handwriting, Guyon called for the original, but she never received it. This leads us to the conclusion that the groups formed around her were divided. There were those who found in her letters proof of heresy and scandalous sexual involvement with her directors of conscience, and those who viewed them as demonstrations of profound religious convictions. The first, headed by Bossuet, ridiculed her intellect and claimed that passages in the letters were tainted with pornographic sado-masochism. The second, consisting of followers of Fénelon, admired her works and her spiritualism.

The intertextual import of these memoirs to paradigms of heroism may be retraced to the implied reader's discourse. These women's writings show evidence of readings limited to works approved by Rome. Guyon gave up novels when she committed herself to her mystical quest. Details of her physical endurance follow the prescriptions of the exemplum, not of *La Princesse de Clèves*. Although she develops the *aveu* theme, she takes it to a mystical dimension which so surpasses the clear simplicity of the social and moral aspects of La Fayette's novel that we cannot compare the two. The memorialists draw superior traits of sinners in need of perfection from the Abelardian discourse of penance.

Religion takes the memorialists away from the intertext of secular women and toward that of men. They echo Christianity's glorifying of the Virgin Mary, which had reached its apogee at the time. The seventeenth century cherished Joan of Arc for her virginity rather than her courage or her cleverness as a warrior and strategist. Dubbing her "La Pucelle" (the virgin), posterity sanctified and represented Joan as the pathetic virgin burned at the stake, not the savior of her country. Indeed, her intact hymen was a point of contention at her trials.[6] In medieval France the act of breaking a virgin's hymen was called "dépucelage," and a young woman whose virginal membrane was still intact was called a *Pucelle*. Indeed, Joan's reputation, as signified by her epithet, rests on her having never been sexually fulfilled, rather than for having enthroned Charles VII. These tales of purity influenced both memorialists who, like her, affirmed that during their formative years they heard male voices herald their potential for greatness. Bourignon chronicles such a persona for herself. She tells of leaving home without her father's permission in response to God's voice instructing her to defend and protect the weak. Like the virgin warrior, she dresses herself as a boy, cuts her hair, and, wearing male attire, runs away from the arranged marriage. Although she regrets the sorrow that her departure causes her father, she is elated by her newfound freedom: "Car je sentais un tel dégagement, & mon ame si libre, que je pensois estre devenüe . . . comme un pur esprit, sans corps" (14). (I felt such a detachment and my soul so free, that I thought I had become . . . a pure spirit, without body.)

The age of reason is also the age of *préciosité*. Physical passion is devalorized not only by the church, but in salons, where the understatement, the litote, is the dominant rhetorical figure of artistic expression. Representation through negation dominates verbal exchanges between men and women. The *précieuse* frees her language of human sexuality to elevate it to the higher sphere of the intellect.[7] This literary trope provides the memorialists with various acceptable forms for expressing their denial of sexuality.

Above all, *préciosité* is a women's movement whose radical feminist aim proposes to valorize women's intellect. To do so, it was necessary to devalue their sexuality. Speaking of sexual desire or love through the litote neutralizes sexual difference and, as a consequence, levels the male-female hierarchy. The search for the essence of love through renouncement of its carnal expression results in the century's adherence to the rules of *bienséance*, abolishing any form of extravagance. (Baroque poetry is its antithesis.) Sex becomes something signified by the negation of its contrary. For example, in Corneille's *le Cid*, love finds its expression in the litote. When Chimène declares: "Va je ne te haïe point" (I do not hate you), it is understood that she means "I love you." To the *précieuse*, love is platonic, immaterial. She claims to negate her physical desire, yet signifies it by its absence. This extended poetic euphemism, shifting passion to a spiritual plane, causes the reader to hesitate, then suspend belief. Ultimately one reacts as one does to the fantastic, namely, by preoccupation.[8]

Neoplatonism, a preoccupation with feigning to give significance, calls attention to whatever the subject of obsession is at the time it comes in vogue. In the salon of the *précieuse*, the subject *par excellence* is the ideal relationship of men and women. Women seize the opportunity to eliminate problems of sexuality and differentiation. Shifting the exchange between men and women to a sphere outside the limits of differentiation is one of the methods open to feminism. (There exist no ideal methods.) The women of the salons generate the sort of undifferentiated discourse of the self which we have already observed in Ahura's and Heloïse's texts. All these women propose a noncompetitive context—and pretext—within which to dialogue as equals with men: Ahura by marrying her brother and speaking through men's voices; Heloïse by affiliating herself with Abelard as his lover, rather than his abbess, and by showing her ability to use his dialectical method; and the *précieuses* by eliminating materiality from the stage of the salon and from the language.

Bourignon, Guyon, and the *précieuses* commit themselves to a sex-sacrificing ideology. Their lives imitates their art. Their commitment to an ideology which glorifies women's intellect takes them to extremes of social behavior. Mlle de Scudéry, acting on her beliefs, forever delays the moment when legitimacy would place her under the dominance of a husband. She prolongs her engagement and never marries her lover. Thus living on words, on a promise, she remains his equal and is never legally dominated as a spouse.

As in salons where an ambiance favorable to equal interchanges was created, Guyon and the great orator Fénelon undertake an exchange of letters and poems wherein the litote dominates. It expresses their spiritual union and is the most suitable rhetorical figure for Guyon's self-annihilating ideology. She and Fénelon greet each other with a refrain on the inexpressible power of their union. Couching their feelings in the legitimate language of platonic love, they open their letters with greetings such as Fénelon's "Je meurs d'envie de vous voir."[9] (I am dying of longing to see you.) In their correspondence, as in that of Heloïse and Abelard, the idea of losing oneself in Christ surfaces, but while Heloïse rejected a discourse which did not express her quest for carnal love, Guyon favors it. Hers is impregnated with liturgical tropes.

Guyon's heroism partakes of the Virgin Mary model, as she calls herself the fecund (albeit asexual) mother of Fénelon. She rarely narrates the events of her relation to her own children in her "real" life to Fénelon. Instead she pens prayers to this imaginary child. In what Kristeva aptly calls a "père-version of language," Guyon, in conflict with Descartes, is carried away by her logorrhea to the edge of "aphasia." She engenders herself powerfully endowed with fecundity by claiming to have been chosen by the Lord to incarnate a new church. She calls her body a Jerusalem, and compares it (herself we could propose) to a spouse coming out of her nuptial bed. The language of spiritual love becomes more and more erotic. Guyon imagines her union in liquidity; she and Fénelon blend together, like basins that flow into one another and rivers that run into oceans. Taking as their theme union in love of God, the correspondents greet each other by stating their inability to express the growing intensity of their love until, finally, their exchanges take the form of poems. He sends her spiritual rhymes bearing titles such as "Perte de l'âme par l'amour" ("Lost of Soul Through Love"), to be sung to the popular air "Les Folies d'Espagne," and she replies with verses of her own titled "Même sujet, même air" (311–12). Guyon blends into nonmateriality. She surpasses linguistic limits by communicating through a third ideal, "un tiers idéal."[10] She is the Heloïse Abelard wishes for but could not change, inasmuch as she refused to communicate through this third ideal, God.

Students of literary movements would benefit from the study of these late writings of Guyon. They indicate how baroque imagery and Jansenism, both antagonistic to the rationalist ideology of her century, go hand in hand. The following statement on "pur amour," for instance, is violently baroque in its imagery:

> Je ne regarde comme pur amour que l'amour impitoyable, destructeur, qui loin d'embellir et d'orner son sujet, lui arrache tout sans miséricorde, afin que, rien ne restant dans ce même sujet, rien ne l'empêche de passer dans la fin. Hors de là il ne peut point subsister. Tout son soin est d'enlaidir, d'arracher, de détruire, de perdre; il ne vit que de destruction. (*Correspondance*, 286–87)

> I only consider pure love a love that is pitiless, that destroys, which, far from serving as embellishment or ornament to its subject, uproots everything without mercy so that, when nothing remains of this subject, nothing may hinder it from passing to its end. Outside, it may not subsist. Its entire duty is to disfigure, tear, destroy, lose; it subsists solely on destruction.

With Fénelon, in the equal exchange of letters, rather than with La Combe, in the memoirs where there is no exchange, Guyon communicates her ideas on the life of the spirit through surprisingly self-assertive statements. During the age of the rational proof of God, she names herself the antirational prophet, boldly claiming that she has been chosen in her century "Pour détruire la raison humaine et faire reigner la sagesse de Dieu par le débris de la sagesse humaine" (*Correspondance*, 43). (To destroy human reason and enthrone God's wisdom through the debris of human wisdom and human reason.) Furthermore, we know that the Bishop de Meaux asked her to write a new autobiography with more details, including gossip from the court. (This is a strange request from a man who freely interpreted holy texts according to his anti-sensual position.) Guyon continues to refuse to organize her text into a history and continues her automatic writing, deliberately carrying to their extreme the antagonistic sentiments of the followers of quietism. Her style of writing is a form of insolence, a rebellion against a powerful man's demands for narratives based on discrete temporal events, and this at a time when, as Marie-Florine Bruneau remarks, "mysticism ceased to be a socially valorized phenomenon."[11] Whatever may have been the directions of her confessors, we know from her own statements that she was determined to improvise, and it is these improvisations which were, as Mallet-Joris observes, "une insulte à la littérature" (538).

When Guyon's representation of an exemplary self models itself on female characters from ecclesiastical discourse who conform to the Eternal Feminine, she gains approval. But when she claims to have been a chosen prophet, she provokes violent reactions from the same readers who had praised her early writings on the method to short oration and admired her definition of pure love. These same readers act against her when she oversteps the boundaries of prescribed female domains. But the writings which cause her to become a martyr are in fact a sort of antiheroism. Associating herself with prophets instead of virgins gives her extraordinary dimensions; she is unlike the docile women who complain and cry as they adhere to their assigned sexual roles. Her acceptance of pain is too radical; she oversteps the rules of feminine compliance and *bienséance*. In a context which extols the supremacy of thought and knowledge over passion, "la pensée et de la connaissance sur les passions," as Kristeva words it, Jeanne Guyon's mystical experience seems archaic, and she becomes "condamnée comme hérétique par une Eglise éprise avec Bossuet de rhétorique mais aussi de raison" (condemned as a heretic by a church enamoured, with Bossuet, with rhetoric but also reason).

When we compare Bourignon's and Guyon's outstanding deeds to those of Heloïse and Ahura, we are struck by a paradox. It is not possible to tell whether Ahura accomplished some fantastic deeds (although her reading the book of the gods was heroic, her *actions* may not have been unusual for a princess), and we know from the correspondence that Heloïse did not perform any extraordinary act. However, both women conceived themselves heroic and convinced their readers through *writing*. The substance of Ahura's valor was writing (the prerogative of scribes) and Heloïse's was subverting Abelard's discourse. Their actions seem ordinary in comparison to men's physical and verbal prowess. The memorialists' attitude toward writing, however, is antagonistic. They neglect artistic endeavor, which is the most important aspect of writing.

But what gesture of nihilistic longing could surpass Guyon's deliberately ignoring the most elementary rules of communication? Her automatic writing is metonymic of her request that her text of the self be committed to the flames. Lacking maternal acceptance and engendering herself in the text *for* her confessor, she defines herself in episodes of sacrificial repression—forever withholding pleasure—rather than in discrete periods of maturation, thus breaking basic rules of storytelling. The reason is that, for Guyon and Bourignon, who strive to leave no trace of materiality, there is no potential for mediation or reconciliation of past and present. For Abelard, who creates a potent virile entity substantiated in his sexual identity by paternal association, for he who tells of past sexual experiences and judges his actions with authority, there is a potential for the conscience to mediate. Such are the paradigms of men's heroism. But for the memorialist who is unsubstantiated by maternal acceptance there can be no reconciliation of body and soul; there can be no integration when the body does not exist as a viable entity from the start.

Guyon escapes into the Pascalian *rien*, but not entirely to disarm her enemies, as Bruneau suggests. Although her discourse occurs "within powers," its stated intent is to reject its establishment.[12] Baroque marginality escapes systems of hierarchies by promoting the belief that existence is senseless and that there exist no objective truths. Consequently, why comply with a society which places women in a submissive position? While mothers in fairy tales are at the height of their popularity (good fairies are recognized as mothers who died in childbirth and appeared to orphans to guide them), while Mme de Sévigné pens letters to instruct her daughter on proper womanhood, and while female voices advise the heroic young woman of La Fayette's *La Princesse de Clèves*, male voices alone guide and advise Bourignon and Guyon. In fairy tales, correspondence, and novels, maternal voices exhort daughters to conduct themselves according to a female ethic developed to comply with societal expectations. They must integrate their sexuality into existing systems, and whether they attain sexual fulfillment in these roles is secondary. In the memoirs of the mystical women, however, the maternal voice is silenced from the start.

As a result, the confessors welcome the writings of mystics who consider a material self—female in their case—unworthy of discovery, of narrating, or even of naming. Kristeva states that Guyon finds nothing to name in herself, "*rien de nominable*" (*Histoires*, 375). The altruistic quest for what Kristeva calls "le 'rien' mélancolique" (381), told in terms of the spiritual rather than of the material life, works against heroism.

Ironically, it is the director of conscience who supports the nonconformist celibate life which frees the memorialists from heroism; that is, he relieves the familial pressures to fulfill gender-dictated societal obligations. But while in one instance he frees them to perform laudable acts, in another he binds them to a doctrine which has an adverse effect, for it defines them in the liturgical discourse of differentiation. More ironically, when the memorialists immolate themselves on the altar where men celebrate through the language of differentiation, they neutralize it. How could the memorialist be the "other" when she is the Echo, unsubstantial? How could the phallus

70

be spoken without differentiation? Even more ironically, it is the confessor who, listening to his echo in the memoirs, cannot understand that the request to burn the book is not a rhetorical trope, but a true wish for privacy. Narcissus does not understand Echo. He publishes it and thus gives her heroic dimensions in history.

A Female Implied Reader: The Daughter in Mme de Sévigné's Letters

The memorialists and Sévigné, although writing within the same historical period, leave women writers with conflicting thematic approaches to the female body. The first, striving for a nonmaterialist life, write of it in the negative, while the second, adapting to the tempered manners of an individual group, confirms its esthetic potential. During the seventeenth century, *préciosité* and baroque, antithetical artistic movements, existed within two artistic and intellectual milieus which, being antagonistic to each other's ideas, engaged in exaggerated explanations to clarify their positions. Likewise, in the present chapter, a juxtaposition of the writings of Sévigné to those of the memorialists will highlight the tropes featured in each. The investigation into Sévigné's works will be brief, as it is only intended to illuminate that of the memorialists.

To highlight the archetypes favored by Greco-Roman male discourse with which the memorialists had to struggle, they will be compared to the antithetical ones featured in Sévigné's works. The original cause of this singular antithesis will be explained in a comparison of two contextual and textual presences: a confessor in the first case and a daughter in the second.

Marie de Rabutin-Chantal enjoyed a liberty that the memorialists never knew. Following the deaths of her father when she was a year old and her mother when she was six, she was brought up by permissive grandparents who adored her. Perhaps, as Frances Mossiker suggests, they felt sorry for the child and "spared her the usual disciplinary measures."[13] Her adult life might well be judged in the same terms. She enjoyed that most enviable state deplored by Bossuet: she was widowed and made financially independent at the age of twenty-five, after only seven years of marriage. Sévigné, a woman of her times, an *honnête femme,* had a great fund of knowledge but never flaunted it. She was accepted and even admired at the court of Louis XIV, where she acquired fame through her correspondence with her daughter. Roger Duchesne is correct in implying that, in the past, the mother's letters to her daughter were preserved only because of their "tendresse," not because of their "valeur littéraire."[14]

Today, critics value them for a variety of reasons: first, they are important records of happenings at the court; second, they enrich the corpus of literary correspondence, which has now become an accepted genre; and third, they contribute to the records of women's works now under study. Retracing their ancestry to ancient narratives—for instance, the myth of Kore-Demeter—we find the point where Sévigné's narratives converge into paradigms of the heroism of women in search of their sameness. As Kore (or Ceres) lost her daughter Demeter (or Prosperpina) to Pluto, so Sévigné lost hers to a husband, the Count of Grignan, who took her away from Paris to his estate in Provence.

Sévigné's esthetic is formed within a close-knit female milieu. What constitutes literature is dictated by a consensual judgment of shared values; a writer is confirmed by her readers. Sévigné's letters were first validated by her daughter and a circle of friends who shared the same values, and, eventually, by a wide public. In past centuries, the reading of correspondence was not always a private enterprise. Heloïse and Abelard's letters were read by the members of their religious orders, and Sévigné's by her daughter, her friends, members of the court, and even the king himself. Hence she widely publicized the ethics of her social group, because, unlike the memorialists, whose acts antagonized their families, Sévigné observes the proper place of women in the social hierarchy.

Her letters to men often suggest some *badinage*. Bussy, her cousin, calls her "Ma belle cousine," and she replies by addressing him (as well as her son-in-law) by his title. "Mon cher Conte" is a form of playful flattery, an acknowledgment of the power of men's titles, their virility. The tone of Sévigné's letters to men, although flirtatious, testifies to her assurance both as a domesticated woman and an *épistolière*. When speaking of her textual revisions she likens herself to a skilled seamstress. When the king, hearing of her reputation, asks for her letters, she does not alter their tone. Communicating publicly is something no *honnête femme* should do, but Sévigné not only boldly accepts, she uses female imagery to tell Bussy that, should her letters be read to the king, they would have to be "raccomodées." The word translates into "darn" in English, but removing the prefix "re" (elided in this word), which signifies to "do again" in French, we are left with "accommoder," to accommodate. Thus Sévigné indicates a willingness to please the king while preserving the gender-specificity of her narratives; she is determined to write as a woman who darns her texture.

While the memorialists' texts originate in a male clerical milieu, Sévigné's is born in a female secular one. For her it is neither an exclusively male nor a sacred enterprise, and she fills it with earthy female imagery. Based on the domesticated body of women, her ethic is unwavering, for it is firmly grounded in the material world. Her address of "mon cher conte" situates her and her reader within the bounds of common activities measured in the conventional time and space of a social situation. While Bourignon's and

Guyon's rhetoric represses the present reality of female sexuality, transforming brief earthly pleasures into eternal spiritual bliss, Sévigné's journalistic style chronicles the body's physical changes, limiting it to the frontiers measured by human perception within which it matures, reproduces, and decays. To address her reader, the memorialist echoes a private liturgical discourse whose asyndetic aspect renders it somewhat illegible. To speak of reality to her daughter, Sévigné mirrors the discourse of female sameness. Her language exemplifies a maternal specificity, and it is now categorized by critics who, to quote Alicia Suskin Ostriker, find that it "appears to derive from physiological fecundity." We may now redefine Sévigné's letters to her daughter as a category of writing which a woman "shares with all mothers."[15] Hers is no longer treated as a writing to be preserved for its tenderness rather than its literary value.

Since the correspondence contains only the mother's letters, it is read, like poetry, as an autonomous text, and the absent daughter is perceived by the reader as an object of desire. In fact, historians often suggest that the Countess de Grignan was distant and cold. But her letters were not preserved and we know her only from the maternal letters. If we create an image of the daughter from the mother's narratives, we may not totally agree with historians. Sévigné acknowledges that Grignan wrote faithfully: daily when they were first separated, and never less than twice a week until her death. We know she used a litote to allude to an inexpressible love for her mother; a brief statement found in one of her few surviving letters makes a direct allusion to the current rhetoric of love which she shared with her, possibly because she cared deeply, *préciosité*, "What have I not lost?" (Mossiker, 497). One could say that only a lover's trope, a litote, could convey the magnitude of her feelings for her mother. On the other hand, one could also argue that Sévigné's passionate letters *did* express unrequited love, that Grignan merely played along, and that its rhetoric of love was meaningless, a mere literary game played in the salons to which both belonged or a narcissistic rhetoric which pleased a closed group. Whatever context generated the correspondence at the time, it now belongs to a literary world which sees the muse-daughter as the object of a maternal quest.

Juxtaposing it to men's texts, we notice that this muse inspires a rhetoric similar to the *courtois* poet's expressions of longing for an unattainable *dame*. Inserting it within a female mythology, we may say without a doubt that it reproduces the Kore-Demeter drama for a female entourage. Sévigné tells Grignan that she admires her letters and that she honors her courage and her reason.[16] She confirms this by reporting an inability to resign herself to the pleasure of reading the letters by herself. She shows fragments of them to her friends, and they say they are charmed by her style. Thus women aggrandize each other's renown. Grignan also shows her mother's letters to her husband and her friends, and she reports that they all appreciate them greatly. By singing each other's praise as writers and by telling the world how they inspire and challenge each other to a strict, disciplined style, they increase their credibility. Both gain in stature as heroic lovers and storytellers. They carefully revise and edit their detailed stories to entertain and instruct each other and their readers on the intricacies of the French court.

Reinforced by her daughter and by a milieu—albeit an elite one—which accepts her, Sévigné frees herself from the rigid rules of classicism and the constrictions of conventional language. Her discourse becomes eclectic—her passages alternating between comic and tragic modes—and her rhetorical figures and tropes find their source in a variety of genres. The most telling aspects of her freedom are her use of earthy imagery and her use of romantic tropes during the reign of *bienséance*. Provoking tears and laughter, she calls for an inter-subjectivity (a shared subjective experience) with her readers. Her description of a fire at her neighbor's house, for instance, blends the tragic and the comic. It begins with details of the devastation and ends with a precise account of the half-dressed crowd of valets, secretaries, and ambassadors who fill the street where she lives. And these earthy physical descriptions are not restricted to strangers; she also mocks her circle of friends, her neighbors, her family, and even herself.

The renown of the letters is due to the fact that, being strictly for the entertainment and knowledge of an inner group, they are well centered esthetically. It is also due to the fact that they circulated among a circle of readers who were eager for gossip and communicated publicly. Sévigné's deference to her readers is one of her shortcomings. She seldom reached beyond her own sex and her own kind. At cross purpose with Bourignon and Guyon, she does not acknowledge the suffering of the lower classes. Today's readers are shocked by her occasional shallowness, especially when she writes of the people who serve her. For example, in the letter on the suicide of Vatel, the chef who killed himself because the seafood the tide had brought did not arrive in time for the king's feast, she reports that the day was a success in spite of the suicide. The nobles had a collation, played, hunted, and dined very well. After dinner they strolled in the park, where they enjoyed the perfumed scent of jonquils. Her concern is for the nobility and their entertainment. The loss of Vatel, Sévigné writes, must be and is instantly "réparé" (I, 236). These passages reveal more about her circle's arrogance than about Vatel's depression.

She also pokes fun at her own kind, but in anecdotes which show a more caring attitude, since she participates in these experiences. When she writes of small humiliations suffered when taking the waters at Vichy and includes herself in the sense of shame, she appears less superficial. Her readers no doubt detected the sexual innuendos in her account of taking the rest cure. It was a substitute for sex and a humbling experience, which she shared with her group of women friends.[17] Her humorous passages poke fun at the foibles of both sexes: men's virility in sexual interplay, as well as bisexual women's debauchery. Others treat of intimate family matters in a comic vein. She is immensely amused by her son's impotence when he first meets Ninon de Lenclos, undoubtedly because Lenclos had been the mistress of his father—her own husband.

Overriding all of these sketches written in the tone of the salon's *badinage* is the esthetic of Sévigné's letters. It restores the readers' trust. They see the correspondence as a work of art, close to fiction and similar to the spontaneous monologues of the I-found-a-bundle-of-letters sort of fiction which became a literary genre in the following centuries, and they forgive her ethical lapses.

Sévigné's narcissistic art for art's sake, first-person point of view gives her text this high esthetic standing. Her correspondence is one of the most outstanding examples of the epistolary genre, which later led critics to award letters the stature of a literature. Now that women's writings are searched for gender-specificity, this maternal narrative voice, depending on a daughter as reader, presents a unique occasion to study an archetypical trope: glorifying the maternal body.

Of great significance is how the mother's art inspires itself by an obsession with the daughter's body. An unhealthy identic symbiosis occurs when the women are together and *not corresponding*.[18] These scenes, alluded to rather than described in the letters, center on the thematics of women's sex and its reproductive functions as maladies. A well-known letter codifies the menstruation as malady trope into a litote. Worried that the Countess de Grignan is again pregnant too soon after childbirth, Sévigné wants to know if she is menstruating. She asks her daughter to let her know how she feels through a code: "Si vous vous portez bien, vous êtes malade, mais si vous êtes malade, vous vous portez bien" (I, 175). (If you are well [not menstruating] you are sick [pregnant], but if you are sick [menstruating] you are well [not pregnant].) In the letters following their stays together, we read how both women fail to preserve any objectivity about each other's bodies. When the Countess de Grignan loses a son at birth, Sévigné believes it is because she herself is sick. In fact, the infant's deformity and sickness are due to the syphilis her daughter contracted from the Count de Grignan. Here the mother seems to be diverting attention away from a disease which contaminated both family lines, the Sévignés and the Grignans. Instead of addressing the real problem, contamination through adultery, she attempts to take control by assuming the blame and thus extricating it from its sexual content. In this case, as in the Kore-Demeter myth, the mother becomes pathologically concerned about her daughter because she has lost control over her. Arguably, these concerns with physical health were provoked by the thought of losing her reader and, consequently, the pretense for writing which was no doubt essential to her.

As we analyze women's writings, it becomes increasingly clear that there is an implicit ethical problem about writing the body. A principle of honesty about it expresses itself in vastly diverse modes. Heloïse's assertions of an ethic specific to her body occasionally infiltrate the male-based rhetoric she learned from Abelard. The memorialists, who also acquired book learning and writing skills under male tutorship, reach beyond the physical to a mystical dimension and, in unorganized narratives, subjugate the material body to place it in an unattainable zone, out of the reach of political forces which attempt to control it.[19] Sévigné, in a woman to woman discourse of tragic-comic episodes featuring the Kore-Demeter prototype of the quest for sameness, develops an Amazonian ethic of mutual protection. The mother and daughter rescue each other's body from the debilitating invasions of sexual intercourse.

The Feminized Hero's Meandering Journey

The *philosophe* is drastically at odds with time-honored paradigms of men's heroism. In the second paragraph of his autobiography, Rousseau categorically declares his non-conformity: "Je suis autre," and a few pages later, he characterizes this otherness by calling himself "efféminé."[1] Indeed, neither the *preux* of *La Nouvelle Héloïse* nor the narrator of *Les Confessions* (the author himself) conforms to standards of heroism canonized in the French romance. Neither claims to possess qualities admired by men.

Important questions remain to be asked of Rousseau's works concerning this claimed difference from men and resemblance to women. His deviation from prevalent models of heroism has been studied, and so have his *ideological* disagreements with his contemporaries; as a result of these studies, a term has been coined for the corpus of his *oeuvre:* "Romantic individualism." What has not yet been categorized and is only now beginning to emerge as a subject of study is how Rousseau's difference expresses itself in gender-specific rhetoric. The present chapter examines this rhetoric in his epistolary novel and in his autobiography.[2]

While storytellers in seminal texts display extraordinary memory and vision, Rousseau instills doubt about the supremacy of the mind and confesses to an inadequate sense of sight. The reference to the rosy fingers of dawn in the first lines of *The Odyssey* is a rich analogy testifying to the poet's faith in language. This anthropomorphic simile accomplishes much in a few words; associating nature and the power of light with the poet's anatomy, it brings the reader out of the sleep of ignorance. But whereas the Greek bard was sure of his role as storyteller, sure of inserting truth in rhetoric—particularly in similes based on the visual—Rousseau is unsure and expresses his doubts in images of darkness. His autobiography brings the reader into the solitary subjective experience of blindness, not into the common objective experience of light. Rousseau constantly iterates his mistrust of the objective stance. Such doubts are often manifested in plays on the verb *voir*, for instance, "Je ne sais rien voir de ce que je vois" (127).[3] This pun translates into "I do not know (voir) how to understand (voir) anything of what I see." Here he not only differs from traditional narrators, he also departs from the model of his contemporaries, the other *philosophes* of the Age of Enlightenment. The latter, although often beginning their inquiries from a position of doubt, had faith in the power of the human mind to find the light.

Before Rousseau the rhetoric of the quest for knowledge centered on tropes of divisions. Narrative voices clearly established distinct identities through the use of double pronouns, "I" and "he." Rousseau's rhetoric obliterates these distinctions between speaking subjects and the objects of their discourse by exploiting genres where narrator and protagonist blend into one subject pronoun, the "I." In his autobiography, in his epistolary novel, and even in his expository writings, the first person dominates. Rousseau's strategies remind us of the ancient Egyptian text, *Ahura's Tale,* where the "I" also dominates, but with the important difference that the ancient text opens itself to a universal viewpoint, while Rousseau's concentrates itself within the perspective of an individual speaker.

He designs further means to destabilize the speaking subject in relation to language by blurring spatio-temporal demarcations. While Homer's narration (the journal of a journey) functions in discrete temporalities and fixes events in defined geographical loci, Rousseau's highlights the flux of movement. When he writes that he can only meditate during his promenade, and when he repeatedly refers to the "march" of his discourse, he evokes a necessary relation, that of movement to narration.[4] His favorite trope, the simulacre of the meditative promenade, represents not only the flux of the human experience in time and space, but also the impossible enterprise of fixing experience in writing.

Over and over again, through rhetorical devices and overt statements, Rousseau indicates his doubts about the potential of the cognitive expression, writing, to illuminate or capture experience. At the end of his autobiography he writes that he has not caught what he calls the totality of his truth, and he sends the reader back to the beginning:

> Si parmi mes lecteurs il s'en trouve d'assez généreux pour vouloir approfondir ces mystères et découvrir la vérité, qu'ils relisent avec soin les trois précédents livres. (697)

> If among my readers some are generous enough to want to delve into the depth of these mysteries and find the truth, may they carefully read the three preceding books.

78

Here, as in other writings, an anti-rational thought is revealed. In the Vicaire de Savoyard's narration it is also explained that *"vérité"* is not found in philosophy but in *"bon sens."* Indeed, the critic should heed the vicar's advice, for the key to understanding Rousseau's concept of self-knowledge leading to *bonheur* (happiness) is encoded within a system of sensory imagery which challenges reliance on reason. One minor topos, the Aristotelian sense of physical *place* to represent a rhetorical commonplace (nature for the maternal body), centers on a mistrust of the visual sense and a fear of the tactile. On the other hand, one major anti-topos, Rousseau's own sense of physical *movement* to represent a rhetorical invention (displacement), centers on a preference for the kinetic.

The *Mal-heureux*

Rousseau is both a man of his time and a maverick. He participates in his contemporaries' rebellion against Christian doctrines, refusing the medieval notion that present gratifications should be deferred and pain accepted to assure life in an eternal future. He also shares their reaction to the previous century's strict rules of Jansenism and *bienséance* and their search for *bonheur,* a happy state on earth and in the moment. He does not, however, express his reactionary attitude in licentious tales. He encodes his concept of happiness in a metonymy, an intuitive experience inspired by Locke's theories of sensations as guides to knowledge: the celebrated promenade. Rousseau's position regarding the rational/sensual conflict is of import to the present study in that he recognizes and exploits the gender-linked dichotomy of the intellectual (masculine) and the natural (feminine) models of the universe.[5]

Like Descartes, he is reacting to seventeenth-century man's alienation from the organic (female) universe of the Middle Ages. But while Descartes seeks solace in the symbolic (the rational expression in language), Rousseau turns to what has been posited as its opposite, the intuitive sensual. Susan Bordo underlines a significant paradox in the development of Descartes' *cogito* which clarifies Rousseau's own (different) quest. She demonstrates that it is an intuitive experience which inspired the Cartesian rational proof of God. Her analysis of the anxiety underlying seventeenth-century man's separation from the organic (maternal) universe of the Middle Ages shows that the *cogito* was motivated by a dream. More specifically, it was a psychological factor—the need for reassurance—that resulted from the fear of alienation, which, in turn, was brought about by a need for reassurance. To counteract the insecurity resulting from his loss of faith in the maternal organic world, Descartes ensured his (and God's) existence in the paternal domain of mathematical formulae.[6] Rousseau's solution is reactionary; the father of Romanticism takes on the mission of refuting the Cartesian model by leaving the male universe of the intellect (culture) and situating himself in a female world of the senses (nature). Advocating his faith in a pre-cognitive stage of self-knowledge, he declares in the first pages of *Les Confessions* that he felt before he thought: "Je sentis avant de penser" (7).

Rousseau directs a great number of his writings against his contemporaries' ethic of scientific productivity. Contempt for their use of time and space is evident in a series of expository writings: *Le Contrat social*, where he formulates new theories of social structures; the *Profession de foi du vicaire Savoyard*, where he canonizes maternal nature and cautions scientists against its exploitation; and *Les Charmettes* and the fifth *Promenade* of *Les Rêveries du promeneur solitaire*, where, in narratives of sensory enjoyment, he develops the prototype of a new model of heroism. Capturing the fluidity of subjective time, Rousseau optimizes his Romantic individualism into an ideal state of *jouissance*, a kinetic sensory experience in maternal nature.

The promenade or "march" of his discourse, his own innovative rhetorical figure, situates the *je* in Kristeva's semiotic order, a "passage" at the limit of the subjective and the social, a "revolution" and a "jouissance."[7] Rousseau's promenade is such a passage; it invites the reader into an ideal world beyond the social limits of measured historical time and into a diffuse female space. The meandering walk replaces the quest-voyage of past stories of heroism which ordered the world on man-made measurements. The journal of the Homeric hero structures his world in time and space according to his extraordinary physical exploits (events), but the autobiographical narratives of Rousseau proceed in a kinetic manner according to immeasurable psychological events.[8] Letting go of organizing consciousness, Rousseau's dreamer moves in a world where spatial and temporal limitations are obliterated. Conceived in the fluidity of the promenade and connected to the deceased mother, this vagabond is a new heroic prototype.[9]

Rousseau's *Les Confessions* has been given special consideration by scholars who cite it as the first instance of autobiography as a genre. But we must note, as Paul Zumthor did, that writings about self take various forms. Abelard's *Lettre a un ami* and St. Augustine's *Confessions*, for instance, are the first stories of the self in which *psychological* factors dominate, while memoirs, a seventeenth-century genre, center more on individuals' *public* life than on their psychology. The uniqueness of Rousseau's work lies in its combining narrations of the *psychological* and sensory aspects of a private life with those of the *public* context within which it occurred. This is the reason why critics often named the story of his life, *Les Confessions*, the first autobiography.[10]

Rousseau expresses the complexity of understanding oneself as a sentient being in a rational world through imagery derived from the senses.

He valorizes sensuality through the kinetic (his original beatific promenade) and elucidates the failure of rational observation through visual tropes. In the autobiographical *La Nouvelle Heloïse*, his *preux* writes in an early letter that he cannot see clearly because there is a *"voile"* (veil) before his eyes. In the penultimate chapters, the truth is unveiled by Julie's *aveu* (the confession of her love for St. Preux to her husband, Wolmar) and he believes he sees clearly. But in the last passages, after Julie's death, her corpse is covered with a *voile,* and, in a further extension of the veiling effect, snows threaten to blanket this ideal world and hide it from his eyes. The *voile* which protects the hero's inner vision of an ideal world by keeping it separate from the civilization in which he actually lives keeps falling. Ultimately, as the coming snows threaten his utopic community, St. Preux leaves. Apparently, Rousseau was attracted to Abelard's letters because he was also persecuted and forced to flee. Abelard left Paraclete, Rousseau Geneva, and St. Preux runs away from Clarens. The fictional hero, like his models, is unable to make himself understood in the world of men, and takes to the road.

Rousseau works out his feelings of antagonism toward patriarchal civilization through a topology polarizing the city and the country, the first representing his *malheur* (unhappiness) and the second his *bonheur* (happiness). His topsy-turvy world reverses the Bachelardian formula of friendly, intimate interiors (civilized cities) and hostile exteriors (savage nature).[11] In the novel, St. Preux refuses to play by men's rules. When the community created for him becomes a social unit governed by the watchful eye of the patriarch Wolmar, its spatial borders defined and the activities of its inhabitants fixed by the temporal units of rituals, something goes wrong and the young man runs away. Rousseau's hero is an outcast in cities and milieus ruled by societal dictates of decorum. Like his model Abelard, who was chased from one abbey to another, and like his creator Rousseau, who had to move from one *château* to another, St. Preux is first expelled by the d'Estange family and, in the end, runs away from the powerful man's estate. Only once and in a natural setting does St. Preux find true *bonheur,* on the lake with Julie in the celebrated boat scene. The attraction to water is so powerful that Rousseau returns to it in the *Fifth Promenade* to retrace the narrative of the lovers' moment of happiness, but now in his own, solitary moment.

St. Preux's flights from patriarchal domains—d'Estange's and Wolmar's—reproduce the author's own escapes from and return to the paternal worlds of Geneva and Paris. In *Les Confessions* Rousseau informs us that his attraction to nature dates back to his difficult relations with the fathers of Geneva and with the intellectuals of Paris. His mythological scheme gives Geneva primary importance; it becomes the ideal site for the development of the theories of Romantic primitivism for which he was criticized. There, where his parents' love had bloomed and where he had been conceived,

81

his *noble sauvage* could live, but there also Rousseau suffered his most stinging rejections. In the first chapters he recounts how his parents were inscribed as citizens and he was not; in the following chapters he directs his efforts to undoing what he considers the wrongful act of the city's leaders, who twice refused to grant him citizenship. To show how his estrangement from the city dates back to his youth and to vindicate himself, he dramatically misinterprets an ordinary scene. One day, at the hour of curfew, he arrives as the city's gates are closing and is not allowed to enter. Interpreting this as a personal rejection, he vows never to return to his master's house and takes to the road. Yet, again and again, he gravitates toward his birthplace.

His first published work, the *Discours sur l'origine de l'inégalité,* is so well received by the patriarchs of Geneva that they announce their intention to bestow the title of citizen on him, but on the condition that he become a Protestant. He complies at first but, as it is against his own principles to appear to be what he is not, he later recants and publishes his true faith in a chapter of *Emile,* the "Profession de foi du vicaire Savoyard." This work causes him to be irrevocably excluded from the group of Geneva's rulers, and, after this last chastisement, he renounces the city forever. Geneva remains, nevertheless, the site of territorial affiliation and rejection where he gives himself tragic dimensions in *Les Confessions.*

Rousseau also devotes numerous pages to the manner in which Paris rejects him. He refers to its *"tourbillon"* and its *"vortex"* (581), associating the city with theories of vortices and repulsions in vogue at the time. This simulacre for opposing forces well conveys his conflicting position in relation to the city of lights. He is both attracted to and driven away by its intellectuals. While he is fascinated by their literary production, he suffers from their gossip. We observe the damage to his self-esteem in the self-deprecating terms defining his presence there. In salons he is a *"balourd,"* and his actions are *"balourdises"* (677). The root of his self-given epithet, *bal,* alludes to the balls (vortices) of social events where he feels *"lourd"* (heavy) or socially inept because he is unable to participate in the flurry of activities—no doubt his uremia contributed to his reluctance—and the last syllable of *balourdises,* "dises" (words said), directs attention to malicious gossip. In his early narratives, Paris is the city of the intellectuals whom he plans to impress with his own intelligence. He delays moving there until he is able to contribute an outstanding cerebral feat. He develops a mathematical formula for musical notes and offers it to the Parisian community of musicians. While some are interested in it, Rameau, the dean of music at the court, informs him that such a musical system has already been invented and that it is not practical. Nevertheless, time after time, Rousseau tries to impress and reports he is spurned by the French. He blames Rameau for not accepting his musical formula, he complains about Voltaire's mockery, and deplores his friend Diderot's lack of loyalty (587). Instead of feeling honored when the king offers him a pension, he feels humiliated, for to receive the pension he would have to spend a day at court waiting his turn for an audience. No doubt the long wait would have been painful for him physically and mentally, and he admits this. Yet, in this case as in so many others, he would rather center on his *malheur* than on his honor. Rousseau's failures in the French and Swiss patriarchies are fundamental to the invention of the metonymy of the promenade, the escape into maternal nature, the "march" of his discourse, a movement away from men's writings of heroic journeys.

Rousseau cannot thrive where life is systematized, and, from the mathematical formula introduced in Paris to the late works presented in Geneva, his failures to gain acceptance in wordly capitals cause him to seek other territories. Beginning with the episode at the gates of the Swiss city, he pleads his cause as an exile from those spaces. It marks the start of his wandering life. This first rejection is cataclysmic. He becomes an outcast when he no longer trusts, and, sleeping alone, without shelter, outside the city's frontiers, the young man discovers nature and acquires a taste for solitary promenades.

Forever searching for a new loci, Rousseau imagines his heroic male away from men's civilized territories and in an impossible female elsewhere. While thinkers of the Age of Enlightenment generally found values lost in tales of antiquity and in newly discovered territories, Rousseau turns to nature for values lost, and he depicts his solitary hero in high places and in a state of mind and being superior to the traditional heroes narrated in territorial journeys.[12] What is worthy of investigation and has not been closely examined in Rousseau's works is how his myopic view of an impossible world affirms what Stephen Kern calls "positive negative space."[13] In a variety of private times and places, above other men and unlike them, often acting like a picaresque hero—but without humor—his man's actions derogate the valorous quest. Obviously not possessing the qualities admired by his group (men), the author himself is unhappy in their presence and, consequently, calls himself *efféminé*.

The autobiography retraces the ebb and flow of his *bon*heur and his *mal*heur (good and bad hours). Announced at the beginning of each new episode, phrases of sorrow become formulaic and more and more poignant. Like bells that toll at strategic intervals, chapter after chapter, they predict forthcoming disappointments and humiliations. The following, for instance, opens the last book: "Ici commence l'oeuvre des ténèbres dans lequel, depuis huit ans, je me trouve enseveli" (*Les Confessions*, 695). (Here starts the tenebrous work in which I have found myself buried for the last eight years.)

Throughout his life story the dark hours predominate over the happy ones, and it is only during his last year, in the *Rêveries*, that he captures his *jouissance*.

Rousseau opens his confessions, like St. Augustine and Abelard before him, by naming his father and his place of birth. In the tradition of men's stories of the self, he defines boundaries of patriarchal time and space to situate himself in history.[14] Unlike earlier writers, however, he immediately follows this introduction with an indicated preference for his mother. He is more sensitive than the rest of humanity because of a non-event shared with her. He was almost not born. He writes: "Ma naissance fut le premier de mes malheurs . . . j'étais né presque mourant" (*Les Confessions*, 6–7). (My birth was the first of my sorrows . . . I was born almost dead.) Strangely, although he characterizes his birth in terms of his own death-like experience, it is his mother who died giving birth to him. After that momentous event of simultaneous birth and death, Rousseau cannot emphasize enough his mother's death: it is the single event that contributes most to making him solitary and sensitive. He points out that her standing in the social hierarchy was higher than his father's and that she was wealthier. He maintains that he is effeminate and sensitive because she marked him so at birth (referring to his uremia), and he declares himself unique because nature threw away the mold after he was born (4). Flawed in his male evidence, the narrator of *Les Confessions* is *mal*heureux, male and unhappy.

He explores this uniqueness in narratives of the epistolary novel by creating St. Preux in his own image—he has him narrate in the first person—and by crossing gender associations to model him on Heloïse.[15] Whereas Abelard, his precursor, asserts his place in the symbolic discourse of liturgy and Heloïse hers in the discourse of love, Rousseau's correspondents often speak the words of the model of the other sex. St. Preux is the one who demonstrates hedonistic tendencies, and Julie the one who shows an untiring penchant for sermons about self-restraint and virtue. Rousseau's contradictory ideology is well understood where it diverges from the gender-linked orientations of the medieval lovers' texts. Abelard's letters offer present physical pain and mental anguish to God in preparation for the end of the world, for judgment day, when he will be justified. Rousseau's eulogies to a fleeting moment of happiness repudiate this eschatological conception of two essential moments—the Eliadan explanation of primitive and medieval societies who believed that the world was created in one moment and would end in another.[16] Rousseau's spatial orientation also differs from Abelard's; while the monk wants to be seen and heard in elite intellectual communities, the *philosophe* moves away from them. Avoiding the world where *paraître* supersedes *être*, he would rather be with plants. During his last years he becomes an herbalist. For him, as for Heloïse, self-knowledge originates in acknowledgment of sensitivity to the physical rather than in intellectual cogitations.

Rousseau is, nevertheless, attracted to the dialectic process through which Abelard expressed his rebellion, and he reproduces it through the exchanges between Julie and St. Preux. Unsure of their potency, both Abelard and Rousseau express doubt and rebel against their contemporaries' assurance of the masculinity of language by indirectly addressing the association of male potency and language. They question the power of language. While Abelard overtly claims to possess the verb and to have faith in his linguistic aptitude, covertly, in the twisted passage where he writes that there is nothing beneath the powerful organ of Echo (his voice), he indicates his doubts about the power of his own words. The metonymy directs attention to a necessary relation, that of his castration and meaningless language. He doubts the authority of his voice.[17] Rousseau's manifest references to Abelard recall this complex allusion to the male sex and language—if only to contradict it. He configures a quest for language which is antithetical to Abelard's. The monk figures himself in a phallic locus where he faces the threat of confrontation with powerful men. By contrast, Rousseau's locus is a maternal impossible elsewhere, a non-confrontation zone of non-events where, as Thomas M. Kavanagh notes, he writes for himself.[18]

The consequences of being as *sensible* as a woman and unlike other men are explored in Rousseau's very first work of fiction. His skepticism about appearances is most transparent in *Narcisse ou l'amant de lui-même* (Narcissus, or the lover of himself), a play which he wrote when he was was only eighteen years old; he preserved it for twenty-three years before finally presenting it to the public, albeit with many notes and justifications. This play explores ethical problems raised by over-reliance on observation and concludes with a moralistic warning about the unreliability of appearances. It makes three very clear statements about *amour-propre* (self-love) and announces the author's famous pronouncement on the difference between *être* and *paraître*, the subject of his first published work, the *Discours sur les origines de l'inégalité*. But more central to the present work is the fact that these statements result from a self-study relying on the visual. The plot is simple; it opens on Valère in front of a portrait of himself touched up by his sister to give him feminine graces. He gazes at this image and becomes so enamored with it that he wants only this woman and refuses to marry his promised bride, Angélique. But through conversations with his family and friends, Valère learns that his self-contemplation has alienated him. In the end, realizing his need for others, he returns to Angélique. To present the moral of the play in a few words, Valère-Narcisse's extreme reliance on appearances causes him to fall in love with a false portrait of himself and keeps him from discovering his inner truth—as well as the outer mysteries of the world. The narcissistic trip into femaleness alienates Valère. The neophyte author should have heeded his own early warnings against crossing the boundaries of gender.

The Incest Taboo and the Challenge of the Symbolic

The principal question addressed in this chapter refers to the intertext of women in Rousseau's works. Attentive to this subject, we examine the fictive material he chooses to imitate them. He turns to Heloïse's letters for a writing territory. His admiration of women, however, is reactionary; it originates in antagonistic feelings about the writings of some of his male contemporaries, not in admiration for women writers. He looks to Heloïse's letters to counter the intertext of men more than to echo that of women.[19] The inattentive reader could be deceived by one of St. Preux's letters to Julie, where he judges Abelard harshly, worries about imitating him, then concludes that he admires Heloïse:

> Un misérable digne de son sort, et connaissant aussi peu l'amour que la vertu. . . . Après l'avoir jugé, faudra-t-il que je l'imite? . . . elle [Heloïse] avait un coeur fait pour aimer. (Lettre XXIV, 51)
>
> A miserable man worthy of his fate and knowing as little about love as virtue. . . . After having judged him, must I imitate him? . . . she [Heloïse] had a heart made for love.

The careful reader, however, becomes aware of Abelard's influence in the novel. The eighteenth-century *philosophe* is fascinated with the writings of the medieval monk. We must note that he pays him homage twice: through imitation in *La Nouvelle Héloïse*, which he structures on an epistolary exchange between lovers, and in *Les Confessions*, which conforms—albeit not very strictly—to the exemplum. Furthermore, it is not to model his thoughts and actions on those of Heloïse that Rousseau looks to the correspondence, but to oppose the ethics of Abelard. His obvious praise of Heloïse deceives. St. Preux claims to be willing to sacrifice all for love, like Heloïse, but he is unable to bind himself to his lover. When legal contracts fail, Heloïse calls herself a courtesan to keep her bonds to Abelard; when he confines her in the abbey, she remains there, his, available to him. By contrast, when St. Preux's inferior social position prohibits him from legally binding himself to Julie, he runs away and consents to return as a friend.

Escaping into the pond of nature, outside the rules of society, the hero gazes at his constant metamorphosis and reaffirms his difference from other men.[20] What he investigates in this heterogeneity are his own saving graces. Content and comforted by his invention of a maternal woman, his ideology remains uninitiated in the problematics of female heroism. Untouched by women's words, from the textual space of his novel, he echoes his own ideas on maternity and individuality through Julie. In the last chapters, her singular preoccupation obviously demonstrates the author's theses on the role of women developed in *Emile;* her single-minded maternal drive—as lover of a man who will give her a son—lacks the fascinating complexities of her purported model, Heloïse. Granted, Rousseau, like his St. Preux, lives women's condition to the extent that he depends on men, his patrons, but there ends his similarity to the other sex.

A struggle to preserve differences motivates Rousseau to deploy his principles of individuality in the novel; all *men* are created equal in his social egalitarian contract. None of his lovers displays Heloïse's integrity. St. Preux is not like her and Julie even less so; her character functions as a spokesperson for the author's ideas. The theses she brings forward were first elaborated in the social contract. These interminable lectures about the failures of civilization do not resemble Heloïse's rebellious protests against the social conventions which deprive her of sexual pleasure as a *woman.*[21] Heloïse rebels against those rules of Abelard and the ecclesiasts which restrict her to celibacy and to the limited intellectual world of a country abbey. She is kept away from the stimulation of literary companions and books. Julie's sexuality is the object of St. Preux and Wolmar. She disseminates Rousseau's ideas in the novel, elaborating his utopic solutions to the ills of a society from which he feels rejected because of his social standing, he who remains without proper territorial affiliation. This woman's narrative voice iterates, a few years later and in a different genre (the epistolary novel), an ideology which was rejected for being too visionary for its time—that contained in the *Contrat social.* Julie restates theories of individualism motivated by a wish for solitude which, in turn, stems from feelings of rejection. It is in an opposite manner that Heloïse reacts to being rejected. Not only does she make no case for the state of individuality Abelard bestows on her by making her an abbess, she reacts by asking for assimilation through a close relation to him. Such is the female specificity which escaped Rousseau when he invented a female correspondent who, he postulated, was modeled on Heloïse.

How cold and how distant Julie seems in comparison to Heloïse becomes clearly delineated when we examine the concrete language which expresses the tactile sensations of sexuality in the letters of the abbess. Heloïse's most striking chronicles are those masochistic and near pornographic ones of sexual desire where, for instance, she calls herself a *fille de joie,* claims to be chained to Abelard, and speaks of nightly lacerating her flesh. Neither Julie nor St. Preux conveys sexual excitement in concrete, mature language. It is merely alluded to in descriptions of adolescent games, where the lovers communicate through hidden letters, in rhetorical figures of metonymy which associate sexual desire with a physical malaise, and stylistically through aposiopesis.

Touching the loved woman is dangerous for St. Preux, for, as he reveals in his own words, he fears the incest taboo. The first reference to incest is overt. Early in the correspondence, St. Preux writes to Julie:

> Je frémirais de porter la main sur tes chastes attraits plus que du plus vil inceste, et tu n'es pas dans une sûreté plus inviolabe avec ton père qu'avec ton amant. (Lettre V, 17)

> I would tremble more at the touch of your chaste attractions than at the vilest incest, and you are not in a more inviolate security with your father than with your lover.

The novel refers to incest a second time in the erotic discourse of paternal chastisement. A letter to Claire from Julie recalls the scene where her father discovered her love for St. Preux:

> Pour la première fois de ma vie je reçus un soufflet qui ne fut pas le seul, et, se livrant à son transport avec une violence égale à celle qu'il lui avait coûtée, il me maltraita sans ménagement . . . je tombai, et mon visage alla donner contre le pied d'une table qui me fit saigner. (Lettre LXIII, 118)

> For the first time in my life, I was hit . . . he [her father] lost control and let himself be carried away by his *transport*...he abused me without reserve . . . I fell, and my face hit the foot of a table, which made me bleed.

Heterosexual pleasure, union with women, is commonly associated in mythological critical approaches with altered physical surroundings and painful states of body and mind—madness, malady, or death—while incestuous eroticism, union with the maternal, is linked to liquids.[22] Fear of incest, as one of the features of narcissism, is also recognized in psychoanalysis to be associated with water. In Homer's text we notice the vulnerability of Ulysses during his narcissistic quest away from home. On Calypso's island, physically incapacitated and mentally handicapped, he is surrounded and invaded by liquids: the sea on which the island sits and the drug Calypso has administered to him. Rousseau's autobiography centers on this watery sex-as-malady trope. An episode during which he visits a prostitute occurs in Venice, the city of canals. Rousseau writes that he examines her body for marks of a fault which would indicate smallpox. This is a well-known euphemism for venereal disease (378). When he speaks of his attraction to Mme d'Houdetot, he mentions that her face was marked by smallpox, "son visage était marqué de la petite vérole" (*Les Confessions,* 520). In the novel, after St. Preux visits Julie while she is ill with smallpox, he is contaminated, but he does not suffer any scarring. St. Preux and Rousseau, like Narcissus, preserve their grace, while Julie and Mme d'Houdetot bear its stigma.

Rousseau's discussion of the novel in the autobiography reveals that it is a veritable pond of narcissism and erotic incest. Looking back to the time he created it, he states that he wrote the scene on the lake to melt his reader's hearts, "fondre son coeur dans l'attendrissement" (519). The lovers are first united in a strange state of mind. Later, on the mountain, for a brief moment they are physically united through a liquid, the miasma of Julie's tears, as St. Preux touches Julie's hand holding the handkerchief with which she has been wiping her face (Lettre XVII). This seemingly insignificant detail acquires meaning when it is considered from the perspective of mythological criticism. In artistic recreations, scenes of incest—primary narcissism—are often depicted in liquids. Several key incidents with Julie involve liquids: the tears in the ultimate love scene with St. Preux, the blood after her father's beating, and, finally, the lake which causes her death when she saves her son from drowning. It is the very lake on which the lovers had been spiritually united in a strange mental state. And all these scenes where men and women touch each other hint at incestuous eroticism: Julie's physical abuse from her father, the chaste touch of her *chevalier* who likens himself to her father, and the recovery of her drowning son from the lake.

Touching is risky in *La Nouvelle Héloïse,* and we understand why when we learn that the text is the reproduction of a family romance, the imitation of nightly scenes where young Rousseau, seated on his father's lap, read novels from his deceased mother's library. Crying together as they read, father and son were united through liquids. The autobiography, where the referential is more assured, tells us how a context enters a text. The preferred literary genre of Rousseau's mother provides a textual space of reincarnation for the author. In fact, he inadvertently reveals the similarities of the plot of his epistolary novel to that of the story of his own birth, when he records how his parent's meeting inspired his first trial at fiction during his childhood.

> Le sort qui semblait contrarier leur passion, ne fît que l'animer. Le jeune amant, ne pouvant obtenir sa maîtresse, se consumait de douleur; elle lui conseilla de voyager pour l'oublier. Il voyagea sans fruit, et revint plus amoureux que jamais. Il retrouva celle qu'il aimait tendre et fidèle. Après cette épreuve, il ne restait qu'à s'aimer toute la vie; ils le jurèrent, et le ciel bénit leur serment. (*Les Confessions,* 5)

> Faith seemed to oppose their passion, but it animated it. The young lover, consumed with pain because he could not have his mistress,

was advised by her to travel and forget. His travels were not fruitful, and he returned more enamored than ever. He found the one he loved still tender and faithful. After this trial, there was nothing left for them to do but love each other for life. They swore to do so and heaven blessed their oath.

Rewriting this love story with himself (St. Preux) as the protagonist, Rousseau faces the incest taboo. As Nancy K. Miller observes, Julie "dies giving herself to Saint-Preux, but in keeping with her character, remaining—as in his dream—beyond his touch in the ultimate nonconsummation."[23] The son can never possess the mother. Lovers touching and even being in each other's presence is problematic. Julie and St. Preux meet between the letters, *hors-texte;* their reports, personal renditions of referential events, are suspect, and the reader wonders what happened in the blank spaces between the letters. These silences between the letters, however, allude to a disobedience of what is unmentionable. In the limbic zone of the non-narrated, the reader becomes preoccupied with what the lovers allude to in the letters: the incest taboo. The novel escapes social reprobation. The prohibition against incest *seems* to be obeyed as the novel leaves maternal Julie to her proper lover, the patriarch Wolmar (in life), and to God (in death). Her remains are left at Clarens.

Rousseau's neglect of the tactile, most of all in the autobiography and in the novel, signifies through preterition. He often builds a love scene to a climax, only to leave unnarrated the moment of physical contact. The attentive reader will observe a repetition of similar patterns in both these works. The following list highlights obvious symmetries. Love scenes between St. Preux and Julie and those between Rousseau, Mme de Warens, and Mme. D'Houdentot—the two women to whom he was most attracted—are identically narrated. The sensory apparatuses which dominate in all these meetings between the various lovers are the kinetic, the visual, and the auditory:

St. Preux-Julie	*Rousseau-Mme W.*	*Mme d'H*
Je vole	Je cours	Elle vint
(I fly)	(I run)	(she came)
Je t'aperçois	Je la vois	Je la vis
(I see you)	(I see her)	(I saw her)
le son de sa voix	Je lui parle	Elle me parla
(the sound of her voice)	(I speak to her)	(she spoke to me)

The lack of resolution in a kiss or an embrace, the non-narration of the sense of touch calls attention to it. Even in his sensual credo, the *Fifth Promenade,* where the narrator describes his *jouissance* and tries to capture the moment through sensual imagery, the tactile is absent.

We may question the original reasons for the need to describe lovers' meetings in this breathless style. Paradoxically, Rousseau unravels his own work by *writing* through rhetorical tropes that the sensual experience escapes language. The "march of his discourse" trope is another attempt to signify how language cannot capture the fluidity of human feelings, that fleeting moment which forever escapes cognitive powers (patriarchal objective discourse). Are his writings promises to an absent mother?

Rousseau spent his last years away from civilization, on St. Pierre Island, where he collected herbs and made laces which he gave to pregnant women in exchange for a letter promising that they would nurse their children. His affirmation of the primacy of the mother-son relationship and his canonization of a benevolent maternal nature tell us that he pinned his hope on the sensitivity inherited from his mother as a possible way of narrating the failure of language (paternal) to express the sensual experience.

Now we understand that his major contribution to society was a valorization of maternity. We see that the maternal woman lives in his narcissistic pond to reflect his difference from men, that his eulogies of women are limited to their sensitivity, and that he excludes their intelligence (Mme Dupin is an exception) because men's writings are his true ideological and ethical intertext. Now that we know he needed to contradict men, let us examine the intertext of women in his works.

His attitude toward women reveals itself in the scenes where he portrays them reading. He enthusiastically welcomes and includes women in the world of literature, where they are passive receptors or reflectors of his sensitivity; that is, he narrates women reading his works. Among the anecdotes which feature women as readers, one contained in his autobiography is most telling. Mme la Princesse de Talmont is his favorite reader. He recalls her fascination with his novel. One evening, as she waited while her horses were being harnessed to take her to the opera, she began to read *La Nouvelle Héloïse*. When the carriage was ready her domestics called her, but she did not reply, and it was not until four in the morning that she finally realized the horses were waiting. She had them unharnessed and spent the rest of the night reading (*Les Confessions*, 646). The style of this anecdote is straightforward. A few pages later, however, ridicule colors a passage referring to a woman writing her own works. Rousseau relates that it was one of his "chances" (*good* luck) to have always had women authors near him, but he was hoping to avoid this "chance" (this time, he uses the word ironically) when he moved to the Luxembourg's domain. He hoped that a certain Mme la

Comtesse de Boufflers, who had the "manie" (bad habit) of writing, would not be present during his stay (54).

He also denigrates women writing in the epistolary novel, where he borrows and distorts the rhetoric of women writers of the previous century. St. Preux's eulogies of Julie imitate both the superlatives of fairy tales and the litote of *préciosité:*

> Je consens qu'on vous puisse imaginer plus belle encore; mais plus aimable et plus digne du coeur d'un honnête homme, non, Julie, il n'est pas possible. (Lettre I, 10)

> I admit that one could imagine you more beautiful yet, but more lovable and more worthy of the heart of an *honnête homme* [with all its implications of the ideal seventeenth-century man], no, Julie, that is not possible.

Imitation is a form of flattery, and here Rousseau contradicts his own confession, that women's bad habits are not worthy of being read; since he imitated women's works, he had evidently read them. He definitely read *La Princesse de Clèves,* as he also infiltrates and subverts its intertext by borrowing the *aveu* theme.[24] Julie confesses her love for St. Preux to her husband Wolmar. But instead of illustrating the complexities of female heroism, Julie's confession exemplifies the novel's propaganda of an ideal society where honesty rules. The *aveu* theme in La Fayette's novel functions in a tragic mode, bringing about the death of a kind husband and the subsequent guilt of his wife. In Rousseau's work it functions in an erotic mode, highlighting an implicit *ménage à trois.* Rousseau was perhaps intentionally ironic, as the outcome of Julie's revelation of her love for St. Preux contradicts the spirit of La Fayette's novel. His heroine's confession results in a subversion of society's dictates, the *ménage à trois,* which supported notions of a utopic egalitarian community. Wolmar forgives, all live happily together (at least for a time), and Julie does not emerge as a heroic character. There is no courage in suffering the consequences of her actions, since there are no consequences. The conflict is neutralized by the utopic solution.[25] The Princess of Clèves's behavior, on the other hand, like Heloïse's, indicates a knowledge that the rules of society are inescapable and that there are no easy solutions, and this gives her actions a heroic character lacking in Julie.

The contextual import of Rousseau's *La Nouvelle Héloïse* and *Emile* to women's behavior is worth noting. Immediately after their publications, these works moved women who had been leaving the care of children to wet nurses, domestics, and tutors to reassert maternal pleasure. Mothers returned to nursing and educating their own children. But the intertextual significance of the novel is even more important. It greatly influenced women writers' narrations of female heroism. The next generation had to confront anew the rhetoric of Judeo-Christian liturgy. Once again, women faced a discourse which restricted them to essentialist positions. Once again, the mother's womb was celebrated as a designated vessel of spiritual birth: the "impossible elsewhere."[26] In the century preceding Rousseau, the *précieuses* had shattered these icons. They rejected all material sexual gratification, including the maternal. After Rousseau, women had to face the challenge of reinserting a non-maternal sexual body into their discourse.[27]

Collectively, the *philosophe*'s works do not provide women with a positive space from which to speak. The effect of the *Discours sur l'inégalité* was considerable, for, although it promoted an ideal of equality admired throughout the world, it failed to accord women the status of speaking subjects in society. It did not give them a voting voice. They were not inscribed in political documents—for example, the American Declaration of Independence—inspired by Rousseau's revolutionary ideas. The aftereffects of his novels were even more considerable: less overt, fictive, they were more manipulative.

The Seduction of the Mother

René Girard theorizes that images of fluidity express conflicts of identity in men. The idea of mixing blood, for instance, raises a fear of loss of individual characteristics and even puts language itself in jeopardy: "Incestuous propagation leads to formless duplications, sinister repetitions, a dark mixture of unnamable things."[28] Kristeva's theoretical *chora* locating the origin of language in maternal impossible elsewhere, a space where the speaking subject splits and becomes other (yet, "he" cannot speak from there) does not contradict Girard's theories.[29] But Rousseau's narrating the narcissistic, incestual scene of giving birth to oneself as a speaking subject in the flux of an a-temporal present contradicts them. He seeks fluid states and experiments with speaking them. When he begins to write this auto-bio-graphy (self-life-writing), his first words, after the proclamation of his difference from men, are that he is "éffeminé." His infatuation with the mother-son relation is blatantly narrated in *Les Confessions*, where he tells how women who do not awaken his sexual desire through some maternal sign leave him cold. Of Mme d'Epinay, he writes: "Elle était fort maigre, fort blanche de la gorge comme sur ma [*sic*] main. Ce défaut seul eût suffi pour me glacer: jamais mon coeur ni mes sens n'ont su voir une femme dans quelqu'un qui n'eût pas des tétons." (*Les Confessions*, 488). (She was very thin, her throat was very white as on my hand [*sic*]. This fault would have been enough to freeze me: neither my heart nor my senses have ever been able to see a woman in

93

someone who had no breasts.) Mme de Warens, the first maternal substitute, is included in joyful anecdotes of childish mother-son games. He eats food she spits out. The decomposed food he shares with "Maman" symbolically violates the incest taboo. The narrator returns to the liquidity of his space of *pretended* un-differentiation.

A passage in *Les Confessions* where he examines his relation to his wife, Thérèse, is most informative of Rousseau's position vis-à-vis women in his life. In a rare moment during which he contemplates his relationship to Thérèse, he makes the startling comment that his promise *never* to marry her was the cause of the permanence of their relationship: "Je lui déclarai d'avance que je ne l'abandonnerais ni ne l'épouserais jamais" (*Les Confessions,* 389). (I told her beforehand that I would never abandon her nor marry her.) This statement deserves consideration, as it tells us how Térèse, his sexual partner and the mother of his children, was indeed a true *neverness,* a reproductive vessel and an echo. A being without significance, either material (she did not mother his children as he gave them away) or symbolic (linguistic), in the atemporal zone of never (Kristeva's "impossible elsewhere"), Thérèse, in Rousseau's imagination, replaces *his* deceased mother, his object. Other revelations about women in Rousseau's exterior life demonstrate how maternity surpassed any other thought in his interior life. He refers to Mme de Warens, his lover before Thérèse, as "Mommy." About his decision to live with Thérèse, he writes:

> Il fallait, pour tout dire, un successeur à Maman . . . il me fallait quelqu'un qui vécût avec son élève, et en qui je trouvasse la simplicité, la docilité de coeur qu'elle avait trouvée en moi. (*Les Confessions,* 389)

> I needed a successor to *Maman* . . . I needed someone who would live with her pupil [himself], and in whom I could find the simplicity and docility of heart which she had found in me.

Rousseau endows Thérèse with superior instinctual knowledge. First writing that she is not intelligent enough to learn the hours on the clock or the months of the year (the male discourse of mathematics), he then adds:

> Mais cette personne si bornée, et si l'on veut, si stupide, est d'un conseil excellent dans les occasions difficiles. Souvent, en Suisse, en Angleterre, en France, dans les catastrophes où je me trouvais, elle a vu ce que je ne voyais pas moi-même; elle m'a donné les avis les meilleurs à suivre. (390)

> But this extremely limited, and even stupid person, if you wish, was an excellent counselor in times of difficulties. Often, in Switzerland,

in England, in France, when I found myself in a catastrophic situation, she saw what I could not see myself; she gave me the best advice to follow.

Locus of instinctual drives, without cognitive processes, without a voice except to reflect the sensory world for him, Thérèse personifies his narcissistic pond. He concludes the brief passage of his reflections on Thérèse by declaring that, after marrying her, he was alone: "Dès lors j'étais seul" (*Les Confessions,* 389).

In Rousseau's scene of primary narcissism (the text of the autobiography), as in Freud's psychoanalytical sessions with female patients (the text of his theories), women are advised to devote themselves exclusively to motherhood; in the case of the father of psychoanalysis, because they have to compensate for their lack of a sexual organ (which can only be replaced by bearing a son), and in the case of the father of Romanticism, because they have a great gift (which is their sensitivity). The rationale Rousseau gives for his proposal that women have a special talent for mothering is at cross-purpose with that of Freud, who states that women are deficient. Notwithstanding this disparity, these men show limited views of women by appealing exclusively to their maternal potential, and this, through seduction and guilt provocation, and more egregiously, by bearing sons only. How narcissism underlies these guides for women's conduct, how both Rousseau and Freud invite women to become slaves of love, is questioned by critics who take an Amazonian stance vis-à-vis the intertext of men writers.[30] They reclaim Rousseau's concept of "*jouissance*" but with a different ideology. As in his case, they depart from a valorization of women's bodies. But while they would also revolutionize society and eradicate its ills, they would do so in a utopic collectivism (which is posited as female). Rousseau would do so in a utopic individualism (male).[31]

The Romantic Hero

When we search for the intertext of Rousseau's writings to men's ancient paradigms of heroism constituted in spatio-temporal narratives—Ulysses' travels—we find no link between them. The storytelling of Homer's hero provides safety, for his tales always end with the discovery of land and the naming of these geographical sites in relation to his story. Ulysses' nightly oral reminiscences—the journal of his journey—capture time and space in language. Later, Homer incorporates them into a poem. Both the oral and the written narrators are sure of their vision, of capturing human experience in language. Rousseau's narrator, on the other hand, is unsure of his vision and keeps returning to the narcissistic, self-reflective pond of introspection.

The epistolary novel provides strategies to avoid authorial control. The author introduces no narrator to imply an omniscient male presence, each letter being narrated in a different, subjective "I." No one mediates between the correspondents. The autobiography also devalorizes controlling consciousness. Here Rousseau often signals the limitations of discursive orders to convey his meaning, calling on his readers' common sensory perceptions. He reports the signs surrounding the discourse rather than the discourse itself by *alluding* to the *existence* of feelings. He states they cannot be fixed, captured in language. (This appeal to the sensual was often mistaken by the Romantics for an appeal to imagination.) In accordance with this view, Rousseau favors the tentative over the authoritative mode: "A measure qu'avançant dans ma vie le lecteur prendra connaissance de mon humeur, il sentira tout cela sans que je m'appesantisse à le lui dire" (40). (As he advances in my life, the reader will acquire knowledge of my humor, he will feel all that without my having the burden of telling him.) When he writes that his humor should be felt without his having to say it, he is neither using a rhetorical cliché nor coining the conventional refusal to describe, but affirming through negation his difference from the rationalists.

We find the definitive formula of this Romantic hero deliberately separated from others in the fifth *Promenade,* where it is transmitted through a landscape drawn from maternal imagery. Rousseau confirms his uniqueness by likening himself to a savage island that is being destroyed, its soil periodically carried away to a neighboring island under cultivation. In a boat (his own space or island), he feels delivered from the disturbances of social life which destroy him.[32] Alone, surrounded by unmeasured liquid, gently swayed by the movement of the water, he experiences fulfillment, a happiness which leaves no emptiness. Here, in voluntary exile, unshackled by human spatial and temporal limitations, he discovers meaning in a kinetic sensation which reconciles the discord between the static and the fluid, lived time and discursive thought.[33]

These narratives of *bonheur* capture the imagination of the next generation of writers, who find in them new literary tropes to express similar *phantasms.* The hero of the Post-Revolution differs radically from the Homeric model which had survived centuries of intertextualities. The *philosophe* undermines the rational (objective) experience of language canonized in Homer's work by looking back to ancient oral traditions, to mythology and the myth of Narcissus. To separate his hero from women, Homer features the trope of the Amazon and the Greek hero and narrates it through figurative delineations of space into nations. Rousseau rejects the Homeric, divisive model. Associating himself with women through his union with maternal nature and conceiving his heroic quest in this negative space, he formulates a new model, one where, as in the myth of Echo and Narcissus, sexual identities blur. His lovers find happiness, as does their creator, in unmarked territories: in nature, outside paternal lands. St. Preux and Julie hide their communications. Their letters are concealed in the trunks of trees, away from the eyes of the Baron d'Estange and Wolmar.

Wandering without a life plan to fill the emptiness of times to come, in maternal nature and away from paternal rule, Rousseau's hero finds his place in the womb-like spaces of primitive huts and caves. The heroes of Chateaubriand, Stendhal, and Constant, to name but a few, are *cadets*—the youngest in the family and therefore without an inheritance—modeled on this new prototype. Before Rousseau, the *preux* was the oldest, who had rights to the family's inheritance and who, after proving his valor in adventures, returned glorious to take his father's place. But the downfall of the monarchy and the death of Napoleon undermined these models of male superiority, and it is now the younger man in the family who becomes the protagonist of novels. Often brutalized or molested by older men as a youth, during his adulthood he finds himself in a disadvantageous position with the strong. Rousseau, the orphan who worked as tutor or secretary in many households (including the Dupins's), claims that this is the reason why he took the part of the weak. This statement further explains why he places his St. Preux in an inferior position, that of a *"petit bourgeois"* without fortune.

Rousseau's refusal to portray male heroism in terms of the valorous deeds admired by his group is of crucial concern to intertextual studies. George Sand responded to his need for solitary introspection in the first chapter of her *Histoire de ma vie:*

> Jean-Jacques était malade quand il voulait séparer sa cause de celle de l'humanité. Nous avons tous souffert plus ou moins en ce siècle de la maladie de Jean-Jacques Rousseau. Tâchons d'en guérir avec l'aide de Dieu.[34]
>
> Jean-Jacques was sick when he wanted to separate his cause from humanity's. We have all more or less suffered from Jean-Jacques Rousseau's malady in this century. Let us cure ourselves of it with God's help.

Yet Rousseau's narratives of happiness caused negative reactions for the very reasons that they were contagious, they were revolutionary, and they precipitated reactions. Taking novelistic discourse out of the objective mode which sexually identifies heroism, Rousseau placed it in a subjective one which undermined such sexual (male) identification, thereby transforming models of male heroism. His writings display an absence of mastery with regard to language and male superiority which injects doubt into the traditionally male-linked scene of writing, the Rabelaisian vanity of associating phallic symbols (abbeys' steeples) with language.

97

■ F I V E

Sand's Early Works: The Object of the Other's Discourse

■

Sand's textual experiments have been the subject of literary criticism only since the rise of feminist scholarship. During her lifetime, while Balzac's exploration of transvestism in *Sarrasine* was widely studied, her own handling of this subject in *Consuelo* was not noticed. While Senancour's quest for the impossible and the bizarre in *Oberman* became a classic, her own trip into the fantastic in *Laura ou le voyage dans le cristal* was ignored. In addition, Hugo's *Preface to Cromwell* (1830) canonized the Romantics' rebellion against rules of the age of Classicism, but Sand's own break with narrative conventions in *Lélia* was not recognized as one of the century's major challenges to novelistic form. Over and above all these oversights was the condescending attitude of critics. Following her death, they merely mentioned her *en passant* in textbook anthologies, although she was an active commentator on the two major movements of her time: Romanticism and Realism. In sum, with the exception of the rustic novels, Sand's works were neglected for one hundred years, from her death in 1876 to the celebration of its centennial in 1976.

Critics are now compensating for the years of silence. In a flurry of activities, scholars have outlined the major characteristics of her writings. The most outstanding one to emerge is her use of the double, what has been called her *dédoublements*. Sand wrote during the century of transformation and antithesis, and a number of critics, taking this as a point of departure, have analyzed the double archetypes of women in her fictive works.[1] Biographers emphasizing this double persona in the author have encoded it in two epithets: *Lélia*, the bold, unsexual temptress of her younger days, and *La bonne dame de Nohant* (*The Good Lady of Nohant*), the kind grandmother of her mature years.[2] These antithetical nominations, one implying she was

98

frigid during the period of her most outstanding works and the other that she was senile in later years, testify to a social context which refused to accept women's sexual desire and credit them with authority. For the present study, the most significant of all Sand's *dédoublements,* even above the adoption of male attire and pseudonym, is the implication of a man narrating her works as she adopts the omniscient style of the nineteenth century.

The present chapter's first question is addressed to this transvestism. Sand's revolutionary experiments were noticed by her contemporaries, and their comments indicate that it was indeed the gender of her narrator which they found most disturbing. Assuming a male identity to tell a story served a double purpose: it gave her authority, and it flattered men into accepting her into the fraternity of writers. But by imitating them she also mocked them. Her male narrative voice is a rhetorical strategy which signals the superficiality of gender markings in fiction. Her narrator seduces readers into accepting her as a man, although she is a woman. Whatever their degree of alertness, her readers were likely to become aware of this transvestism at some stage of their reading. When they did, they were shaken in their beliefs in discursive conventions. Her contemporaries responded to her experiments with disparagement and admiration. Whatever their reaction, it is easily noticed that most of their statements were somehow directed at her sexual identity. Beaudelaire called her a monstrous woman, and Vigny accused her of lesbianism (because of her friendship with his mistress, the actress Marie Dorval). Balzac, Hugo, and Flaubert, on the other hand, accepted her as a colleague, but called her a great *man.* One may logically suggest that, since these men were all writers, they were reacting to her imitation of their voice—the century's omniscient male narrator—more than to the pseudonym which was only a signature. Narrators certainly possess more powers of suggestion than mere names. Sand's textual transvestism, more subtle and cunning, is more disturbing than the signature. She narrates in the voice of writers of her time who, with the exception of Flaubert, took an omniscient stand vis-à-vis their narrative.[3]

Today's woman author acknowledges that when she first places her pen on the page to write in French, the gender she will give her narrator is the principal issue she must address. Marguerite Duras, for instance, states that one must pretend to be a man to have access to writing. The first woman who wrote, she says, played the naughty child, and Colette, among others, "clowned to amuse the men," because it is "the first work to be done."[4] Nineteenth-century authors did not openly discuss the problematics of women writers. Sand published no statements testifying to her struggles with gender and narrative voice, but in her autobiography she offhandedly refers to her invention of a male narrator for her early *Lettres d'un voyageur*:

A l'époque où j'écrivis ces lettres, je ne me sentis pas trop effrayée de parler de moi-même, parce que ce n'était pas ouvertement et littéralement de moi-même que je parlais alors. Ce *voyageur* était une sorte de fiction, un personnage convenu, masculin comme mon pseudonyme, vieux quoique je fusse encore jeune; et dans la bouche de ce triste pèlerin, qui en somme était une sorte de heros de roman, je mettais des impressions et des réflexions plus personnelles que je ne les aurais risquées dans un roman, où les conditions de l'art sont plus sévères. (*Oeuvres autobiographiques, I,* 7)

At the time I wrote those letters, I was not too frightened to speak of myself, because it was not openly and literally of myself that I was speaking then. This *voyageur* was a sort of fiction, an accepted character, as masculine as my pseudonym, old although I was still young; and, in the mouth of this sad pilgrim, who in fact combined all the characteristics of the hero of a novel, I placed more personal impressions and reflexions than I would have dared in a novel, where artistic conditions are more strict.

Although she does not openly state it, her use of the masculine ''voyageur'' tells us she was aware of narrating as a man. This transvestism is more prevalent in the early works, where, indeed, a lack of confidence moves the neophyte writer to self-effacement. In her later publications, a self-assured writer shows herself by addressing her readers directly.

Les Couperies: Narrative Voice and the Creative Process[5]

One of Sand's very first works of apprenticeship, *Les Couperies,* penned in 1830 and published posthumously, shows a concern with voice. It features two narrators, a woman and a man.[6] Its self-conscious format can be well understood in comparison with a work of visual art, Velasquez's *The Maids of Honor.* Within the large canvas depicting the maids we see two small frames, one of a doorway opened to the outside light showing a painter with his easel, and the other of a mirror reflecting the faces of the king and queen. The casual onlooker would assume that the painter in the first small frame could be Velasquez, and that the king and queen in the second could be the ''real'' parents of the princess. Critics would eye these frames differently. They would propose that the first experiments with varieties of light and the second represents the parents who commissioned the painting. The critic's eye would also see a composition *en abîme,* the painter painted painting, the creator of the work within the work. Similarly, in Sand's *Les Couperies* a young man begins to narrate a story, quotes another story from a book written by an old woman, then ends his story. Both texts are in the first person, but one is told in the masculine and the other in the feminine. To the casual reader the inserted narrative in the feminine appears to be told by the implied author, who is a woman (Aurore Dupin). To the critical reader it is an experiment with narrative voices. As Velasquez includes the painter and his potential viewers in the small frames, so Sand narrates a writer *en abîme*, as well as a potential reader of her work: the writer, a woman, and the reader, a man (the young man who quotes her written story).

This essay of Sand also shows her early preoccupation with authorial presence and gender. The young man's story has no plot; he simply tells how he climbed to the top of a mountain to dream and saw an old sibyl. At first, believing she is a ghost, he questions the reality of her presence:

> Est-ce là une femme? . . . Un de ces êtres qui inspirent l'amour et l'éprouvent? peut-être, ce fantôme a été la beauté . . . devant ce temple ruiné, les mortels ont plié le genou. (*Oeuvres autobiographiques, II*, 575–76)

> Is that a woman? . . . One of those beings who inspire and feel love? perhaps, this ghost was beauty . . . in front of this ruined temple, mortals bent their knee?

Here Sand addresses the problematics of representing women in language. Then, after the young man acknowledges her presence, he and the old sibyl have a philosophical conversation about *bonheur* (happiness), and she asks him to read from a small book that she is holding. The booklet, entitled "Le Livret de la vieille," is the text *en abîme*, told in the first person feminine. This story was written in 1830, but the narrative moment of the young man's story is 1880. The present of the old's woman's story, however, is 1830, the referential time of writing. Aurore Dupin was then twenty-six years old, and she was not yet known as George Sand. Hence, at the time of writing, 1830, Sand invents a future time where young men read old women's books.

What does this reveal? The sibyl's story tells of an escapade with three male friends. During a *promenade* in the country they climb a mountain, the one where the young man and the old woman are presently speaking, reading, or dreamily gazing at Sand's favorite landscape, *Les Couperies.*[7] In her tale the old woman and three friends act out novels: one where the young men will be soldiers and she a nurse and cook, and another where they will defy the world and sell theriac, a mind-altering drug. When the young man finishes his reading, the old sibyl says that she was too choked up with food and laughter to speak at the time of these escapades and that it is only later, when writing, that she found her voice. What she could not tell her friends is Rousseau's formula for happiness. She learned to defy years of sorrow by looking to brief moments of *bonheur*.

In Velasquez's painting, a visual experiment, the painter makes himself *seen* as creator of the work through his medium, by painting a smaller frame for his portrait. In Sand's essay, a textual experiment, the writer makes herself *heard* through her medium, the larger text, as she narrates in her own voice, the feminine. Both feature a creative presence *en abîme*. In the Velasquez painting the creator is represented in the second degree; Velasquez paints a painter in the frame. In Sand's essay the creator is represented in the third degree: the author gives voice to a young man, who, in turn, gives voice to a woman (her story is contained within *his* story). In *Les Couperies*, as in *Ahura's Tale*, although all narrators speak in the first person pronoun, the "I's" are not of the same gender. In the Egyptian story three scribes speak as "I" for Ahura, and in Sand's, although both the young man and the old woman narrate in the first person "I," one voice is in the masculine and the other in the feminine. An extraordinary effect is created by this polyphony as the different voices take the reader out of the measured time of traditional (Homeric) storytelling. The Egyptian princess traverses centuries of life when she asks the third scribe to reunite her soul, her body, and her family. Sand's text also crosses time boundaries; meeting in the simultaneous temporalities of narration, a young male narrator and a young woman writer are reunited in a future time of artistic creation. Storytellers meet in a simultaneity of moments; since in both texts time is not immutable (it *is* subject to change) and, therefore, cannot be fixed or categorized, no one may be identified by this time. In this zone of the non-identifiable, speaking through a multiplicity of voices, blending the masculine and the feminine, the women give themselves authority (masculine) while preserving their specificity (feminine).

In the century of the restrictive Napoleonic code, how will Sand find a way to give herself authority in her own voice, how will she encode a woman's body in narratives? These concerns generate much of her early production. How will the old *voyageur* engender a woman in a first person narrative?[8] How will Aurore speak about being a woman after the creation of the old traveller and the adoption of the pseudonym "George"? Throughout her works she solves the problem of voice and gender through constructions similar to *Les Couperies*, featuring narratives opening into other narratives. Like Chinese boxes, they surprise readers and cause them to wonder about narrators and gender, and, consequently, about the sex of the implied author, in real life a woman.

Indiana: Female Heroism in the Masculine, *Une Chose Problématique*[9]

Sand leaves no doubt that the narrative voice of her first solo novel (1830) implies a man, not a woman writer.[10] "He" speaks the language of the omniscient nineteenth-century narrator who addresses readers directly to make sociological comments about events. At first glance these interjections seem to indicate that the novel's mission is to criticize the mediocrity of the bourgeoisie, but a closer investigation reveals a more complex project. Sand, wearing the mask of the conventional narrator of her time, doubles her authority. She speaks in the voice of the dominant social class *and* gender. Through him she criticizes men as writers of novels and women as readers of the genre. To criticize effectively, her narrator must depict both sexes with a mixture of admiration and pathos. Accordingly, his ironic interruptions of the narrative must point out clever parodies of both male heroism and female (docile) *heroinism.* Once his credibility is established as an elite thinker and a member of the superior sex, he gradually allows himself to plead the cause of women. First he asserts his understanding of the power of rhetoric:

> Rien n'est si facile et si commun que de se duper soi-même quand on ne manque pas d'esprit et quand on connaît bien toutes les finesses de la langue. C'est une reine prostituée qui descend et s'élève a tous les rôles, qui se déguise, se pare, se dissimule et s'efface; c'est une plaideuse qui a réponse à tout, qui a toujours tout prévu, et qui prend mille formes pour avoir raison.[11]

> Nothing is as easy and common as the way we dupe ourselves when we do not lack wit and know all the finesse of language. It acts as a queen of prostitutes who descends and ascends to all roles, who dresses up and disguises herself. It is double-faced and self-effacing, a suitor, a *plaideuse* [both a woman who pleads and/or a defense lawyer], who has an answer for everything, who has foreseen all, and who takes a thousand shapes to be right.

He also makes arrogant statements to demonstrate first-hand knowledge about members of his sex:

> Le plus honnête des hommes est celui qui pense et qui agit le mieux, mais le plus puissant est celui qui sait le mieux écrire et parler. (*Indiana,* 213)

> The most honest of men is the one who thinks and acts best, but the most *puissant* is the one who knows best how to write and speak.

The double meaning of *puissant* (powerful and potent), associating men's sex with linguistic power, is an open challenge to Sand's contemporaries. In fact, her imitation of men's language is so striking and disturbing that after reading a few pages of *Indiana,* her editor accused her of making a *pastiche,* an imitation of Balzac.[12] She was confrontational and Amazonian, yet he called her Echo. In fact, the novel does echo the intertext of men, but it imitates to subvert.

The Sandian narrator begins with open invectives against women. To distance himself from them and to place himself on the side of men, he makes derogatory declarations about his female protagonists. A variety of interventions, ranging from boorish statements about women to confessions of ignorance about them as a group, place him on the side of men. In the first case he, the superior narrator, denigrates Indiana: "Honte à cette femme imbécile!" In the second, through repetitions of the ubiquitous nineteenth-century "je ne sais quoi," he claims to lack knowledge of women's ways. Later, the same stylistic device is used to compliment women. During a conversation between Noun, Indiana's illiterate Creole maid, and Raymon, a jaded socialite, the narrator interrupts his story to declare that he, now the inferior narrator, is unable to repeat what the maid said because of his inability to capture her eloquence: "Elle dit les mêmes choses, bien mieux cent fois que je ne pourrais vous le redire" (84). This understated praise of women grows as the novel progresses. During Noun and Raymon's last conversations, he underscores her fine speech by underplaying his own. He cannot transcribe an important soliloquy, he claims, because he lacks the secret inspiration which comes to virginal souls from profound sorrow: "Où trouver le secret de cette éloquence?" (84).

The first peripeteia of the novel includes Raymon de La Ramière, a Parisian for whom Indiana eventually leaves her brutal husband and for whom she risks her life. Endowed with unusual linguistic skill, Raymon is a twin of the Sandian narrator. Readers are warned that they may be deceived by the words of this libertine:

> Ce Raymon, dont vous venez de suivre les faiblesses et de blâmer peut-être la légèreté, est un des hommes qui ont eu sur vos pensées le plus d'empire ou d'influence . . . vous avez été entrainé . . . par le charme irrésistible de son style, et les grâces de sa logique courtoise et mondaine. (113)

> This Raymon, whose weaknesses you [readers] have just witnessed and whose superficiality you have perhaps damned, is one of those men who have had the most empire or influence on your thoughts . . . you have been carried away . . . by the irresistible charm of his style, and by his courteous and worldly logic.

This brief dissertation is charged with satirical allusions to the scene of courtly poets and their listeners. Courting through syllogisms is oxymoronic, for true love, as understood by the Romantics, is antagonistic to games of logic. Linguistic play is not serious, not a carrier of truth. This interruption, addressed to readers in general, contains a subliminal message to women only. Courtois poetry is a form of flattery, a lie, in sum, a literary convention of which they should be aware.

The novel subverts all forms of stereotypical heroism. Chivalric enterprises, in word and deeds, are parodied in the first chapter; the two most important men in Indiana's life, her lover Raymon, and her husband Colonel Delmare, are caricatures of *chevaliers.* Raymon is first caught climbing the walls of the Delmare estate on his way to the room of their maid Noun, and the colonel shoots him in the buttocks with salt. Risking his life for the love of a maid and getting shot in the backside, Sand's romantic lover makes a ridiculous entrance. Firing a gun loaded with salt to defend his estate, the *paterfamilias* also appears foolish; the inoffensive missile is an obviously pejorative allusion to a lack of military *and* sexual prowess. This initial incident, skillfully narrated in a pseudo-serious tone, challenges the reader's sense of humour and calls for an intelligent awareness of the intertextualities of male heroism.

The trope of chivalric heroism, first travestied outdoors in physical confrontations over territory, continues to be misrepresented as the novel moves to the salon and to scenes of political verbal competition between the men. The Parisian is invited to stay at the Delmare estate until his wounds are healed, and the two men, along with the family friend Ralph, spend their evenings discussing politics. In these scenes, through pedantic interruptions, the narrator garners credibility as a social commentator and member of the dominant group of men. The trope of courtois poetry is further exploited as the novelist introduces a critique of female heroinism in conversations between Raymon and the two women. Both Indiana and Noun are deceived because of their willingness to risk all for a love that is assured through Raymon's words. It follows, as foreshadowed by the first chapters of the novel, that in verbal exchanges women are no match for the potent seducer. When Noun writes to Raymon to entice him to come back to her (after he has turned his attention to Indiana), she borrows her mistress's perfumed stationery. The uneducated Creole's message is, however, ineffectual. The narrator calls it a chambermaid's letter, full of grammatical errors: "Hélas! la pauvre fille à demi sauvage de l'île Bourbon ignorait même qu'il y eût des règles à la langue" (53). How could Noun's worth be approved by Raymon, how could the unlearned islander's letter be acknowledged by the sophisticated Parisian? Noun, pregnant with Raymon's child, drowns herself.

Indiana and Noun are pitted against Raymon and the narrator. In both cases they interplay as readers and writers. The two women, readers of novels and listeners of courtois flatteries, share a common ethic: unlike the inconstant narrator and Raymon, they are true to their word. The women keep a serious tone, while the men treat love with irony. Raymon writes to Indiana of his undying love when the Delmare household has to return to Bourbon Island—the island of Bernardin de Saint-Pierre's prototypical Romantic lovers, Paul and Virginie—where Noun and Indiana had been brought up because of the colonel's disastrous financial dealings. Indiana answers with a letter also swearing her love. Risking everything, she leaves her husband for him, but when she arrives in Paris, she finds that Raymon has not joined action to words. He has already married a bourgeois woman, Laure de Nangy. Like Noun, Indiana attempts suicide, but she is saved by the silent family friend Ralph.

Sand's narrator infiltrates the interchanges between lovers to remonstrate against female *heroinism*. Both he and Raymon caution women about the poor examples of womanhood one finds in novels: the narrator in interpolations to the readers and the latter in direct interrogations. Raymon asks Indiana where she has learned to dream of love, in what novel for "femmes de chambre" (210) she studied society. In the end she has learned her lesson, and she agrees with him:

> J'avais appris la vie dans les romans à l'usage des femmes de chambre, dans ces riantes et puériles fictions où l'on intéresse le coeur au succès . . . d'impossibles félicités. C'est horriblement vrai, Raymon, ce que vous dites là! . . . vous avez raison. (240)

> I had learned life in novels written for chambermaids, in these laughing and puerile fictions where our interest is involved with success of the heart . . . in impossible felicities. It is horribly true, Raymon, what you say! . . . you are right.

Noun, a pathetic victim of women's lack of book learning and worldly education but a valorous one, kills herself rather than suffer the dishonor of bearing an illegitimate child. Furthermore, her suicide teaches her educated mistress a lesson. After she discovers that Raymon is married, Indiana attempts to drown herself and becomes aware of her resemblance to Noun. In the end she realizes that she, like the Creole Noun, does not belong to the bourgeois milieu where she has been transplanted by her marriage to Colonel Delmare, and she decides to spend the rest of her life on Bourbon Island, working with an underground network to free slaves. She is thus given greater heroic dimensions than Noun; for she is virtuous in the true Roman meaning of the word, virile and stronger.

Sand added a conclusion to this first ending to broach anew the problematics of women and language. Initially the novel ended with Ralph rescuing Indiana in Paris and bringing her back to the island, where both leap into a cascade. In the added epilogue Sand shifts to the epistolary style as her narrator, now a tourist, writes a letter to J. Neraud (a friend of Sand in real life) telling him how he searches the island for Indiana but has difficulty finding her. (The reader deducts she did not die after all.) The islanders, he reports, have never heard of her. Finally he locates her deep in the island and learns that she and Ralph, her loyal friend, are living as husband and wife, but without the vows of marriage. He discovers in conversations with Ralph that she is devoting her life to freeing slaves. In this epilogue the problem of woman as speaking subject resurfaces in the speech of men.

In this novel the implications of a male author and his lack of knowledge about women are two strategies which bring the casual reader to a vague awareness of narrating and gender. The novel overtly critiques writers (men) and readers (women) of novels. Here Sand is the first to exploit the Paul-and-Virginie brand of heroism later satirized in Flaubert's *Madame Bovary*. The disastrous consequences for two women readers who let themselves be defined by the language of Romantic love is illustrated in two exchanges: one between Raymon and Noun and the other between him and Indiana, both of which end in attempts at suicide.

The final chapter of Sand's *Indiana,* like that of La Fayette's *Princesse de Clèves,* brings attention to the hero's extraordinary deeds without elaborating them. We witness another litote as Sand twice signifies through lack of elaboration: through the inability-to-describe tropes of the narrator and through the final silence of the women. Expecting to read Indiana's direct discourse—her own words quoted—in the end Sand's reader is as disappointed as La Fayette's. Indiana's presence is problematic, "une chose problématique" (343), the narrator hears from the natives. It is Ralph who tells him that Indiana is working underground, not Indiana herself. This novel, like *La Princesse de Clèves,* ends in the confines of a silent place, but such perplexing silences speak louder than words. In the end the women are no longer defined by the language of Romance and novels (men's intertext). We are left, however, with one major disparity between the two novels. Through numerous constructions *en abîme,* where women at the court tell stories to warn the hero, La Fayette narrates in the first person feminine, but Sand has yet to find strategies for a first person feminine narrator in this early novel.

Lélia: Narcissistic Subject?[13]

To do away with the controlling narrator of previous novels—the one who speaks through the mask of omniscience—and to feature first person female voices, Sand has to undermine principles of sexual identity. In *Lélia* she works out a partial answer by experimenting with androgyny. First, the epistolary form allows each correspondent to write in the first person masculine or feminine; second, all of them claim at one point to be Lélia, blending sexual identities; and third, to further challenge identity markers, Sand titled her novel with a feminized version of Lélio, a male character from Italian drama. Thus, the protagonist(s) is sexually undifferentiated.

107

Sand is notorious for playing games with gender and identity, games which extend beyond her *nom de plume*. Scholars are familiar with the variety of sobriquets with which she signed her correspondence. In *Lélia* she invents latinized names: Lélia the woman artist, Sténio the poet, Pulchérie the courtesan, Magnus the mad priest, and Trenmor the reformed libertine. All of them speak in the first person. Three of the most striking aspects of this polyphonic novel to be analyzed here are the disintegration of Lélia in the dialogical discourse of heterosexual desire with men, her reintegration in the monological discourse of homosexual desire with a courtesan, and the collapse of the text into one person's metaphysical search—Lélia's.[14]

The novel is a unique text, an anomaly, an undeniable expression of the realities of a moment of crisis. A look at the personal problems motivating the creation of this fractured novel is fundamental to its understanding. During the three years prior to its publication, serious problems had arisen for Sand, who had just left the home where, as dictated by the Napoleonic code, she had been a ward of her husband and treated as a minor. The years following her move to Paris were the most turbulent of her life. The termination of her relationship with her lover and literary collaborator, Jules Sandeau, followed by the success of her first solo novel, *Indiana*, added enormously to her preoccupations.

These conflicts are not treated in her *Histoire de ma vie*, but in the novel *Lélia*. In the autobiography, when she arrives at a stage in the story of her psychic development where, in the tradition of women's memoirs, the private and the public are in conflict, she opts for the narrative of her public and excludes any reference to her intimate life. These moments of silence in the autobiography, these "feminist withdrawals"—to use Elaine Showalter's term—generally occur shortly after the narration of her marriage to Casimir Dudevant.[15] At this point she leaves the candid, self-revelatory anecdotes of her youth in favor of more deliberate analyses of her place in the public world. It is in other genres that we find evidence of the private struggles so crucial to her artistic development.[16] Indeed, scholars have often conjectured that there exist major lacunae in Sand's autobiographical narratives of the period of her life from 1820 to 1839. These are filled in by *Lélia*, first published in 1833 and re-issued, in revised form, in 1839.[17]

This metaphysical novel is undeniably laborious. Its disregard for spatio-temporal logic, its lack of plots and transitions, and its polyphony are only understood as symptomatic of a moment of crisis. Astonished by her own creation, Sand explains in her autobiography that all its characters are fragments of one personality: her own. Retrospectively, she unifies them according to her ages.[18] But her chronological approach only leads away from the more complex system in which she casts the drama. The key to the novel's mystery lies in another suggestion, this one found in her correspondence, where she reveals that it is ''un livre assez obscur pour moi-même.''[19]

It must be acknowledged that textual experimentation was not unusual in the 1820s; the transgression of spatio-temporal limits and the transformation of Sand's speakers into one character (Lélia) were well within what had become by 1833 an accepted topos of Romanticism. In *Lélia* Sand returned to the fractured narrative modes of *Les Couperies,* and this time, through the use of metaphors, she amplified the illusion. In the early work she achieved temporal infinity, and in *Lélia* she extended it to spatial infinity. The temporal illusion is first created through the collapse of past and future anterior into the present of a text. The spatial illusion is achieved through a kaleidoscopic effect, that is, when different characters, looking at themselves in mirrors and lakes, become one. Lélia is locked in a time warp without the divisions of human history. The first scene opens onto a search for origins, and the last closes with the statement that her life has lasted ten thousand years.

The novel, a narcissistic work, centers on a woman's *impuissance.* She struggles with the problems of creative processes which bring production to a halt. The double meaning of *impuissance* (sexual frigidity and lack of power) associates sexual desire with writing, raising anew problems of narrating and gender. Lélia's status as a problematic hero is established in the very first lines of the novel, where Sténio the poet asks who she is, an angel or a demon. Lélia, appropriating language as arrogantly as Ahura, replies that she has stolen the power of the gods and that she is the Verb. While the poet casts her in the conflictual angel-demon (Echo-Amazon) archetypes, she recasts herself into Medusa, inventor of language. Against these spectacular backdrops, wearing theatrical costumes, Lélia poses and soliloquizes dramatically.

If we view the story of Lélia as more than one doubling, ''dédoublement,'' we find that the novel deploys three major conflictual archetypes of women: Echo, object of others' discourse, a wind spirit who would have no reflection in mirrors; Amazon, subject of her own discourse, who speaks in women's enclaves outside the open space of male-female interchange; and Medusa, the powerful mother who created the alphabet and gave the consonants to Hermes. In the presence of men, Lélia's discourse does not stray from the revolt against tradition which had become an established Romantic rebellion. In her dialogues with Sténio the poet, for instance, she is Echo, the subject of the other's discourse; in the presence of Pulchérie the courtesan, she is an Amazon; and in scenes with Magnus the priest, she is Medusa.

Problems of sex and artistic creation are explored in interminable soliloquies, where characters, seemingly engaged in conversations, do not truly address each other. The most significant soliloquy is located deep within the text, in a scene with the courtesan. Pulchérie is the most positive fragment of the author; she *is* the woman author chased from her own discourse. Her name obviously celebrates women's sensuality, Pulchérie being also Zinzolina, Spanish Arabic for the reddish violet color obtained from sesame; this color of blood shades their conversations. A marked shift in atmosphere takes place in the key scene. Here the two women meet, as the novel moves from its cold, theatrical, nocturnal environment to a natural outdoor setting, where diurnal imagery awakens the senses. Waterfalls, birds, bells, dogs, and voices in song are heard as Lélia and Pulchérie, in close intimacy, discuss women's problematic relations with men. Their dialogue touches on shame and bondage. Lélia confesses her dissatisfaction with heterosexual love, telling Pulchérie that after the "brutal act," she lies waiting in silence by the man who sleeps and snores contentedly while she remains unsatisfied. Then Lélia explains how a married woman prostitutes herself and how she herself had effaced her existence behind that of another. She feels shame at having voluntarily participated in the master-slave relationship of wedded couples. In this scene, Lélia uses the discourse of feminist critics who first coined the term *heroinism* for women's collusion with the destructive patterns of sanctioned marriages.[20] Yet, associating the married woman and the prostitute, Lélia subverts the discourse of marital love, and this in an age when the Napoleonic code divinized marriages.

The conversation with the courtesan then shifts from a rejection of heterosexual marriage to an exploration of homosexuality. Pulchérie tells of a dream. Although the dream is told in the first person, the "real" author is removed from this scene. George Sand—who was closely associated with the character of Lélia by posterity—cannot be accused of homosexuality, since it is the courtesan who speaks. The women are sleeping next to each other by the lake of poetry (its association with poetry is evident, as Sténio the poet dies on its shore). When they awake, the courtesan, sister and double of Lélia, tells that she dreamed they were kissing, but upon awaking and looking into Lélia's eyes, she felt a guilt which had not been not there during the dream. She then asks Lélia to look into the mirror of the lake, inviting her to know herself. She is more beautiful because she resembles a man, Pulchérie says. An important event takes place here as Lélia, who has almost no physical presence throughout the novel, shrugs her shoulders, using body language rather than words to communicate her rejection of the mirrored male persona.[21] Whatever we may conjecture from Lélia's gesture after she looks at her image in the narcissistic lake of poetry, we must acknowledge that a problem with her male persona is at issue.

This scene, linking artistic expression to homosexuality, parallels another which links it to heterosexuality. Later, the identical sisters, Lélia and

Pulchérie, decide to teach Sténio the sensual, liberating love which had temporarily freed the two of them in the dream. One evening, during a masquerade, Sténio is tricked into thinking that Pulchérie, hiding behind a domino, is Lélia. He follows her into a cave where she gives him the kiss of a mother and lover, "un baiser de mère et d'amante" (112). He believes that he has made love to Lélia but discovers in the morning that it was not she, because the women have concluded that Sténio cannot possess Lélia (125). The poet cannot possess the woman. These two love scenes, one homosexual and the other heterosexual, explore allegorically a possible reintegration of the irreconcilable "moi" fragmented by the discourse of love, the artist split by the poet's original question about angels and demons (Echo and the Amazon). Ultimately Lélia rejects both heterosexuality and homosexuality. Isolated and unable to look into the mirror of introspection, she expires at the hands of the priest.

In scenes with Magnus, Lélia confronts the destructive forces of liturgical discourse and takes on the persona of the archetypical Medusa.[22] On one occasion, Magnus enters her chambers with the intention of making love; seeing only her back, he comes closer. When she turns toward him, he sees that she has transformed herself into a laughing Medusa, and he runs away. Nevertheless, the victory of Medusa, possessor of the Verb and inventor of the alphabet, over the priest is a brief one. She is silenced forever by this mad priest, who strangles her with a rosary. The demise of Lélia clearly imputes the heterosexual discourse of liturgy.

On the last pages, in a sort of epilogue, Trenmor, the reformed sinner and mediator of lovers' quarrels, narrates. A clear personification of Sand's old *voyageur*, he teaches the cadence of lyrics. Trenmor survives to tell of a possible reunion of the writer and the woman. The three literary faces of Sand's "moi" referred to in her correspondence—Lélia, Sténio, and Magnus—die, but a metaphysical conceit foretells the return to earth of Lélia the woman and Sténio the poet. Trenmor sees an arc in the sky, its two legs originating from each side of the lake where Sténio and Lélia are buried. In the great mirror of heaven the woman and the poet are joined symbolically— through substitution—and they find peace in death and defeat.

Pulchérie's survival promises integration as she kisses both Lélia and Sténio. The novel, an endeavor to reconcile the writer and the woman in the language of the dialectic of love, will be revised and published again. The two kisses foretell the revisions of the next edition of *Lélia* six years later; this time the reintegration of the artist and the woman is spoken in Lélia's own words.

Artistic creation as a necessary relation to Lélia's sexuality is encoded in the theme of Lélia's *impuissance*, that is, her sexual frigidity. A metonymy enhances the complexity of this *necessary relation*. Lélia, the author

111

en abîme, cannot create because of her sex. A rhetoric for the female body is lacking for the nineteenth-century woman writer.[23] How does the artist create without what Patricia Meyer Spacks calls the anger of having to imitate that renders her impotent?[24] How does Sand confront the intertextual discourse of men without either echoing or opposing it, two reactions which would engage her as object or *revers* in her own discourse?

The 1833 edition of *Lélia* was followed immediately by acerbic reviews and articles, one of which even provoked a duel.[25] This violent reaction of the public, along with other events of Sand's intimate life during the next six years, led her to modify the novel considerably for a new edition in 1839. By that time she had overcome the stormy and notorious liaison with Musset, which had begun two days before the publication of the first novel and ended later in Venice. She had also terminated another liaison with Michel de Bourges, her lawyer; if we judge from her correspondence, this relationship was a more mature and sexually satisfying one. Through legal battles (which Bourges won for her), she regained all that she had lost—her domicile in Nohant as well as custody of her two children—when she moved to Paris to become a writer. This liaison ended in 1837, and Sand subsequently met Chopin, who was to live with her eight years. The court proceedings for the divorce had been scandalous, and Sand evidently did not want to raise the public's furor against her one more time with the same controversial Lélia in whose character the public recognized the author. These complications, along with her maturation as a woman and as a writer—she published a dozen novels and *Les Lettres d'un voyageur* during the six years following the first *Lélia*—explain the modifications she made in the second.

In 1839 she removed some of the most angry passages of the first *Lélia,* adding more optimistic and socially acceptable ones. These contain significant changes, as Sand, having found a public voice in which to speak her own views, created a new persona for Lélia. While in the previous edition her hero rejected her century, in the new one she incarnates it. She has the stature of charismatic figures of her time, personifying both the Romantic poet and the female messiah whom the St. Simonians were expecting. A female counterpart of Chateaubriand, a *belle ténébreuse,* Lélia preaches from mountain tops, her long hair flowing in the wind.[26]

The last chapters contain the most significant revisions. Sand places Lélia in the convent which Sténio had visited in the 1833 edition and gives her the poetic passages he had declaimed. Here, superimposing her new edition onto two female intertexts, those of Heloïse and La Fayette, Sand creates new myths of women. Lélia is a courtesan and a messiah. This time she discovers that she is joined to Pulchérie through a familial link; they were born of the same mother, Zinzolina (Pulchérie's other name in the first edition). Lélia is also ordained into a religious order in this new version. As the ceremony unfolds, it is revealed that she is the daughter of Zinzolina, that she was born in Spain, and that her original name is Lélia d'Almovar. It is then proclaimed that she is also "Annunziata," a female Christ figure. Now she becomes associated with new myths, as the puzzling angel-demon muse, subject of Sténio's questions in the first edition, is revised. During the ceremony of ordination, her gestures symbolize purification and rebirth. Shedding the skin of the *impuissante*—Sand replaces the black velvet cape of the 1833 edition with the vestment of the mythical Amazon, white linen—she frees herself from symbols of submission. After her ordination as abbess of the convent, she uses the power of her position to reverse ceremonials, just as Heloïse had subverted liturgical discourse. She removes a veil instead of donning one and speaks to the bishop as an equal. In this respect she is not unlike the earlier Lélia, who signaled rebellion by not bowing her head in church; the new Lélia, however, uses her oratorical skills to articulate her beliefs in words. Within the locus of the sorority, she comments on how the feminine operates in culture. The lessons embodied in the interruptions of *Indiana*'s male narrator are now clearly enunciated in the feminine by Lélia. A long diatribe on Don Juan admonishes women to be on guard against the perils of the discourse of Romantic love. Nevertheless, even in this more optimistic edition, Lélia, like Heloïse and the Princesse de Clèves, exhausts herself in the end and looks for peace in the silence of a convent, where she expires.

Both editions of the novel open with Sténio's question about angels or demons, but only the second closes with Lélia's reply that she is the Verb. In 1839 Sand replaced the Judeo-Christian mythologies of the earlier edition with those of ancient Greece. The final scenes contain significant revisions on the subject of the Verb, but this time it is manifestly linked to sexual *impuissance*. The death scene in the first edition associates Lélia's artistic *impuissance* with Roman Catholic myths created by men's desire, that is, with an oppressive, patriarchal, cultural heritage. In the second edition a new scene is superimposed on this first one. This time desire is associated with Prometheus instead of Magnus, as Lélia identifies with the Greek god and states in a lengthy monologue that Prometheus, whom she personifies, is "le désir impuissant" (541). This time her death is caused by her efforts to solve an inner crisis rather than by exterior forces. She loses her life after verbally exhausting herself in an interminable monologue about artistic creation, not after being strangled by Magnus. Again her voice is silenced, but in this last address, where she finds an audience, she answers Sténio's original question and reunites the angel and the demon into one desiring, Promethean woman. Lélia creates new myths, but both narratives of archetypes, liturgical and pagan—those of Magnus and Prometheus—render her *impuissante,* and she expires at the end of both versions of the novel.

In neither edition do we find evidence of a female intertext which would provide a paradigm of women's *jouissance* without implying mystical eroticism or physical and moral debasement.[27] But in the conversation with Pulchérie we do find a new, if somewhat utopic, text. Because it is the most significant, the crucial scene of the first edition remains unaltered in the second. In the deepest center of both versions, in the imaginary atemporal zone of dreams, in a space and time which pre-date sexual identity, Lélia meets her sameness, Pulchérie, and the two explore dark aspects of the male discourse of sexuality and the latency of a female one. Pulchérie holds up a double mirror to Lélia to show her both the beauty of her male reflection in the lake of poetry and the *jouissance* of her female one in her physical touch: kissing her sameness. Lélia replies with indifference to the first (the male persona) and shame to the second (homosexuality), and it is this second, the more powerful reaction, which is significant. Only in a dream, when morality is relaxed, do the women meet without shame. They enter the invisible zone of touching, the zone where Luce Irigaray writes of love of others as love of the self, "je t'aime, je m'aime" (I love you, I love myself), and where Kristeva proposes that one is not yet thought of as different.[28] There Pulchérie, feeling no shame, teaches self-love to her double, Lélia.

The kiss of the courtesan, like the wand of the fairy, unseals Lélia's lips and momentarily delivers her from her *impuissance*. In nondifferentiated language, she speaks of her own artistic prostitution and of colluding with those who cause her frigidity. In the second edition, in the gynocentric milieu of the convent, Lélia articulates her belief that women must deliver themselves from the dark aspects of the Romantics' rhetoric, Don Juan's words of love. Sand encodes the investigation of the forces which hinder creative processes for Lélia in the trope of desire—all the characters desire Lélia and are fragments of her personality—and all want to possess her (to know her). The most meaningful in terms of the search for the self are Sténio the poet and Pulchérie the courtesan, since each personifies one of the double forces which neutralize her. Lélia must face the prostitution of being a woman artist who looks like a man and a woman engaged in a sexual relationship with an unloved husband, two conditions which stultify and suffocate her. Sténio the poet desires Lélia but cannot possess (touch) her, as his differentiated language is disintegrating. Pulchérie also desires Lélia, but her nondifferentiated discourse of sexuality is aberrant. Nonetheless, she is the one who holds the promise of reintegration. Her two kisses, one for Lélia and one for Sténio, are metonymic of the integration of the woman and the artist. If Lélia learns to accept (embrace) both of these forces, she will become morally and physically integral.

■ S I X

Sand's Mature Works: The Interior Quest

Throughout her works Sand struggles to devise ways of narrating women, from the early *Les Couperies* to the late *Contes d'une grand-mère*. The previous chapter demonstrated how this problem was broached in *Indiana* and *Lélia* through negative narrational strategies. In the first case an omniscient narrator inveighs against heroism, and in the second a woman warns against collusion with destructive patterns. The present chapter proposes to demonstrate how Sand found new strategies for the deployment of the feminine in the novel of the *cantatrice* and in the story of her life.

The pervasive concern with voice in Sand's writing is nowhere more manifest than in *Consuelo*, where the protagonist is an artist, a *cantatrice*, and where a woman's genre, the fairy tale, is subverted.[1] Lélia, who was also devoted to art and who ultimately expired from vocal exhaustion, is reincarnated in Consuelo. Lélia's attempt to express herself in the admirable oratorical style of Corrine was a failure.[2] Her creative urge was diffused, and her text, lacking a spatio-temporal order, reflected her confusion. Consuelo is Lélia cured of her impotence. Her creative drive is well focused.

If in *Indiana* it is Raymon (a male character in a novel titled with a woman's name) who is the double of the omniscient narrator, in the *künstlerroman* it is Consuelo, a female protagonist who is the double of the maternal narrator. A fairy tale opening compels the reader to think of narrative voices and speaking subjects in the feminine. Although Sand valorizes woman as hero in countless novels entitled with feminine names, *Consuelo* (followed shortly by the autobiography) is the first work which brings the reader to imagine a female protagonist as well as a female authorial presence.

In this work, where the hero's most outstanding characteristic is a powerful voice, the reader may imagine that she, Consuelo, is the author (Sand) *en abîme*.

Consuelo: Female Heroism in the Feminine

A *roman feuilleton, Consuelo* was first published in installments in the *Revue indépendente* and later in the *Revue des deux mondes*. The serial format, designed for ritualized readings, places the reader in a familial nineteenth-century scene, that of nightly storytelling. In fact, Sand assigns the role of child to her implied reader and that of mother to the narrator. Through endearing addresses, such as "chère lectrice" and "lecteur bien-aimé," she reassures them as if they were children.[3] While they are naive and fearful, she is knowledgeable:

> Nous nous débattons parfois contre ces chimères et ces terreurs de la nuit, tout en nous disant qu'elles sont l'effet du cauchemar, et en faisant des efforts pour nous réveiller; mais un pouvoir ennemi semble nous saisir à plusieurs reprises, et nous replonger dans cette horrible léthargie. . . . (I, 367)

> We sometimes fight against nightly chimeras and terrors, telling ourselves that they are merely the cause of nightmares, and we struggle to wake up; but an enemy power seems to take hold of us again and again, and immerse us again into a horrible lethargy.

Music, the universal language, dominates the novel. Consuelo is a singer in search of a harmonious life, and her quests are encoded in the polivalent metaphor of music. The conflicts of the two quests specific to *Ahura's Tale,* one for love and the other for knowledge, are encoded at the start in two types of music and in the sites where it is performed: sacred music in churches and profane music on the operatic stage. An orphan without any means of support other than her own skills, Consuelo must earn her living in a man's world. She aspires to become a singer, an independent individual committed to vocational, sexual, and maternal fulfillment, but she is trapped in a culture which regards women who perform on the stage as prostitutes.

Consuelo's search for harmony begins in Venice, where she sings religious hymns. When this first quest fails, a second, interior one follows, as she moves to the deep underground labyrinths of Bohemian forests. A third quest, a monolinear one this time, takes her out of the darkness and into the enlightened cultural centers of Europe. Consuelo's major undertaking is to harmonize the overwhelming conflicts which constantly threaten to silence her. The narrator undermines intertexts of docile virgins waiting for their prince and mature women devoted entirely to motherhood. The opening chapters parody fairy tale portrayals of docility and contradict Rousseau's praise of maternity as a woman's only vocation.

The first pages of the novel challenge fairy tale descriptions of heroines with parodies of its rhetorical tradition.[4] Described in a litany of superlatives, Sand's hero is unlike heroines of fairy tales: not regal, she is small, "une petite personne" (I, 8); her skin is not snow-white, but yellow as a candle, "jaune comme un cierge" (I, 11); her body is not pretty, but rather unengaging and unexciting, "sans aucune séduction" (I, 14); and her hair is not golden, but outside any code of feminine beauty: short, thick, and combed back, "cours, épais et rejetés derrière" (I, 14). She is first seen squatting like a mouse in a corner of the *scuola,* thoroughly absorbed in the study of music. Another tradition of fairy tales is subverted in this episode when Consuelo is jilted. Her fiancé, Anzoleto, a tenor who prostitutes his art by singing for effect rather than perfection, leaves her for an attractive singer of lesser talent. Consuelo's looks fail to secure her a husband, but her singing gains her public recognition.

Sand places Consuelo in the Venetian schools which Rousseau admired, but only to reverse his description of the students in *Les Confessions.* He writes that he is so impressed by their singing that he falls in love with them, even though they are *"laiderons"* (ugly creatures).[5] The narratrice also calls Consuelo a *"laideron,"* but only to make her subsequent transformation more dramatic. When she sings, she is a beauty. Sand had evidently noticed the specious links between ugliness and artistic talent in Rousseau's autobiography, and in this novel she demonstrates the complications of the demon-angel archetypes of Romanticism:

> Un feu divin monta à ses joues, et la flamme sacrée jaillit de ses grand yeux noirs, lorsqu'elle remplit la voûte de cette voix sans égale et de cet accent victorieux, pur, vraiment grandiose, qui ne peut sortir que d'une grande intelligence jointe à un grand coeur. . . . Le Comte, ne pouvant maîtriser son émotion, s'écria: "Par tout le sang du Christ, cette femme est belle! . . . c'est la poésie, c'est la musique, c'est la foi personnifiées!" (*Consuelo* I, 74)

> A divine fire covered her cheeks and a sacred flame was seen in her large, black eyes when she filled the vault with this voice without equal, with a victorious, pure, and truly grandiose accent; one which only occurs with the union of great intelligence and a great heart. . . . The Count [Zustini], unable to restrain himself, shouted: "By the blood of Christ, this woman is beautiful! . . . She is poetry, she is music, she is faith personified."

Sand's fairy tale variants show a pedagogical intent.[6] Her hero provides new models. Subordinating the quest for marriage to the quest for career, her story takes the focus away from the book of domestic learning and shifts it to the book of worldly learning. Vladimir Propp's study of tales proves that their structures are constant, and it is indeed this consistency, the accepted tropes of female heroinism, that Sand exploits as the axis of her variants. Consuelo's achievements are not to be recognized in the confines of home, but in public arenas. She displays outstanding characteristics, and, as with heroines of fairy tales, men compete for her; in her case, however, the stake is artistic achievement rather than physical beauty. Consuelo is not passed on from father to husband (because of her potential to continue the family line by bearing children), but from music master to impresario because of her musical talent. To subvert the pedagogical discourse of fairy tales, *la plus belle* is replaced by *la plus studieuse*. Consuelo is a stranger in her milieu, an exception, unlike other girls; the young *"choristes"* do not recognize in her a girl of latent heroic dimensions. They ridicule her because she prepares herself to make a living from her art instead of learning to attract a marriage partner.

As in fairy tales, Consuelo's conflicts arise when she reaches sexual maturity. She is warned that she must preserve the sacred aspect of her art *and* her virginity, and the two become inextricably associated in her mind. Her maestro advises that she must forgo sexual pleasure to attain artistic perfection: "Je ne te veux ni mari, ni amant, ni famille, ni passions, ni liens d'aucune sorte" (I, 147). He exhorts her to keep her virginity by telling her that she will lose herself if she gives herself to a mortal being: "Le jour où tu te donneras à un mortel, tu perdras ta divinité" (I, 147). Consuelo, who must question these societal restrictions being passed on to her, feigns not to understand him:

> Mon maître, lui repondit-elle, vous êtes grand, mais je ne le suis pas assez pour vous comprendre. Il me semble que vous outragez la nature humaine en proscrivant ses plus nobles passions. . . . Peut-être vous comprendrais-je mieux si j'étais plus chrétienne: je tâcherai de le devenir, violà ce que je puis vous promettre. (*Consuelo* I, 147)

> My master, she replied, you are great; but I am not great enough to understand. It seems that you outrage human nature by proscribing its noblest passions. Perhaps I would understand you better if I were a better Christian: I will try to become one, here is what I can promise.

In a conversation between her two mentors, it is clearly enunciated that Consuelo's choices do not include domestic duties. The impresario Zustini asks Porpora to give him his talented pupil for his theater, but the maestro replies that he prefers to make a good nun of her, "une bonne religieuse" (I, 69). The antithesis of the angel and the demon first surfaces here in two opposite choices of careers. While Porpora recommends that she dedicate herself to sacred music and sing in convents and churches because he views his pupil as a good nun, Zustini asks her to sing profane music on the operatic stage, for he sees in her a fallen woman. He calls her a devil. When he finally hears her sing and sees her at the same time (previously he had heard her voice but had not been able to see her, and he thought her voice belonged to her beautiful rival Clorinda), he exclaims: "C'est toi qui es le diable en personne!" (I, 84). But the narrator introduces the reader to Consuelo's determination not to let artificial conflicts distract her from the genuine ones. She hears from Porpora and Zustini that purity of art and body are interdependent and that she should decide which one will be sacrificed, but the reader is informed that she disagrees with their premise. During a public performance, the *narratrice* interrupts her story to tell her reader that Consuelo's real beauty has no relation to either physical traits or virginity:

> La beauté s'observe, s'arrange, se soutient, se contemple, et se pose pour ainsi dire sans cesse dans un miroir imaginaire placé devant elle. La laideur s'oublie et se laisse aller. Cependant il en est de deux sortes; l'une qui souffre et proteste sans cesse contre la réprobation générale par une habitude de rage et d'envie: ceci est la vraie, la seule laideur; l'autre, ingénue, insouciante, qui prend son parti, qui n'évite et ne provoque aucun jugement, et qui gagne le coeur tout en choquant les yeux: c'était la laideur de Consuelo. (*Consuelo, I, 14–15*)

> Beauty observes, arranges, supports, and contemplates itself. It poses itself, so to say, endlessly into an imaginary mirror placed in front of itself. Ugliness forgets itself and lets itself go. However, there are two kinds: one, often raging and envious, suffers and protests ceaselessly against general reprobation; this is the true, the only ugliness: the other, ingenuous, without worry, will commit itself and neither avoid nor provoke judgment and win the heart while shocking the eyes: such was Consuelo's ugliness.

Out of the convent and onto the stage, the hero of the novel must learn why, in the public eye, artistic expression and the gratification of her sexual body—the *souillure* of the lower order—interfere with each other. In the Venetian episodes she first realizes that allowing these conflicts to occupy her thoughts stifles her. She learns through allegory that both her maturing sexuality and her art cause jealous quarrels and that there exists a mysterious association between sex and artistic expression. She loses both her fiance and her position at the theater. Anzoleto, jealous of her success, leaves her and her singing career in Venice ends in a furious *cabale*. As a result, the Spanish orphan leaves the city with a talismanic letter from her master Porpora and undertakes a search for inner knowledge.

The mysteries of Venice, locus of the first scenes of the novel of initiation, are encoded in a network of sounds. Cacophonic during the day, but harmonious at night when the *avocato* sing in accord with ringing clocks, whispers, and kisses, the Italian city confuses Sand's hero just as it did young Rousseau and Balzac's Sarrasine.[7] Consuelo is also duped because, like Balzac's Frenchman, she does not understand the cultural undercurrents of the city. Deceived by her unfaithful fiancé Anzoleto (obviously a male counterpart of Zulietta, the courtesan who confounded young Rousseau), she leaves Venice and heads for Bohemia. In the castle of the giants, sounds are stifled. The owners, the Rudolstadts, have not spoken to their neighbors for ten years, and they hide a mad son who is given to periods of mutism. Unlike Lélia, Consuelo becomes silent when the progress of her career ceases, but also unlike the previous hero, she listens rather than raging and lamenting.

While the Homeric hero both fears and is attracted to female voices, Consuelo is drawn to the silence of men. Although Consuelo is attracted to men, she cannot commit herself, for marriage impedes her career. As in the case of Homer, when Sand's hero enters a zone inhabited by the man who will attract her, she depicts her in tropes of silence. But in contrast to the bard's story, these episodes *are* narrated. Prolific paragraphs describe Consuelo's arrival in the castle of the giants. Foreboding sounds announce her: the tolling of an enormous bell; the squeaks of the bridge; and one single, dramatic clap of thunder. Misunderstandings, all of them cast in the metaphor of sound—including human voices—mark her stay with the Rudolstadts. Members of the family are introduced according to their languages and their appreciation of music. Consuelo speaks Spanish, Italian, and French, but her knowledge of German, the language of the Rudolstadts, is limited. As for them, not only do they not know Spanish or Italian, they do not know much about music. Amelia, Albert's promised fiancé, sings off-key, and the baron prefers hunting fanfares above all. Only the mysterious Albert is able to communicate with Consuelo, for he speaks Spanish and knows the language of music. Her double, he speaks her language, is a musician, and, although older (thirty years of age), is still pure. The family has named him its *"souffre-douleur"* (I, 191), and he also personifies Consuelo's suffering. He is overcome with moments of madness, during which he hears voices from the past and relives anterior lives; he disappears for days, during which the family helplessly cries and prays; and it is given to Consuelo, as implied by her name, to save and console him. To find the mysterious madman, she must travel a long distance through dangerous underground labyrinths.

In this key episode, Sand, working anew on the palimpsest of genres where women are child-like, uses the motifs of fairy tales in which women's (and children's) inadequate footwear designate fragility and vulnerability. Grace Stewart retraces this trope to the *künstlerroman*, a genre where

120

"the feet and legs of female artists receive inordinate attention."[8] She finds that no fully integrated human being, no creature both artist and woman, is depicted in the novels under her scrutiny. I do, however, locate in my own study of Sand's portrayal of the female artist the very tropes and motifs Stewart locates: the preoccupation with planting one's feet firmly on the ground (117); the conflict which female artists face between the selfless role of the heroine and the self-expressive role of the artist; and the conflict of the artist-self as a monster. In Sand's novel, moreover, these tropes signify the very process of the struggle for integration which no human ever totally achieves. In other words, Sand displays these as motifs of a process, not a state of being.

Consuelo fabricates boots to travel in the slippery tunnels of the labyrinths. As in fantastic fairy tales, a magic object, the sound of Albert's violin, guides Consuelo through the meandering paths of the labyrinths. When the hero overcomes her weaknesses, the storyteller borrows from medieval archetypes, comparing Consuelo to Bradamante and to Joan of Arc, who dreamed of liberating her country: "Jeanne d'Arc avait rêvé et entrepris la délivrance de sa patrie" (I, 257). Before she descends underground, Consuelo must decode a phrase in a foreign language. She does and, after hours of travelling through tunnels, enters Albert's inner sanctum with the use of magic keys, finds him raving incoherently about his ancestors, and spends the night consoling him and watching over him. She cures him through such a lengthy logotherapy that, in the morning, she loses all energy and he has to carry her back. In the labyrinth, Consuelo faces the monstrosity of being a woman artist, and after she awakes from the illness (during which she aborts a monster, symbolized by bleeding), fortified by Albert's faith in her, she undertakes the search for world knowledge. She leaves Bohemia for the open road. Once again a variant of a female trope is introduced, for, if Consuelo needs to be accepted by Albert as a worthy woman-artist, it will not happen through revelation or by the removal of an exterior artifice—a donkey's skin or a layer of ashes. She will be the agent of her own transformation. The solution to her conflicts lies not simply in gaining recognition from the social group for artificial conformity, but in undertaking a journey of self-discovery. The significance of these borrowings lies in the outcome, as it is at the end of the search that Sand introduces her variant of fairy tales. She reverses the sexual identity of the savior: Consuelo is the strong one and Albert the one in need.

Showalter comments that Sand was a heroine to British women writers not "because she transcended femininity, but because she was involved in the turbulence of womanly suffering." Although I am generally in agreement with her findings, I disagree with her proposal that it was Sand's life which influenced British writers. It was her novels. What is important in

Showalter's work is that she draws our attention to major similarities in French and English women's narratives of male and female heroism. I find that Sand's portrayals of heroism, like Charlotte Brontë's description of Jane Eyre, neutralize traditional narratives of strength and weakness. My own revisionist readings of Sand's works were motivated by Showalter's proposal that Rochester's blindness, for instance, is an "immersion of the hero in feminine experience" and by her suggestion that the "woman's man must find out what it is to be a woman" (152). My readings have determined that several of Showalter's observations, for example her conclusion that Brontë treats the heroine as an equal rather than as a "sensitive fragile fool who must be sheltered and protected" (143), support my finding of similarities in women's works across the Channel. It would be difficult to find one of Sand's female heroes who, even if she is fragile, does not overcome her weakness and demonstrate some—albeit often silent—inner virtue.[9]

Albert and Consuelo are obviously destined for each other, but one peripeteia after another impedes their union. The marriage-career conflict is not settled until volumes later, for in the Bohemian episodes Consuelo's ears are still ringing with the admonitions of her master. As in the Homeric quest, the hero learns about the world outdoors, in daylight and on the road. During the peregrinations which follow, she learns that marriage is not only an impediment to women's artistic drive, it is a sorry way of life. She sees that intelligent women who marry waste their energy performing what she considers meaningless domestic duties. Her political perspicacity sharpens. She observes that some of the stumbling blocks to women's selfhood are universal, and she considers her orphaned state a blessing. It makes her an exception. She also indicates that her desire for Albert is not to be acknowledged at the moment, because men are subject to a madness which she must learn to understand. She crosses the gender of the mad-woman-in-the-attic trope. In one of her inner dialogues, Consuelo worries that her lover-to-be and her maestro are threatened with loss of reason: "Albert et le Porpora sont . . . également menacés de perdre la raison ou la vie" (*Consuelo*, II, 315).

The novel moves back and forth between episodes which tell of the female hero's quest for world knowledge in the historic linear mode and her search for inner knowledge in underground explorations. Consuelo's travels to the musical centers of Europe alternate with interior, narcissistic voyages of self-discovery, and she becomes more integrated with each adventure. The urgency of society's demand that she be docile to father and husband weakens as her artistic career grows and as she places herself in situations where she lives the man's condition. Like her creator, Consuelo discovers a simple solution to the obstacles a woman meets during her career: she lowers her voice and disguises herself as a man. On the open road, with her fellow student Hayden, she experiences the superficiality of gender barriers by transforming herself into a *chevalier,* complete with boy's attire.

If Sand masculinizes her female hero, she also feminizes her male one. She demonstrates how Albert discovers his true mission when he alters his male behavior. He is cured of his madness when he nurtures and supports Consuelo. The prototype of many of Sand's male protagonists, Albert, a mild man, takes his mother's name and gives away his "patrimonie" (I, 192). His mores become as pure as those of a "young girl" (I, 194), and he unshackles himself from the "l'antique ardeur chevaleresque" (I, 199).

For Consuelo the artist, the risk lies not in listening and reading, but in infiltrating the world of men—by singing profane music on the public stage, speaking democratic ideals, and, finally, keeping a journal of the journeys of a female composer. Consuelo usurps the prerogative of the Homeric hero. When she is incarcerated for speaking her democratic political opinions, she fills her solitary hours by composing music and recording her deeds in a journal. Later, in the penultimate chapter of the *roman feuilleton,* she is accepted into the prestigious religious sect of the *Invisibles,* honored as a female hero. In this episode, she returns underground once more and faces centuries of ancestral traditions. By looking at artifacts and skeletons—as a scientist would, rather than by reading history, as women did—she sees concrete evidence of her heritage of tyranny. When she reaches the inner sanctum of the sect, a mysterious person called Wanda, her voice lowered with age, initiates her into the secret society of the *Invisibles.*

Sand returns in the end to consider the hermeneutics of artistic creation as prostitution, a concept first introduced in *Lélia* and then in the Venetian episode of *Consuelo.* At first, Consuelo had been neutralized to silence by her lack of knowledge. Now, at the completion of her quest, she has learned that to become heroic, women must be educated about the true meaning of prostitution. She reverses the fundamental assumption that it is sexuality for profit and pronounces it a waste of women's creative drive. Women, she concludes, sacrifice their talents to no one's profit. She discovers that the truth of artistic profanity about which Porpora had warned her had more relation to gender than to sexuality. It was society's view of women's artistic productions as prostitution which she had to face and overcome. Wanda, endowing Consuelo with heroic dimensions, informs her that she is an exception, one of only a few women to become members of the sect, for ordinary women are too weak (uneducated) to join them. She admonishes Consuelo:

Quoi que de cyniques philosophes aient pu dire sur la condition passive de l'espèce féminine dans l'ordre de la nature, ce qui distinguera toujours la compagne de l'homme de celle de la brute, ce sera le discernement dans l'amour et le droit de choisir. La vanité et la cupidité font de la plupart des mariages une *prostitution jurée*. (*Consuelo*, III, 384).

Whatever cynical philosophers may have said about women's passive condition in the order of nature, discernment in love and the right to choose would always distinguish the companion of a man from that of a brute. The vanity and cupidity of most marriages make them a *sworn prostitution*.

Women, implies Sand, must be educated to their sexuality. The problem lies in who will expound this pedagogy. Who will speak of woman's sexuality? How problematic this was for Sand becomes evident when we examine the voices who speak these lessons. Albert and the androgynous Wanda speak words Lélia had spoken in the earlier novel. Albert is the one who states that the sacrament of marriage is only profitable to men. Sand's shifting of these words from a female to a male protagonist indicates that after the scandal of *Lélia,* she has become more cautious. She attributes controversial ideas to her male characters, for then readers are less likely to ascribe them to the author.

Nowhere in Sand's works is this struggle with voice and author more fully elucidated than in the novel of the *cantatrice*, where she underscores problems specific to women writers. Is giving authority to men's voices collusion? Is it selling out? Is conforming to literary traditions a woman writer's true prostitution? Narrative after narrative, trope after trope, Sand masculinizes her women and feminizes her men. If her heroic woman needs to be validated by a man, her heroic man is her complement; his function is not only to validate her, but to do so in a non-dominating manner. Sand subverts through her portrayal of Albert. His divergences in ways of interacting with women are striking. He takes them out of the essentialist prison, where tales of Homeric and *chevaleresque* quests have placed them as silent mirrors of men's desires, and gives them heroic dimensions as speaking subjects. Consuelo, he claims, possesses extraordinary gifts of music and poetry: "La femme douée de génie et de beauté est prêtresse, sibylle et initiatrice" (*Consuelo*, I, 385). (The woman of genius, endowed with genius and beauty, is a priestess, a sibyl and an initiator.) Likewise, their son sings her praise. Writing lyrics to her compositions and accompanying himself on the guitar, he sings a ballad to "La bonne déesse de la pauvreté" (III, 551). Through narratives of the Medusa-Hermes archetype, Sand undermines patriarchal history: in a sibylic gesture of genius and beauty, Consuelo initiates her son into her art. She gives away the alphabet (the voice) to her son, but preserves her creative genius by composing the music.

Consuelo is finally united to Albert in this episode, when all conflicts are reconciled and when she has accomplished her destiny as an artist and an individual fully integrated into an egalitarian society. On the road, in Rousseau's zone of the promenade, in indefinite spaces between patriarchal cities, she and Albert live the rest of their lives as equals and without the sacrament of marriage. In Venice Consuelo had openly stated her doubts about any association of artistic perfection with virginity. In Bohemia she worked out how she had internalized these values and then aborted them. And finally, when she accepts herself, Albert accepts her and they are united.

Sand's concern with gender is clearly indicated in this text, which features a patrilineal as well as a matrilineal heritage. Albert received instructions on the ideology of the sect of the *Invisibles* from his mother, Wanda, and it is he who, Christ-like, addressed crowds on the road to promulgate their ideology. Consuelo's mother was a *zingara*, a goddess of song. She passed her talent on to the future generations through Consuelo who, in turn, passes it on to her son.

Histoire de ma vie: **The Quest for the *Femme Perdue***

Problems of narrating women constantly manifest themselves in Sand's writings. The epilogue of *Consuelo* contains a startling comment about narrative voice and female heroism. Following the revelation that Consuelo has lost her voice, the narrator tells readers that humans lack the imagination to understand why: "Ici il y a une grande lacune, à laquelle notre imagination ne peut suppléer" (III, 531). Imagining and narrating women becomes troublesome in the autobiography, where a woman, Aurore Dupin, has signed the cover of her life story with a male pseudonym, George Sand.

In the preface to an edition of critical works on women's autobiographies, Domna Stanton observes that for writers the act itself has to be broached in a context of sexual identity.[10] For George Sand the question of referential status of narrative persona to author presents an unusual obstacle. How will "he," George, speak in the first person for "she," Aurore Dupin? "His" discourse is already established; he has shown himself as the omniscient narrator of the novels. It is Aurore's discourse that is problematic. How will a female speaking subject be given authority? Will Aurore be disclosed by George in a discourse of self-revelation modeled on the writings of women or men: from the letters of Heloïse and the memoirs of the mystics or from the confessions of Abelard and Rousseau? Also, how will her female specificity be narrated within the context and intertext of her own repressive century? These are the questions that the remainder of this chapter means to address.

As in the story of Ahura, who had said something to gain the approval of her father (the man in power), Sand addresses great writers in order to be accepted into their brotherhood. Like the Egyptian princess who said something extraordinary, Sand challenges the ideas of literary figures of the past. George models "his" first three chapters on the personal expository style of Montaigne and Rousseau, claiming "her" (Aurore's) place in a line of autobiographers. Then, in the next eleven chapters, Sand turns over the narrating task to the voices of a woman and a man: Marie and Maurice Dupin, Aurore's grandmother and father. Sand transcribes their correspondence during the Italian campaigns. Gradually, in brief passages between letters which pre-date her birth, a discourse for Aurore engenders itself. In the next twenty-five chapters, the first-person voice takes over, narrating in the episodal style of traditional nineteenth-century novels and disclosing, in the feminine, the author's childhood and adolescence. These central chapters provide valuable information about the development of a woman writer. The final chapters, bearing titles which announce private anecdotes ("My Literary and Intimate Life," for example), pattern themselves on the style of St. Simon's and Manon Roland's memoirs.[11] Portraying public figures of her time distances the author from her own life at the referential moment of writing. Hence problems of narrating Aurore, the mature woman writer, surface in the opening and closing chapters—when the time of writing, referential time, meets the time of the narration—but not in the central ones which concern her youth.

The prefatory chapters of *Histoire de ma vie* feature time-honored tropes of transformation; here Sand inaugurates her investigation of the problematics of identity principles. She frames her investigation within the ideologies of two philosophers from previous centuries. She adopts the notion of perpetual movement promoted in the essays of Montaigne and the *promenades* of Rousseau. A master of narrative strategies, Sand transposes traditionally gender-linked relations of dominance and submission between implied writers and readers by narrowing or increasing the distance between them through two alternating discourses. A maternal one brings writers and readers closer to each other, and a paternal one distances them.

When addressing Rousseau, the tone is intimate and maternal. Taking hold of the mother-son relation he so praises, Sand stages a familial scene and reverses his model, giving the mother (herself) the role of powerful speaking subject and the philosopher (Rousseau) the role of reader. She responds to his persona of wild child in need of consolation by retrieving a pet name given to him by female intimates. She calls him an *ours*, a sort of gruff but lovable bear. Holding the pen, she comments on his model of autobiography. To intimate revelations of his fate as an orphan in exile, she responds with words of consolation; to what she calls his confessing Madame de Warens while he confessed himself, she responds with words of reprimand. Didactic editor of his works, she shows forbearance after reading that he stole

126

from Francueil (Dupin was also called Francueil), stating that he never mentioned anything about the *philosophe* stealing from him. She scolds Rousseau for his misanthropy and tries to redress his rejection of his children. Following the lead of Mme Dupin de Chenonceaux, who supported them during his life, she would sustain them by being their textual grandmother. In fact, she once sketched a play about one of his children, whom she placed in a crowd during the Revolution. One could suggest that Sand wished to reclaim for the child the place his father had denied him in history.[12]

Nevertheless, her disapproval of his misanthropy is surpassed by admiration for his eulogies of motherhood. Sand relates anecdotes which associate her with the great *philosophe* through the sensual. Reacting affirmatively to his praise of women's immense capacity for sensitivity, she includes him in her family's history through tears. She describes how her grandmother invites him to dinner after a tearful reading of *La Nouvelle Héloïse*. Rousseau arrives, enters the vestibule, looks at her, and bursts into tears. She also begins to sob, and they sit a moment, staring at each other in silence. After this awkward introduction, they move to the dining room, but the mood does not shift. The dinner is a sad disaster, and Rousseau leaves quickly, without saying a word. In this anecdote Sand touches on the very essence of the ideal interaction with Rousseau's deceased mother, exemplified in the familial nightly scenes where he and his father read novels from her library and cried together. Sand regrets having to scold him: "Pardonne-moi Jean-Jacques, de te blâmer en fermant ton admirable livre des *Confessions.*"[13] (Forgive me Jean-Jacques, for blaming you as I close the admirable book of your *Confessions.*) Most of all, she responds to his statement that not enough has been said about the relationship between mothers and sons by devoting five hundred pages to the correspondence of her grandmother and her father.

Of interest to the study of intertextuality is how these chapters transform the prescribed usage of male and female discourses by giving the submissive role to the son and the dominant one to the mother. In Sand's case this subverts men's narrations of competitive battles over objectified women, but in Rousseau's case it does not. In spite of all their contractual pacts, men in his works are engaged in a competition. What is iconoclastic in Rousseau's intertext is the subversion of patriarchal narratives of heroism.

Both Rousseau and Sand invent familial scenes to neutralize sexual desire. In the *Contrat Social,* a reasonable rhetoric binds the individuals of Rousseau's ideal community; but the passionate rhetoric of the participants' desire in the *ménage à trois* of *La Nouvelle Héloïse* subverts the very notion of the contract. Although life at Clarens, like the idealistic arrangement suggested in the essay, is governed by a contractual, linguistic pact, although the men's rivalry seems neutralized by their sworn friendship, a drive stronger than friendship, desire for Julie—the mother of St. Preux's biological child and Wolmar's step-child—disrupts the order of the group. Rousseau demonstrates the failure of his own social ideals as he fictionalizes a group whose cohesion depends, after all, on two men's desire for a woman, that is, on competition. Maternal Julie dies, the ideal community is threatened by snows, and the two men part. Seen through the eyes of St. Preux, the orphaned lover, Julie's death causes the reader to cry over her but with him. The nineteenth century no longer weeps over the death in battle of Roland, the victorious *preux,* but laments instead Rousseau's St. Preux's loss of a maternal lover.

Sand also recasts the family into an order which would neutralize the rivalry of sexual desire. Like Rousseau, she rebels against society's encoding of the family within a frame of patriarchal legitimacy, but not, as he claimed, because it disfranchises the individual; what she borrows from him are revolutionary ideas about the power of maternity. Favoring solidarity rather than individuality, she portrays groups gathering together through mutual nurturing. After him and because of him, the mood is propitious to proclaim a manifesto for metagenisis. That is, in her ideal social order, the family would coalesce through the maternal propensity for nurturing rather than through competition.

An unprejudiced discourse reflects Sand's wisdom at this stage of her life. She dialogues as an equal, and in the feminine, with Montaigne as well as Rousseau. Both teacher and student, she gives Montaigne a lesson on women and friendship and takes one from him on writing and time. Her discourse is generally in amiable agreement with Montaigne's, but it becomes confrontational when addressing his pronouncement that women are incapable of the lofty status of friendship. His assertion that women lack intellectual strength motivates a vindication of women's writings. She replies with praises of women writers. She contradicts his statement that women lack intellect by claiming to be the descendant of an intelligent woman, thus praising both her own writings—she is after all an author herself—and Madame Dupin's, the wife of Francueil, for whom Rousseau served as secretary. One of Dupin's essays, Sand insists, takes precedence over Montesquieu's *L'Esprit des lois* because, although it may be "inférieur" in form, it is "supérieur" in content (*Oeuvres autobiographiques,* I, 42).

In the last pages of this first chapter, having acknowledged her debt to both Montaigne and Rousseau and having annotated their ideas with a mixture of defensiveness and self-assertiveness, Sand develops a thesis of her own. This is buttressed not only by their concepts of the *branloire pérenne* and the *promenade,* but also by her own contemporaries' concept of Romantic metempsychosis. She recasts Montaigne's notion of the changeability of the "I" of today, his claim to "paint the passage," as well as Rousseau's notion of the fluidity of his discourse about himself, the *promenade,* into a trope of her own.[14] Observing birds' power of flight (the way they communicate through harmonious sounds, fly to save each other, and form family units through spontaneous adoption), she proposes aviary heroism as a paradigmatic axis for human heroism. Although she mocks it, she suggests a process of metempsychosis between birds and humans. She and her readers may have once been members of the plumed species. Aviary virtue may be observed in those who communicate harmoniously and respond nobly to everyone's needs, states Sand, who favors adoption over blood lines. (A number of her novels feature spontaneous adoption.) Like birds, humans may fly free of the restrictions of patriarchal family structures based on blood lines.

Montaigne's and Rousseau's individual experiments to escape the self-imposed limitations of humanity stress isolation. Both the essayist's and the *philosophe*'s tropes represent states which free but isolate them. The *branloire* as well as the *promenade* are metonymies for transient states through which they would escape the ephemeral order of a universe measured spatio-temporally: men's cities. Sand, however, experiments with the metonymy of flight. She signifies through a trope of necessary relations, joining and preserving the individual within the group rather than isolating him or her. The flight to communicate and nurture proposes to free humanity from self-imposed limitations. Following the example of birds and reaching beyond legitimate ties, humanity could free itself through spontaneous adoption and expand the concept of the legitimate—and thus blood-related family—into a fuller spectrum. But the flight to communicate and nurture, a revolutionary concept, was dismissed through faint praise, when posterity baptized Sand the good lady of Nohant, "la bonne dame de Nohant."

All these tropes—Montaigne's *branloire,* Rousseau's *promenade,* and Sand's flight—arise from analyses of the "moi." Montaigne's *branloire,* a metaphysical search for absolute knowledge of one's place in the universe, originates with himself; in prefatory advice to the reader, he says "je suis moi-même la matière de mon livre" (I am myself the matter of my book). This astonishing statement translates into "me-same" (the English "myself" is not a proper equivalent). As Kristeva points out, the concept of "self" does not lend itself to translation, as a different word has not been coined in French for the psychological concept of "me"; it remains "moi."[15] The play on "Je suis autre" on the first page of Rousseau's *Les Confessions* translates into "I am other" and, like his *promenade,* signifies a narcissistic search for autonomy through knowledge. Sand's flight, also a quest for knowledge, is a thetic rhetorical trope also founded on "moi," but here on "moi-nous" (me-we or us). To Montaigne's and Rousseau's rhetorical figures of narcissistic evasion, one stoic, the other hedonistic, Sand proposes one of metonymy for altruistic and hedonistic evasion: nurturing.

The intertext of Rousseau as it transpires in Sand's works differs from the way it manifests itself in her contemporaries' writings and makes her a maverick within the generation of the Romantics to which she belongs. Rousseau's sensory *promenade,* a reaction to the Age of Enlightenment, became one of the Romantics' favorite tropes, and their heroes isolated themselves in the passive sensual *jouissance* of his immeasurable time and space. Later, but still in Sand's time, other exponents of Rousseau's narratives of fluidity achieved by breaking down sensory barriers, also impressed flights of fancy upon the imagination. The Symbolist poets, who pursued the idea into the "correspondences" of the objects of their sensory apprehensions— sights evoked sounds and vice-versa—devoted poems to birds as symbols of themselves. But while the Romantics and the Symbolists favored symbols (substitutions) Sand preferred metonymy (relations). For instance, she designates the generative power of motion toward a union—a necessary relation outside territorial nomenclatures.

Her use of aviary tropes, so popular in her century, differs from that of her contemporaries. The albatross in Leconte de Lisle's and Beaudelaire's poems is symbolic; it substitutes the haughty qualities of great birds for the superiority of the poet. In Lisle's poem, the victory of the proud albatross leads nowhere, in nimbus; in Beaudelaire's poem, the great white wings of the albatross cause his downfall. In the end, like the first *Lélia* of Sand's years of *impuissance,* the Symbolists' albatross loses himself in the "gouffres amers de l'univers" (abyss of the universe). In contrast to the defeatist and isolationist pantheism of the Symbolists and of her own early novel, the rhetorical figure for the power of flight in Sand's autobiography stresses the unitarian optimism of interrelation. This contrast explains why her later writings about spontaneous adoption and anonymous families of peasants provoked violent reactions in readers who no longer saw in her the Lélia of early years. They re-named her the "bonne dame de Nohant," the kindly grandmother of later years. They saw in the mixing of families an invitation to what Girard refers to as a female, nondifferentiated, primeval state, and they rejected it.[16]

Among the ideologies which influenced Sand, the most constant was Rousseau's spirit of egalitarianism. She disagreed as he did with existing family structures, but if she were to engage him in a dialogue, she would surprise him by regrouping people not into the frame of a social contract, but into the cohesive nurturing of the mother-child relationship he praised so highly.

Once Sand has established her position as an authoritative thinker and writer, responding to the discourse of philosophers and poets, in what discursive categories will she encode her personal life? The autobiography departs from the language of her own familial history, that is, from stories she has heard and from documents and correspondence she has read (the first from the maternal line and the second from the paternal). Two separate mythologies, one from the Delabordes and one from the Dupins, provide two rhetorics for the split of Aurore and George. To recuperate Aurore the woman, daughter of her mother, within the text of "George" the writer, descendant of her father, Sand encodes her double identity in the *peuple*-aristocrats conflict of the French Revolution: the common people—Delaborde, her mother's side—and the aristocrats—Dupin, her father's side. Casting Sand's own conflicts within those of the two factions of the Revolution, the autobiography integrates the oral tradition of the common people with the written one of the nobles, resulting in a valorization of the common people without a rejection of the aristocracy. A woman speaking as a man abolishes the power base from which traditional narrators speak and situates the speaking subject both in the historical time of men (George's) and in the universal time of living the women's condition (Aurore's).[17]

Sand first abjures the paternal and conjugal titles (the noble *particule* de): "Mon nom n'est pas Marie-Aurore de Saxe, marquise de Dudevant, comme plusieurs de mes biographes l'ont découvert, mais Amantine-Lucile-Aurore Dupin" (*Oeuvres autobiographiques,* I, 13). (My name is not Marie-Aurore de Saxe [her father's ancestors], Marquise Dudevant [her husband's], as many of my biographers have discovered, but Amantine Lucile-Aurore Dupin.) She also sabotages the paternal family's claim to an aristocratic lineage by placing the Dupins in the margin of history. Retracing their bastardy, she states that her father was a "natural" grandchild—a euphemism for an illegitimate son—of Auguste II, King of Poland (1679–1733).

After thus reviewing her ancestry on the Dupin side, she affirms a more legitimate parentage on the maternal side:

> On n'est pas seulement l'enfant de son père, on est aussi un peu, je crois, celui de sa mère. Il me semble même qu'on l'est davantage, et que nous tenons aux entrailles qui nous ont portés, de la façon la plus immédiate, la plus puissante, la plus sacrée. . . . Je tiens au peuple par le sang, d'une manière tout aussi intime et directe; de plus, il n'y a point de bâtardise de ce côté-là. (*Oeuvres autobiographiques,* I, 15–16).

> We are not only our father's child, we are also a little our mother's. It even seems that we are even more so, and that we hold on to the entrails which have carried us in a more immediate fashion, in the most powerful, the most sacred manner. . . . I am linked to the people by blood in a way that is just as intimate and direct [as the one to royalty] and, furthermore, there are no bastards on that side.

Unlike her predecessors St. Augustine and Rousseau, who link themselves to the maternal through the liquidity of milk and tears, she does

131

so through blood. Thus her mother-child bond, pre-dating breast feeding and crying, is formed before birth, before one is separated from the mother and inserted into historical time, when, as Kristeva proposes, someone is there, but no one speaks. Sand and Kristeva glorify this pre-linguistic state; Sand writes that it is more immediate, powerful and sacred, and Kristeva that it is more assured, for it is not subject to rhetoric.[18] Combining maternal and paternal discourses, Sand situates herself in the monumental time of living the woman's condition.

What better relation of power for a woman than that of mother and child? Sand transcribes and romanticizes five hundred pages of her grandmother's correspondence with her father during the Napoleonic campaigns. She writes: "Quel beau sujet de roman . . . si les principaux personnages n'eussent été mon père, ma mère et ma grand-mère!" (I, 77–78). (What beautiful subject for a novel . . . if the major characters had not been my father, my mother and my grandmother!) But what difficulties these five hundred pages reveal about writing the self in the feminine. Sand first gives authority to women by mocking the discourse of dominance and submission of the romance, giving Marie Dupin the mentor's role and Maurice that of a submissive *chevalier*. After hesitating to insert a woman, herself, into George's narratives in the prefatory chapters, Sand finally gives birth to Aurore in the spaces between their letters, *en abîme*. Buried deep within the five hundred pages of the transcribed (and revised) correspondence of her father and her grandmother, we find the first hesitant recordings of Aurore, the woman, by George, the historian-autobiographer.

Sand's critics have deplored her revisions of the correspondence without closely examining its significance. The romanticized letters of the son and his mother serve a double purpose. They draw attention *away* from Maurice's illicit liaison with Sand's mother, Sophie, the garrison woman who was with him during the campaigns; if this story were told, it would have to be narrated from the father's perspective and in the differentiated discourse of heterosexual desire. Instead, the correspondence highlights a mother-son discourse which empowers the woman.

In addition, the correspondence takes the Italian campaigns out of their marital context, where groups are organized for confrontation, and shifts them to a familial one, where groups are gathered for cohesiveness. During the gestation period that is the transcription of the correspondence, Sand is de-engendering herself. That is, George has to give birth to Aurore in a discourse that will integrate "his" male persona. Aurore is also conceived in Rousseau's territory of conception, Italy, but while he insisted on affixing his identity to documents in Geneva, Sand renounces documented proofs of her citizenship. Conceiving Aurore between the letters ruled by the maternal,

Sand prepares her reader for a woman's discourse forged from a principle of cohesiveness, and the tension of such a discourse is maintained by its inherent risk of neutrality.

Such a risk is taken in androgynous narratives. Sand writes of her grandmother taking the tenor part in songs, of her grandfather enjoying embroidery, of her physical resemblance to her father, and of her grandmother saying that he looked like a pretty girl in his adolescent years. We must note the most outstanding expression of her ideal—an androgynous deity which she located within the central chapters of her own story:

> Corambé se créa tout seul dans mon cerveau. Il était pur et charitable comme Jésus, rayonnant et beau comme Gabriel; mais il lui fallait un peu de la grâce des nymphes. . . . Et puis, il me fallait le compléter en le vêtant en femme à l'occasion, car ce que j'avais le mieux aimé, le mieux compris jusqu'alors, c'était une femme, c'était ma mère. Ce fut donc souvent sous les traits d'une femme qu'il m'apparut. En somme, il n'avait pas de sexe et revêtait toute sorte d'aspects différents. (*Oeuvres autobiographiques*, I, 812–13)

> Corambé was created by himself in my brain. He was as pure and charitable as Jesus, as brilliant and handsome as Gabriel, but he needed some of the grace of nymphs. . . . And also, I needed to complete him by occasionally dressing him as a woman, because what I had best loved and best understood until then was a woman. So it was then often bearing the features of a woman that he appeared to me. In short, he had no sex and took on many different aspects.

Metonymic of the necessary relation of female sexuality to the creative act of writing, Corambé is a two-piece puzzle which, locked together, *signifies* an absence. Koram—Latin for "in the presence of"—is linked to "B," the letter Sand always omitted when she first recited the alphabet, and thus "B" represents absence. Corambé, as we see, has a necessary relation of the mysterious power of creation: the absent mother. Moreover, she is the woman for whom Aurore first invented novels; Corambé the androgynous deity expired, Sand tells us, when she began to write novels.

Where the Homeric narrative expires, in the sacred female locus, Sand's narratives originate. Where Ahura's narratives express risk, especially during the quest for the book associated with the power of the gods, Sand's do likewise. Her punitive god is society, which associates writing with prostitution. What stands out here are problems of profanity in writing. For Sand, prostitution is collusion with society's myths forbidding women from writing—that is, being ashamed of writing and hiding the text in a drawer. She solves that problem through a rebellion similar to Heloïse's, by publicly embracing the courtesan, her mother and herself. The first revolutionary acts of Aurore resurface in the chapters of her youth, where the writer acknowledges that her mother the courtesan was her source of inspiration. Sophie was her original reader, the one who listened to and encouraged her childish stories. When enclosing her between four chairs, "entre quatre chaises," she listened to the child's inventions. Aurore's oral storytelling ceased after her father's death, when she was four and lost her mother. She was left with her grandmother, because Marie Dupin and Sophie Delaborde were convinced that the child would receive a better upbringing in the Dupin's home in Nohant than in her mother's apartment in Paris. Aurore's mental inventions continued, but since she had lost her reader she kept them to herself until a traumatic scene focusing on her mother stopped them. Her grandmother, scolding her because she is playing with the Berrichon children, tells her that she is behaving like her mother and declares that she will become, like her, a lost woman, "une femme perdue." As a result, Aurore wonders if there could be in her mother's present life some new secret which no one wants to tell her: "Il y avait, dans la vie actuelle de ma mère, quelque secret nouveau qu'on ne voulait pas me dire." A burning emptiness ensues, "un vide cuisant," as she internalizes the secret. Aurore loses the sources of life, fixes "un seau" (a seal) on her lips, and refuses to eat. She is taught early that women's sexuality is unspeakable and reacts with silence.

Sand narrates anew the revisionist mythology contained in the dialogue of Lélia and Pulchérie. Here again a mode, a shade, is found for the relation of two women. A color, red, appears: "Rougirai-je d'être la fille de ma mère?" (Must I blush because I am the daughter of my mother?) Then Sand infuses a hint of physical life into Aurore by likening her to a neglected fruit, one which is not nurtured: "Si ma mère était méprisable et haïssable, moi, le fruit de ses entrailles, je l'étais aussi." (If my mother was despicable, so was I, fruit of her entrails.) Finally, the psychological implications are narrated: "Je ne m'aimais plus moi-même." (I no longer loved myself.) The outcome is self-hatred and mutism, the end of fiction: "Plus de roman. . . . Corambé était mort" (*Oeuvres autobiographiques,* I, 856–67). (No more novels. . . . Corambé had died.) Literally, "entrailles" finds its equivalent in English "entrails," but when used figuratively in French, it signifies feelings of affection.

After this episode, she forges a discourse for "moi-toi" which associates mother and daughter. It begins in silence. Aurore's grandmother, finding her behavior too unruly, places her in the "Couvent des Anglaises," where young women's bodies are covered and their actions controlled, and where lessons are taught behind bars because men are forbidden. Within this enclosure, within walls, Aurore knights herself "chevalier de ma mère," and begins the quest for the *entrailles,* where she was created. These chapters of a girl's pubescence, again framed, *en abîme*, within those of the historical chronicles of George which open and close the autobiography, combine the texts of George and Aurore (the flashbacks of her adolescent years).

Aurore's search for self-knowledge takes place in the unnamed, dark, underground world of a convent, itself contained in the wider zone of men's city. Sand reveals in this autobiographical writing the origin of the *dédoublements* of several of her heroic women which we explored earlier, particularly in the atemporal zones of the narcissistic novel, *Lélia*. The convent girls are divided into two camps, the angels and the devils. The angels conform, and the devils disobey by defying the restrictions imposed on their nascent sexuality. Aurore, an angel at first, soon begins a solitary rebellion. She makes a mockery of the nun's attempts to control her words; she bites her lips, holds her nose to keep from laughing, and puts her bonnet on her ear to protect herself against a "niaise" and "ridicule" religion. When she shocks the sisters with this sort of pagan behavior, they begin to scold her, and she joins the "*camp des diables*" (I, 879). All the convent girls are taught to deny the body, but only the devils mock these teachings. During the day they pretend to block their noses and their ears, and at night they engage in underground activities: readings of Ann Radcliffe and a quest called "*délivrer la victime*" (I, 886).[19] This silent game dates back centuries. Its time is dark (the girls move at night when the nuns sleep), and its location is bloody— they travel through the "terror-filled" cells which served as caches for nobles during the reign of terror. The interior voyage promises to reveal "la clef du monde de ténêbres, de terreurs, de mystères" (I, 886). It is a mockery, a pseudo-quest, but one of great urgency, for it promises freedom from constraints. The devils know that the victim they seek in the thickness of the walls does not exist, and they laugh so that they almost break their jaws, "à se décrocher la mâchoire" (I, 881), because there is in this mania of looking for the victim something profoundly stupid, but also, Sand writes, something heroic.

This mouse-size epic is of great value to one who needed all the romantic aspects of this situation to fight against the convent's regimen: "Il me fallait bien toute cette situation romanesque pour lutter contre le régime du couvent qui m'était fort contraire" (*Oeuvres autobiographiques*, I, 893). The interior quest for the victim, the mutinous reaction against society's sanctions of sexual impulse, is a healthy outlet, for it releases anger. When the chevalieresque adventure for the non-existent victim stops, a period of mysticism and anorexia ensues. Aurore finally has to collude with the system which oppresses her by devoting herself to prayers, and her grandmother, concerned about her physical and mental states, takes her out of the convent. Paradoxically, this period of abstinence and total devotion to religion generates Aurore's creative forces, and she begins to write.

135

She keeps a journal and composes satirical essays for her mother and her grandmother. These first writings reconcile the angel, Marie Dupin, a stoic aristocrat, and the devil, Sophie Delaborde, a hedonistic commoner. These essays, satirizing women's bodies—those of the old countesses who peopled her grandmother's salon—find their intertext in the writings of Marie Dupin. During the Revolution she had written bloody couplets about Marie-Antoinette and her entourage. Aurore had read them. The revolutionary spirit of these couplets is contagious; it liberates Aurore's pen, and she writes about women's bodies, albeit in a parodic mode. Marie and Sophie are united in their enjoyment of these essays, the first recognizing her written couplets and the second her own oral satires of the decrepit countesses of the Dupin salon. The mother, however, detects a false note in the language of the Dupins which her daughter is using. Literary conventions are foreign to the language that she speaks and that she has taught her child, and she asks her if she is going to start speaking that way. These maternal warnings anticipate problems of voice and gender—those of the tired old traveller of the *Lettres d'un voyageur* and the omniscient narrator of her first novel, *Indiana*—which the future writer will have to overcome.

The last of Sand's journals, the autobiography of her mature years, reconciles the two maternal figures into a powerful Medusa. As in the transcription of the letters of her grandmother and her father, where the mother-son were equalized in the relation which Rousseau praised, Sand-Aurore's maternal voice meets a child-like implied reader. A powerful maternity dominates over a child-man who has not yet reached the force of his maturity, his difference. In these narratives of her own quest, told in a woman's voice, she reclaims Medusa's reputation as inventor of the alphabet.

Sand is the first established woman writer to provide insights into the association of artistic creation with a silent space of confinement and to link it to repressed sexuality. But while writing of a female body's freedom as a sort of *jouissance* was possible in autobiographical narratives of her youth, it was problematic in novels, where it could not be encoded in the Eternal Feminine tropes of Romanticism. The search to give a voice to the lost sexual woman is affirmed in the self-intertextuality of the autobiography, which is a product of the writer's own works. In numerous texts, within a historical time, *en abîme*, a woman breaks her silence and then becomes silent again. In the early *Les Couperies*, a woman's story is framed within the historical time of the man who begins and ends the essay. This process is repeated in *Indiana*, where an omniscient narrator opens the novel, quotes a woman's words, then reports her silence in the closing epilogue. It continues in *Lélia*, in conversations between *Lélia* and the courtesan. Deep in the center, both break the silence to reveal the cause of Lélia's *impuissance*, but then the artist is silenced again by the priest, and Magnus the mediator closes the narrative.

136

In the second *Lélia*, where the protagonist dies from vocal exhaustion, a phoenix represents the project of still another heroic woman to rise out of her ashes. It continues in *Consuelo*, written shortly before the autobiography, where the hero sings and then loses her voice. Sand's *oeuvre* works on this ebb and flow: a woman loses her voice at the end of the novel and another one finds hers in the next work. As they progress, however, the narratives grow more and more *au féminin*. The *Histoire de ma vie* summarizes this progress and finally brings Sand's narrative voice to the height of maternal fecundity.

Interrogative and Analytical Quests

To articulate the conjunction of maternity and ethics by disavowing existing determinations of the specificity of sexual difference is a task both Cixous and Kristeva assigned themselves in two brief autobiographical writings analyzed in the present chapter. Their stated aim is to revolutionize our view of the relation of a woman (speaking subject for Kristeva) to language—although according to Lacan this would be a malapropism. Writers and theoreticians, both women become engaged in the debate over language and differentiation and respond to its participants: Cixous by celebrating the transformative power of women's *corps cosmique;* and Kristeva by conceptualizing a semiotic order which preexists birth, established at a time when one is not yet a speaking subject and, therefore, not yet differentiated in the symbolic order. Both are aware of writing in an age when, viewing the text as a spatial territory, critics have emptied it of its contextual referentiality. Both understand how impossible it has become to speak of sexual identity when the representation of an individual's reality "outside" the text has been invalidated. When Lacan theorizes that language is a process of differentiation and that woman is that necessary difference, how can woman speak?

Cixous, founder of a now extinct feminist studies program, writes within a militant ideological context whose participants refuse to comply with any generic discourse. A disregard of conventions is willful and intrinsic to her writing. Like Guyon's *écriture automatique,* her text resists the discursive categories of literary criticism, but, unlike the memorialist, her experiments have a practical aim. She invites readers into the problems of spatial thinking and language by announcing this intention in her title. "La venue," or the coming to writing, implies the initiation of a process, the text being written, rather than the finished product. Cixous, looking at the inertia of a completed text, decides to bring it to life by infusing it with the energy of creating. She works at bringing an authorial presence back into the text. The key terms in her word plays, her parodies, and her *écriture* are: "emplacement," to indicate processes; "corps cosmique," for the dominance of a living maternal body over the inertia of a fixed text; and "souffle" (breath), for the vocal energy of the narrator. All are interwoven into a complex tapestry, which resists the unraveling of canonized literary criticism.

In her study of Guyon, Kristeva writes of the hysteric's feeling of having a futile, vain discourse, and she points out that feminism has made a militant ideology of this feeling of futility by declaring all discourse "phallocratic."[1] She states her position vis-à-vis the issue by defining it in linguistic terms. Adding neologisms of inclusion to it, she calls for new ways to think the speaking subject—one of which would be to displace it into a temporality yet to happen, the future anterior. To disrupt the ideology of a fixed symbolic, she posits motherhood's splitting as a different notion of identity.

Although both women challenge the standing order of critical thinking and its language, their discursive modes are at variance. They share an aversion to the fixed and the final, but Cixous's mode is interrogative—she worries that the question might find its answer—while Kristeva's is analytical: she works at studying the essential features of writing and their continually shifting relations, thus avoiding foreclosure.

Kristeva, keenly aware of her own rhetorical devices, often apprises her reader of them. At odds with her own theoretical writings, she views the autobiographical text as a space of possibilities wherein she may insert her own notions of identity, one of which is to think the speaking subject in a new way. Alternating between "I" and "we," pronouns which only a mother could articulate, she narrates her quests in the singular and in the plural: individually and within groups. She states that she is in search of territories which "match her states of mind."[2] Consequently, her autobiographical text delineates itself into two territories of temptations—the "I," interior, solitary, and sacred; and the "we," exterior, collective, and profane. The "I" seeks itself and the "we" quests for knowledge of the world. Kristeva creates a metaphor for her quests by naming them seductions and herself a sinner, guilty of seducing and of being seduced.

No imitations, no parodies, no confrontations occur during her investigation of discursive categories to speak the self. Working with the tools at her disposal, she rules over them. Cixous, however, parodies the language of the confessional and confronts the confessors, threatening to show them her "sex/te." She dishonors those who codify the meaning of words in processes which she calls "emplacements." By combining them into neologisms, such as "homm(icil)e" and "ani(male)," she multiplies their significance. Kristeva, on the other hand, analyzes language from the perspective of both the confessor and the sinner—she studies, then practices psychoanalysis. She also combines words to extend our awareness of their instability, favoring minute segments, particularly prefixes, such as *trans, inter, un, dis,* and, most tellingly, *irr* and *in*. These signify the *irr*educible nature of writing and express the idea that words are *in*essential markers.

As with Sand, who was in search of the voice of a *femme perdue*, in games of transvestism Cixous and Kristeva abolish the spatio-temporal constructions separating accredited narrators from protagonists. Both view essentialism as a male construct derived from canonized writings which oppose men's existential journeys to women's stillness. Obfuscating identity principles—such as those of narrators and protagonists—they extricate implied authors, narrators, and protagonists from their textual prisons, thereby implicating a contextual possibility.

Cixous's *Emplacement*

Reproducing the two effects achieved in the stories of Ahura and Sand, the monophony of the three scribes and the polyphony of narrative personae *en abîme*, Cixous subjects her discourse to a variety of personal pronouns. The voices speaking as I, she, you, and we feature both monophony and polyphony. Her "we" invites the reader to participate in a practice of intersubjectivity, a process of splitting and reintegrating wherein the distinct "I" and "you" constantly reunite:

> Il y a toujours en moi quelqu'un de plus grand que moi . . . que je ne cherche pas à égaler, un corps, une âme. . . . Un texte . . . auquel je veux livrer passage, auquel je m'enchante d'avoir à donner l'infini. Hélène Cixous, ce n'est pas moi, c'est ceux qui sont chantés dans mon texte, parce que leurs vies, leurs peines, leur force exigent qu'il retentisse.[3]

> There is always within me someone greater than I . . . whom I do not try to equal, a body, a soul. . . . A test . . . for which I want to make room, for which I am enchanted to have to give the infinite. Hélène Cixous, that is not I, it is those who are sung in my text, because their lives, their sorrows, their strength demand that they echo.

Narrative voices as they imply identities—in sum, all categories of narrating which organize the text to give someone authority—are constantly in play in a game which Cixous encapsulates in the concept of "emplacement." This word indicates her preference for processing the new in relation to what is already in place or for preserving rather than substituting. In this autobiographical text about writing, she bridges the distance between writer and readers by inviting her reader to speak into her text; "j'écoute," she writes (47). Elsewhere, she calls for "writing by the voice."[4] Warning against identity principles, "méfie-toi des noms" (54), she refuses a cultural heritage which divides, that is, appropriates territories by naming.

She also disavows principles of authorship by claiming that her discourse is generated by a non-identifiable "souffle." Like the air and the wind which are unmeasurable by the human eye, breath "illusions" the powers of life. In its most commonplace interpretation, the "souffle" has the potential both to animate and destroy fires; it represents an energy analogous to the illusive creative powers of human imagination. The "souffle," which is Echo's element, narrates for Cixous. In "Le rire de la Méduse," she speaks of the ancient Echo archetype by claiming that she is a *"donneuse"* (the term has a double meaning, that of informer and giver).[5] Echo told Juno of her husband's infidelities and repeated the words of others. Indeed, air (souffle) is the element of the invisible wind spirit, who mimics to perfection because her separate identity is unspeakable. As Suleiman writes: "In good Derridean fashion, she [Cixous] points out that the bisexuality she had in mind was not that of the hermaphrodite . . . but rather the bisexuality of a 'dual' or even multiple subject. . . . "[6] Indeed, when Cixous says "I" the reader is often led to conclude she means "you."

In the undifferentiated element of the "souffle," playing on the polyvalence of "voler," which signifies both to fly and to steal, Cixous claims to have stolen the power of flight. Revising ancient archetypes, in "Le rire" she likens herself to both Echo the wind spirit and Hermes the winged messenger. Woman is not afraid of flight, of the adventure into the anonymous flux. In another writing she proposes that women must disorder things; they must not flounder in the ancient order.[7]

Cixous claims a new, non-ordered identity which contains all her others. She is and she is not Hélène (la belle) and Cixous (l'étrangère), the exile from the Algerian city or Oran. As in Heloïse's address to Abelard, the barriers between I and you break down. When the order of identifying is nullified, when there is no difference, nothing is *propre*. Here, "propre" has a triple meaning: property, proper noun, and clean.

National identities also become the subject of Cixous's subversion. Writing of air and flying takes her beyond frontiers, but it also isolates her. Calling herself "la belle Hélène" takes her across the ages to ancient Greece, away from France, the territory where, being a woman and a stranger, she is doubly alienated. Like Rousseau, she may not claim a place in France's political and cultural hegemony, but, unlike he who affirms his difference and his right to independence through his hosts' political rhetoric, she, who abhors difference and independence, questions her legitimacy through parodies of the French language. She writes: "En français je vole, je suis voleuse. Pas d'hommicile fixe" (Venue, 42). A thief (voleuse), homeless (no domicile), and homicidal (hommicile alludes to homme and homicide), she again steals the features of Hermes, the Greek archetype claimed by the French. As he stole the alphabet given to him by Medusa, so she arrogantly appropriates herself the right to invent new words and to murder grammatical rules. Moved to fly through the frontiers of language, her practice of writing will happen somewhere else, she says, "ailleurs," somewhere other than in the territories subordinated to the domination of philosophy. For Cixous the "somewhere else," the reaction to exclusion, differs from Rousseau's. Rather than creating a marginal "other" in a promenade, she employs the image of the texte-corps. She writes that its zones inhabit her, situates herself in the center of her text, and places it in the center of herself.

The image of the writer as a cosmic body dominating La venue à l'écriture implies tactics of convertibility, as in the ancient metaphysical doctrines of microcosm and macrocosm. The cosmic body, an individual entity, recapitulates the universe. It constitutes itself through a multiplicity of voices which, working in relation to each other, relay the narrative of a universal female entity. Cixous's is an esthetic re-examination of the equation of ethics and maternity. It provides a new way to valorize femaleness in the practice of écriture.

The body, synecdoche of the text, is a "corps sans bord," a "contrée sans limite" on which Cixous writes with small milk jars (Venue, 45). The surface of its territory is black, and the trajectory of its exploration is the color of milk, as indicated by the white ink which marks it. Its interior is colorful; a red current of energy constituted of blood and lava flows underneath. The imagery of this body-text re-states the theme of the souffle, the energy which simultaneously gives the text its life and threatens to destroy it. For her, writing is not the Romantic jouissance of being one with maternal nature—away from patriarchal domains and contained within the borders of an island. It is the gargantuan pleasure of filling the earth with a great mass and of being in the center of "la mèr/e" (the mother and the indivisible liquidity of the ocean). Cixous's concept of pleasure is similar to Abelard's enjoyment of polemics in the "father of himself" debate. In the women-to-women language of Sévigné to her daughter, Cixous features the "mother of herself" theme. She writes of "s'accoucher." She thus combines and re-combines the two genders to militate—against differentiation, identity, and even nations.

Her strategy of "emplacement" redresses the traditional essentialist association of the mother's female body with nature—patriarchal site of constraint and exploitation—by expanding it into a broader realm, a cosmic one, where mundane questions of politics are not taken seriously. A rhetoric in her *écriture* of the self which dominates over narrative of events makes it clear that it has become a problem of language. Imitation and subversion of other writings make up the story of Cixous. Her puns demonstrate how she cannot get hold of her subject. Her parodies touch on a variety of discourses; for instance, in a section called *"Confession,"* she mocks Christian liturgy and psychoanalytical jargon. She confesses to having an *"animale"* which inhabits her and which she is forbidden to touch (*Venue,* 40). The pun combines the meaning of three words, "mal-animal-male." Cixous is alluding to woman's sexuality which, in Christianity's (male) view is a *souillure* (mal) of the lower order (animal). She claims that the old wolf, the "Suroncle," has ordered her not to touch it. (This is an obvious allusion to the "surmoi," the French word for superego, and to Freud, whom she often calls "oncle.") Speaking the language of the psychotic, she accuses Freud of trying to separate her from her sex.

Although, like the memorialists, she creates the space of her text as ethereal and indivisible, she questions this invention. She worries that she may have imaged herself spatially into a void. Her body has already been used as imagery for the unknown, and she is concerned that she may be simply echoing the discourse of the Freudian dark continent and of the Cartesian doubt: "Comment aurais-je pu dire 'je suis'?" (*Venue,* 32). The text-body becomes a space in which to lose, but not isolate, herself. In "Le rire" she also wonders whether she is creating a lacuna, a Pascalian void, this time a zone of non-communication where, like Echo, her discourse would meet the deaf ear of Narcissus, a "sourde oreille masculine" (43). Yet her laughter is at times tinged with hysteria. Her puns may provoke a laughter of alienation because she has placed herself in an Amazonian enclave. Cixous's superimposing, her "emplacement" of her own images of motherhood upon patriarchal writings, signifies that it is writing—that which is traced and fixed—which will preserve her voice. She retraces the symbolic to an original site of nondifferentiation. Taking a playful stance vis-à-vis Freudian and Lacanian politicians, Cixous makes it impossible for them to engage her in debate, except in her playful language of undifferentiation.

Kristeva's Displacement

By contrast, Kristeva's autobiographical writing shows an aversion toward the sort of aposiopesis we find in Cixous's writings. She also is in search of ways to speak of the *femme perdue;* she treats it in a style which, although dissimilar to Cixous's, is similar in intention.[8] She profiles a yet-to-be-born entity, one which *is* yet is not. In the language of theory rather than that of fiction, she also writes of herself through and beyond temporal frontiers. Theorizing a pre-linguistic stage in a future anterior time, the semiotic, she gives the maternal new meaning, but without denying its affiliation with the paternal. Kristeva proposes thinking the speaking subject in new ways; unlike Cixous, with whom one could not dialogue without using her own inventive language, theorists could communicate with Kristeva in the language of Freud and Lacan. Kristeva's semiotic order, her major contribution to thinking the speaking pre-linguistic subject in new ways, is only understandable in the psycho-linguistic language within which she defines it. The semiotic can only take place in the symbolic.

In "My Memory Hyperbole" Kristeva's road to self-discovery is fraught with temptations to commit common sins, and the first of these temptations is Paris. She writes that she was attracted to the city of lights because there marginal phenomena become "actual fields of *study*" (265). Like Rousseau, she arrives with a trunk full of the product of her own efforts, a thesis on Céline, to impress French intellectuals. Like the *philosophe*, she also would show her ability to master by encoding and decoding. While he contributed a mathematical formula for music, she brings critical formulas for the study of avant-garde literary tests. Rousseau's guilt at leaving Geneva, his site of affiliation, drives him first to Paris, and he isolates herself from the Parisians to preserve his individuality. What she calls her guilt also brings Kristeva to isolate herself, but not to preserve individuality; she is within a group that is isolated. She states her intent to narrate the "I" in the "we" when she writes of spending her first night with radical Eastern European émigrés. They attend midnight mass on Christmas Eve in Notre-Dame cathedral. Thus it is within the patrimony of Paris and on the date of Christ's birth that she gives herself birth, fully grown in the sacred inner sanctum of the cathedral. There are no narratives of her youth in Bulgaria.

Her quests alternate between interior and exterior locales. She succumbs to a second "seduction" at the café Deux Magots, facing St. Germain-des-Prés, where she is introduced to the *Tel Quel* group. She describes their meetings in erotic terms, speaking of their "existential passion" (266), of her having admired a large picture of Sollers published in *Clarté*, of their narcissistic coupling, of his logical firmness, and of Beatrice and Dante. With the group she undertakes a quest *à plusieurs*, a collective enterprise motivated by narcissism. She views the group's appreciation of its own work as "crimes committed in common" and as a quest for "libidinal or sublimated gratifications" (268–69). Their crimes include the displacement of Sartre and existentialism; a shifting ideology which takes them from structuralism to the deconstruction of phenomenology and post-formalism; and a "perverse relation" with the Parti Communiste Français. Analyzing society from their psychoanalytical point of view, the group concludes that they are observers of the truth of Freud's statement that "society is a crime committed in common." They see in the PCF the "reality of a machine serving as conveyor between the ideal (May 68) and the individual" (273).

In spite of her claim to speak for "nous," by repeatedly referring to her individual private guilt Kristeva reveals that she does not truly believe she incorporates any group. She recounts her own intellectual activities within marginal groups in marginal terms. For instance, she writes that she lands "at the door," not inside the buildings where she meets Goldman and Barthes, and that she experiences a displacement during the revolutionary spasms of the group. Displacements, dividing her and leaving her an outsider, are fundamental to her position vis-à-vis her work at the end of this quest with the *Tel Quel* group. Finally, when the group comes to see religion as a "discourse for analysis" (273), she begins her own private analysis of the power of the sacred (268), and she is horrified. The axis of Kristeva's thought at this stage is described in the following paragraph:

> Psychoanalysis—as the locus of extreme abjection, the refuge of private horror that can be lifted only by an infinite-indefinite displacement in speech and its effects—represents for me today the logical consequence of my initial questioning, which it still allows me to pursue. Leaving aside the uncertainties of the perversities of analytic institutions, I see psychoanalysis as the lay version, the only one, of the speaking being's quest for truth that religion symbolizes for certain of my contemporaries and friends. My own prejudice would lead me to think that God is analyzable, infinitely. . . . (267)

Kristeva cannot deliver herself from the private guilt. Although she tries to escape what she calls an unbearable state of inner solitude, she returns to that painful inner experience. This realization of private guilt, this inner quest, is followed by explorations of the exterior world. "Displacements in speech" of psychoanalysis become another seduction; this one takes Kristeva to a new field of study, linguistics. She invites one of the fathers of that science, Benveniste, into her inner quest, making "an important place" (267) for him in her thoughts. With him she starts an external quest *à deux*. The "displacements" in speech grow into "linguistic knots" on which, she theorizes, the power of the sacred is built.

A term first derived from Georges Bataille's *l'Expérience intérieure,* the inner experience had been debated by the *Tel Quel* group when discussing Freud's thoughts on the alterity of the subject in language. After her meetings with Benveniste, Kristeva views the internal experience in a new way, as both the problem of the alterity of the subject in language and that of *being* the subject of another's discourse. This discovery or, to be more precise, this acceptance of both alterities, coupled with the death of Benveniste, leads Kristeva to theories of abjection.

145

Accepting the other as an "unavoidable necessity," she delineates an interior search for the degree zero of the symbolic. At this stage, Kristeva plans to displace the paternal and find the roots of the "internal experience" in the potential of the female body (274). A new seduction presents itself in "the characters of Chinese texts," and she leaves for China. Thinking now of politics as a modern religion, she speaks of sexual politics. The trip moves her to publish the result of an analysis of women in China.[9] Buttressed by readings of Marx and Lévi-Strauss, this study brings Kristeva to a political conclusion: the reproductive potential of women's bodies is regulated because of the need of the group to perpetuate itself. In spite of the inquiry into the condition of Chinese women, Kristeva's "I" continues to sketch a self in the discourse of analysis. The inquest into feminism leads her not to an experiment with *écriture féminine,* but to the abject, which is gradually working itself out into a mood propitious to thinking the speaking subject in new ways.

The seduction of Chinese texts and the analysis of the women's condition bring her back to the state of abjection which preceded the trip. She says farewell to the politics of communism and feminism, stating that she despises "isms." Exception should be made, however, for eroticism, which "shapes each person's biography." Kristeva then adds that "only a novel could restore the wild indecency of it" (275). After the Chinese experiment, she returns to the inner quest:

> I can say, however, that for most of the Paris-Peking-Paris travelers (Roland Barthes, Philippe Sollers, Marcelin Platynet, Francois Wahl, and myself), this arduous journey, one that from the outset was more cultural than political, definitely inaugurated a return to the only continent we have never left: internal experience. (275)

At this stage a new seduction presents itself, as Kristeva's inquiries into language finally take her to a new geography—that of the mind—and to a quest for knowledge (*à deux*): the "psychoanalytic adventure" at the Institute of Psychoanalysis with Lacan. Once again, during this trip into linguistics and psychoanalysis, she probes her inner self. Analyzing her own actions and reactions, she discovers the "wildness of the speaking being and of language." While Lacan obtains inner strength from divisive analytical processes, Kristeva is devastated. She remarks that her analyses of language unveil a "background of desire and hate" which is "like a power of horror, like abjection," and she avoids following Lacan to his "painful end" (275). Nevertheless, she learns that combining linguistic and psychoanalytical approaches reinforces the position from which she speaks of humanity, that of the speaking subject.

146

Kristeva once stated in an interview that, in order to become autonomous, "it is necessary that one cut the instinctual dyad of the mother and the child and that one become something other."[10] But what is the process of becoming something other for a woman writer? Is it acceptance of abjection? This question becomes the subject of her subsequent studies of the power of horror, narcissism, and abjection. She explores these in what she often refers to as "spaces" where texts meet excessive use of the illogical. For instance, her fascination with the semiotic—that is, for her, the pre-linguistic—directs her to analyze the "*père-version*" of Guyon's memoirs.

Territories which promise to match her states of mind continue to seduce Kristeva. She finally accepts an invitation to lecture at an American university, where she finds, as she had in Guyon's text, that words are "inessential masks." Here also she is fascinated with the "unanalyzable" and the "irreducible" (276). Following her inner configurations, she situates herself in Greenwich Village, within a small marginal enclave which is itself within a larger cultural center, New York City. She observes that America *is* her state of mind. Distanced from her European scenes of eroticism, Notre-Dame and the cafés of Paris, she finds a new challenge. In a site where something remains to happen, she may locate the pre-linguistic which she had searched for in her analysis of the maternal. In the space of this "challenged giant," she feels closer to truth and liberty, for in this locus there "is no adherence to a culture, be it local, regional, French, Latin, or Mediterranean" (276). She sees the future anterior promise she seeks in America: "I dream that our children will prefer to join this David, with his errors and impasses, armed with our erring and circling about the Idea, the Logos, the Form: in short, the old Judeo-Christian Europe. . . . If it is only an illusion, I like to think it may have a future" (276). At this point, Kristeva locates the perfect metaphor for her state of mind; maintaining herself in a position of ambivalence—a lucid consciousness of illusions—she pursues her interminable combat with what cannot be analyzed.

Cosmic and Multileveled Trajectories

Kristeva's invitation to think the speaking subject in new ways, reinforced by her writing this subject as both an individual "I" and a "we," comes together with Cixous's glorifying of women's energy and power. Both speak the subject in a new way to undo the case for gender identity: Cixous through *emplacement,* Kristeva through displacement. Cixous's pleasure, her *jouissance,* lies in speaking the language of madness by "emplacing" herself in it through a variety of subject pronouns. In a different vein, Kristeva's positive narcissism lies in theorizing and in mastering meaning: displacing herself into a group named "we."

147

Writing of women's *jouissance* and of the pre-linguistic are risky ventures. Cixous's is a profane version of the seventeenth-century memorialist's *écriture automatique*. If, as Kristeva suggests, Guyon's text of the self is a *"père-version"* of language, Cixous's is a *mère-version*. Her disorganized text is a metonymy of the chaos of pre-birth, the disorder that is also the *souillure* which Guyon chases from her memoirs in the seventeenth century. Guyon's discourse of mortification makes her text, like herself, a sacred tabernacle for the father confessor. Cixous's own text is also a site of celebration, but a pagan one: that of a "ventre enchanté." The memorialist's body is unspoken in spiritual terms, but Cixous's, in the final defiance of her writings, is kept alive in its materiality by being named. Guyon's masochistic statements abnegate the present, while Cixous's affirm the moment. She takes her woman's body-text out of the Judeo-Christian spatial thinking, which polarizes the finite and the infinite, and into a chaotic, cosmic zone of flux.

Cixous is aware of the risks of speaking the woman's body, yet she takes a chance. She would attempt to name while avoiding the trappings of differentiated identities. Writing is not a simulacrum of Penelope's unraveling of her woven text. Writing is not to erase and write over. It is "emplacement," an addition rather than a replacement. Her text, Cixous states, is a narrative of deferment, forever seeking not only to delay a final answer to a fundamental cosmic question, but also to suspend the question itself. Her interrogation instructs the reader that she fears a reply: "Quel malheur s'il arrivait à la question de rencontrer sa réponse. Sa fin!" (What malediction if the question would ever meet its answer. Its end!)

In a comparative study of Kristeva, Cixous, and Irigaray, Stanton concludes that the first two writers share modes of discourse.[11] For both, as Stanton points out, the mode is revolutionary. Nevertheless, the rhetorical devices and the tactics through which revolution is communicated vary greatly. Certainly, as the present study has demonstrated, Cixous's trajectory is cosmic while Kristeva's is multi-leveled, interior and exterior. Yet both avoid polarizing through images of processes, those of "emplacement" and "displacement." Both view themselves as inventors and thieves of language, thus associating themselves with the archetypes of both Medusa and Hermes. Cixous, searching for a language to place women's bodies in the first person feminine, invents tropes of her own, and like Kristeva, demonstrates that she also wonders whether the speaking subject needs to be thought of in new ways. Cixous overcomes her timidity vis-à-vis language by taking the authority of naming. Naming, she states, does not do violence, it preserves life— "garder en vie." What she does name is her female body, calling it a core and a "venture enchanté" (*Venue,* 11). Kristeva, facing the pain of seeing one the subject of the discourse of others, suggests a discourse of "univocity." She empowers herself by first confessing that her searches for a theoretical foundation are seductions and then by becoming the analyist, or the one who, as Singer writes in her study of Foucault on sexuality and power, judges the sexual discourses of others and acts "therapeutically, punitively, managerially, on the basis of the discourse produced."[12] With the same intention, that is, that of writing the female body, Cixous creates a close-knit text which provides no room to engage in patriarchal logic. As Singer points out: "Feminine writing is not simply a consequence of the existing power deployment, but is precisely that which cannot be anticipated or realized within its operative logic" (147).

Thinking of the subject in a relation, united with others yet speaking in one voice, these women take us back to *Ahura's Tale*. Thinking in new ways, Kristeva situates her autobiographical text in her own monumental time, a time which crosses the territories named by men in stories of journeys—those of ancient Egypt and Greece—and the time of living the women's condition—that of Ahura's narratives, which speak across centuries. As Tina Chanter writes, monumental time combines spatial and temporal concepts, the first "traditionally associated with the feminine sensibility, with maternity," and the second "attributed to masculinity, to the father."[13] This concept, coupled with that of the semiotic, leaves woman at the threshold of nature and culture, that is, of birth and language.

Can we think the speaking subject in new ways? Can we master the meaning of mythology? Is Medusa sharing her invention with Hermes or is she losing her vowels (voice) to a thief? Or is she herself the thief? The autobiographical texts of Cixous and Kristeva keep these questions alive. For the theorist, Kristeva's concepts of the semiotic and of monumental time would constitute productive possibilities of deployment for a theme now popular in feminist theories: thinking the speaking subject in new ways. One could argue with John Lechte's conclusion that Kristeva's work is unsatisfactory for those who have put their faith exclusively in politics because "politics becomes the sphere of a dangerous dogma when it refuses to acknowledge that the social contract is always under threat from jouissance and thus always in the thorns of being negotiated, and re-negotiated."[14] Kristeva's work *is* political in that it takes the question out of politics, thus subverting the very idea of being political about feminism. Because she couches her arguments in the discourse of the theoretical, she provides the very foundation of a feminist political debate. Now when feminists discuss Kristeva's theoretical engendering of articulation (language) in a semiotic pre-linguistic order which, in turn, can only occur in the symbolic order (language), they can speak of the symbolic in nondifferentiating terms.

NOTES

Notes to Introduction

1. *Webster's New Twentieth Century Dictionary of the English Language* (Unabridged, 1951) retraces the origin of the word weaving to the French term for text: [Fr. *texte*, textus, woven; also fabric, structure, text, from *texere*, to weave.]. We see here a clear association of the act of weaving with the act of storytelling or writing. Anyone who has noticed this, and who has also observed the continuity of imaging in the tapestries of the unicorn lined up at the Cluny Museum in Paris, realizes that weaving can be a form of storytelling. The point here is that Penelope's daily weaving is a metaphor for her life (her story) and that her nightly unravelling while Ulysses is narrating his story to entertain his hosts is metonymic of how women's words are encoded in men's writings. This process of revelation through mystery, this signifying of the abstract (women's words) through the concrete (the woven tapestry), this obvious substitution of the container for the content, is an important aspect of language and sexual politics.

2. The term *revers* is derived from Luce Irigaray's study of the writings of Plato and Freud, *Speculum de l'autre femme* (Paris: Minuit, 1974). A different view of sexual identity in representation of characters in fiction is also suggested by Anne Robinson Taylor, in *Male Novelists and Their Female Voices: Literary Masquerades* (Troy, N.Y.: Whitston Press, 1981). She sees a reversal of representation in fiction. What the female character sees in a man is what the author sees in a woman.

3. One canonized definition, for example, retraces heroism in storytelling to places and time. It names four main periods in four principal territories: (1) ca. 2,000 B.C., the Middle and Near East (Sumer and Egypt); (2) ca. 1,000–400 B.C., Babylon, Greece, and Palestine; (3) the Middle Ages (Europe); (4) modern times, that is, 1750 to the present day (no locale). It also retraces all the earliest written narratives ascribed to men: the Homeric poems, the odes of Pindar, the annals of Charlemagne, the medieval romances, and others too

151

numerous to list. See Alex Preminger, ed., *Princeton Encyclopedia of Poetry and Poetics* (Princeton: Princeton University Press, 1965).

4. Michel Serres, in *Hermes: Literature, Science, Philosophy*, ed. J. V. Harari and D. F. Bell (Baltimore: Johns Hopkins University Press, 1982), refers to Ulysses' stories as the journal of his journeys. My work is also inspired by Stephen Kern's *The Culture of Time and Space: 1880–1910* (Cambridge: Harvard University Press, 1983).

5. Rachel M. Brownstein, in *Becoming a Heroine: Reading About Women in Novels* (New York: Viking Press, 1982), finds that novel readers, like novel heroines, are often women who want to become heroines. I agree that the self created in autobiographical narratives is a creation of the novel-reader-become-writer who wants to distinguish herself from other women and become a hero. However, I do not totally agree with her suggestion that women often validate their uniqueness by being "singled out among all other women by a man" (xv). I would add that they also validate their uniqueness by undertaking the self-sufficient quest for knowledge.

6. As Nancy K. Miller writes in *Subject to Change: Reading Feminist Writing* (New York: Columbia University Press, 1988), the attempt is problematic: "What we might wish for is a female materialism attentive to the needs of the body as well as the luxuries of the mind. Can we imagine, or should we, a position that speaks in tropes and walks in sensible shoes?" (76).

7. Some French philosophers—Derrida, Lacan, and Deleuze, in particular—have challenged most traditional approaches to the text. Calling into question the reliability of "representability," they brought about what Alice A. Jardine calls "the demise of experience"; see her *Gynesis: Configurations of Woman and Modernity* (Ithaca: Cornell University Press, 1985). It would seem that, in this modern mode, any critical inquiry addressed to the mimetic function of the text would be retrograde. The writings of these philosophers have serious implications for modern feminist criticism.

8. The problem of referentiality in autobiography has been the subject of numerous studies. Major critics fundamentally agree with Valery's statement that all writing is autobiographical. Lejeune's definition of the genre as a sort of referential contract between a writer at the border of the text and referential readers is presently the most widely accepted theory. The following have provided background for my study. They are listed alphabetically. Michel Beaujour states that a self-portrait is the secret project of all autobiography ("l'autoportrait est le projet secret de toute autobiographie"); see *Miroirs d'encre: Rhétorique de l'autoportrait* (Paris: Seuil, 1980), 9. Elizabeth W. Bruss, inspired by Searle's theories of speech acts, organizes a schematic table of linguistic markers sensitive to the context in *Autobiographical Acts: The Changing Situation of a Literary Genre* (Baltimore: Johns Hopkins University Press, 1976), 31. Beatrice Didier undertakes a *socio-critique* in *Le journal intime* (Paris: Presses universitaires de France, 1976). George Gusdorf's approach is ethical; he views the genre as an "examen de conscience"

in *La découverte de soi* (Paris: Presses universitaires de France, 1948), viii. Philippe Lejeune first coined the term "pacte" or contract in *Le pacte autobiographique* (Paris: Seuil, 1975). Georges May approaches the genre in its diversity in *L'autobiographie* (Paris: Presses universitaires de France, 1979). George Misch's book is the seminal work on the genre; see *A History of Autobiography in Antiquity* (Cambridge: Harvard University Press, 1951). James Olney focuses on the spiritual mind of man in *Metaphors of the Self: The Meaning of Autobiography* (Princeton: Princeton University Press, 1972). John Pilling studies English, French, and Russian writers in *Autobiography and Imagination: Studies in Self-Scrutiny* (London: Routledge & Kegan, 1981). Jean Rousset uses a structuralist approach to the autobiographical novel in *Narcisse romancier: Essai sur la première personne dans le roman* (Paris: Librairie Corti, 1973). William G. Spengemann compiled an annotated bibliography on the genre in *The Forms of Autobiography: Episodes in the History of a Literary Genre* (New Haven: Yale University Press, 1980). Karl Joachim Weintraub studies the individual in society in *The Value of the Individual: Self and Circumstance in Autobiography* (Chicago: University of Chicago Press, 1978). Altogether, these studies have contributed to my reading autobiographies from a gender-specific perspective. The single most influential work was Lejeune's. His situating the "I" at the border between text and extra-text helped me bridge the gulf between texts and authors created by structuralism.

9. The concept of archetype as it functions in my study is inspired by my discussions with French scholars working on mythological approaches to various disciplines. Gilbert Durand's definition is particularly cogent: "Precisely, it is both a psychic force and a major symbolic source, one whose pregnancy, universality, and perennity may be assured." See *Figures mythiques et visages de l'oeuvre: de la mythocritique à la mythanalyse* (Paris: Berg international, 1979), 99. I also work with the idea that archetypes, unlike symbols, are created in narratives. Pierre Alboury first established this difference between symbol and myth, stating at the outset of his work that unlike symbols, myths require narratives. See *Mythes et Mythologies dans la littérature française* (Paris: Armand Colin, 1969).

10. How men's stories of the self stress autonomy and how women's narratives are considered anomalous because their stories of the self are different is the subject of Carol Gilligan's *In a Different Voice: Psychological Theory and Women's Development* (Cambridge: Harvard University Press, 1982). This study was instrumental to the basic formulation of my own theoretical framework. Susan Bordo's work on the ideas of Descartes in his *Meditations*—to be elaborated in chapter four—was also important to the development of my theories. See "The Cartesian Masculinization of Thought," *Signs* 2, no. 3 (1986) 439–56.

11. The first reference to this term is attributed to Ellen Moers. It will be discussed in chapter five. See *Literary Women: The Great Writers* (Garden City,

N.Y.: Doubleday, 1976; Anchor, 1977). Patricia Meyer Spacks, in *Imagining a Self: Autobiography and Novel in Eighteenth-Century England* (Cambridge: Harvard University Press, 1976), also explains how women's heroism differs from men's; she notes that within an atmosphere of social instability, the female hero must remain the same, her moral responsibility depending on a consistent identity.

12. This version is taken from Robert Graves: "Mercury, or Hermes, or Car, or Palamedes, or Thoth, or whatever his original name was, is given poetic sight by the Shrouded Ones (his mother Carmenta, or Maia, or Danae, or Phorcis, or Medusa.)" *The White Goddess: A Historical Grammar of Poetic Myth* (1948; New York: Farrar, Straus and Giroux, 1966), 230–31.

13. For a comprehensive investigation of the problem of referential logic and ethics, see Barbara Johnson, *The Critical Difference: Essays in the Contemporary Rhetoric of Reading* (Baltimore: Johns Hopkins University Press, 1980).

14. Several writings on the subject of the metaphor associating writing and prostitution support this theory, and they are worked out in chapter five. For specific works on the subject, see Ruth Bernard Yaezell, ed., *Sex, Politics, and Science in the Nineteenth-Century Novel: Selected Papers from the English Institute, 1983–84,* New Series 10 (Baltimore: Johns Hopkins University Press, 1986).

15. Reading Julia Kristeva's works as I researched texts from ancient times to the present gave me a sense of direction. The development of my own theories are fundamentally influenced by the evolution of her thoughts from linguistics to psychoanalysis. Kristeva was first attracted to the structuralists' refusal to accept traditional reliance on factors outside the text. Like Derrida, she used this position as a point of departure for further theories, but whereas he was inspired to "deconstruct" phenomenology, she directed her effort to analyses of the crises which determine the transformations of discourses during its history. She first investigated the creative process of writing in "Le texte clos," *Languages* 12 (1968): 103–25. She elaborated it in *Semiotikē: recherches pour une sémanalyse* (Paris: Seuil, Tel Quel, 1969. Reprinted in 1978. Paris: Seuil, Tel Quel). In the latter, through the neologism "semanalyse," she defined her method as a conceptual ensemble which leads to the discovery of mutations particular to the historical becoming of a text and to its impact on signifying practices. In agreement with the Saussurian model, she viewed the sign as doubly oriented: first, toward the signifying system in which it is produced, and second, toward the social process in which it participates. Later, departing from Bakhtin's dialogism and moving away from the traditional authorial center, her exploration of spaces where texts meet excessive use of the illogical inspired another neologism, "intertextuality." In *La Révolution du Langage Poétique: l'avant-garde à la fin du XIXe siècle, Lautréamont et Mallarmé* (Paris: Seuil, 1974), she defined a process by which sign systems transform themselves into each other. Kristeva's concern with psychic pain and its linguistic expression was well within the ideological

framework of the leading French thinkers of the 1960s and 1970s. Freud's discovery, elaborated by Lacan's introduction of the "other" in the mirror stage, propelled Kristeva, along with the *Tel Quel* group, to speak of the necessity of this other. In a number of works she developed a unique construct of narcissism as both the most archaic death-drive which precedes identity (sign, order, or belief) and the motive for revolutionary action.

Notes to Chapter 1

1. An early version of my preliminary work on narcissism was presented at a conference and published. See "Mythologies de l'amour," *Le Mythe ét le Mythique* (Paris: Albin Michel, 1987), 193–202.

2. Unless otherwise specified, what I refer to as ancient narratives are taken from the anthology of Thomas Bulfinch, *The Age of Fable or Beauties of Mythology* (New York: Tudor Publishing, 1935).

3. In her study of Freud's works, *L'énigme de la femme dans les textes de Freud* (1980; Paris: Editions Galilée, 1983), Sarah Kofman concludes that his theories are motivated by his own horror of women's genitals. In his proposal that women need a son, she sees a projection of his own unacceptable need for women and demonstrates how the mother-son relationship became an obsession in his last texts.

4. I was particularly interested in Gilligan's rebuttal of Erik H. Erikson's theorizing in *Identity: Youth and Crisis* (New York: W. W. Norton, 1968) that women were incapable of reaching the highest level of moral categories of human development; see *In a Different Voice*. I was also helped in my attempts to clarify the term "self" as used in literature by the ideas of Judith Kegan Gardiner in "On Female Identity and Writing by Woman," *Critical Inquiry* 8 (1981): 347–63.

5. Julia Kristeva, in *Pouvoirs de l'horreur: essai sur l'abjection* (Paris: Seuil, 1980), associates language with "la lutte pour se séparer, c'est-à-dire, devenir sujets parlants et/ou sujet à la loi" (the struggle to separate from the mother, that is, to become speaking subjects and/or subject to the law), 113. Hereafter all translations are mine.

6. Feminists in different fields of study have addressed this question. Evelyn Fox Keller, in *Reflections on Gender and Science* (New Haven: Yale University Press, 1985), demonstrates how some scholars couch biased views in biological determinism and argues, as I do, that it is a form of narcissism; it "is not simply that the dream of a completely objective science is in principle unrealizable, but that it contains precisely what it reflects: the vivid traces of a reflected self image" (70). Her comments on the "modes of access to knowledge as masculine" are as applicable to critiques of canonized literary theories as they are to scientific ones. "Masculine here connotes, as it so often does, autonomy, separation, and distance. It connotes a radical rejection of any commingling of subject and object, which are, it now appears,

quite consistently identified as male and female" (79). Although when reading Fox Keller we come to understand where gender-based thinking leads science, we may suggest alternatives to her vision of a gender-free science "premised on a transformation of the very categories of male and female, and correspondingly, of mind and nature" (178). We may suggest that it might not be necessary to transform them if they were simply not categorized according to gender.

7. Kristeva's concept of narcissism surpasses traditional definitions. It is developed in both *Pouvoirs de l'horreur* and *Soleil noir: dépression et mélancholie* (Paris: Gallimard, 1987).

8. See Edward Tripp, *Crowell's Handbook of Classic Mythology* (New York: Thomas Crowell, 1970), 41. My research on French documents turned up very few studies on the Amazons. The editors of the *Grand Dictionnaire Universel du XIXᵉ Siècle,* Tome I, do not trouble themselves to find any quotable sources. The entry reads: "Nom donné par les anciens à des femmes guerrières qu'ils disent avoir habité les rives du Thermodon, en Carradoce et avoir étendu leurs conquêtes jusque dans l'Asie Mineure." (Name given to women warriors whom the ancients *say* inhabited the shores of Thermodon, in Carradoce and spread their conquests as far as Asia Minor [my emphasis].)

9. In *Le mythe des amazones dans la mosaïque antique* (Beyrouth: Dar el–Machreq, 1975), 8.

10. See, in particular, A. Reinach's comments in "L'Origine des Amazones," *Revue de l'histoire des religions* (Paris: Ernest Leroux, Editeurs, 1913), 31: "Ainsi, la légende amazonienne s'est enrichie au contact de toutes les guerres nationales que les Grecs ont soutenues contre les barbares du Nord et du Levant. Elle en est devenue comme le résumé et le symbole. Avoir combattu les Amazones,—ou, puisqu'elles étaient femmes, avoir pu conquérir la ceinture de ces vierges indomptables,—ce fût l'exploit que tout héros grec dût avoir accompli pour paraître vértablement héros national." (Consequently, the Amazonian legend is enriched by national wars where the Greeks came in contact with barbarians of the North and the Orient. It became the sum and symbol of wars. For all Greek heroes to become veritable national heroes, they had to engage the Amazons in combat—or, since they were women—they had to win the belt of these indomitable virgins.)

11. Quoted from Charles Villier, "Le Courrier des Départements," *Histoire des clubs de femmes et des légions d'Amazones: 1793–1848–1871* (Paris: Librairie Plon, 1910), 237.

12. Paul Diel, *Le symbolisme dans la mythologie grecque: étude psychanalytique* (Paris: Payot, 1952), 207.

13. See Jacques Lacan's *Ecrits I* (Paris: Seuil, 1966), 157–58.

14. This quote is from Jardine's *Gynesis,* 164.

15. This definition is found in *Princeton Encyclopedia of Poetry and Poetics.*

16. Both French and American feminist literary criticism originate in a fundamental sense of mission which focuses on difference. The initial stages of my research were inspired by Simone de Beauvoir, who was the first (in 1949) to work out a feminist version of the concept of "alterity" in *The Second Sex*, trans. H. M. Parshley (New York: Knopf, 1957). Other early feminist writers in France are analyzed and their writings reprinted in *New French Feminism: An Anthology*, eds. Elaine Marks and Isabelle de Courtivron (Amherst: The University of Massachusetts Press, 1989). Major early American works were also relevant to this chapter. Refer to *Nature, Culture and Gender*, eds. Carol P. MacCormack and Marilyn Strathern (Cambridge: Cambridge University Press, 1980); *Sexist Language: A Modern Philosophical Analysis*, ed. Mary Vetterling-Braggin (Totowa, N.J.: Rowan and Littlefield, 1981); and *The Voyage in Fictions of Female Developments*, eds. Elizabeth Abel, Marianne Hirsch, and Elizabeth Langland (Hanover, N.H.: University Press of New England, 1983). For a study of resistance to codification, see Cheri Register's "Literary Criticism," *Signs* 6, no. 2 (Winter 1980): 268–82.

17. See *A History of Autobiography in Antiquity*.

18. Refer to Petrie W. Flinders, ed., *Egyptian Tales: Second Series XVIII to XIX Dynasty* (New York: Frederick A. Stokes, 1896), 87–141.

19. It is interesting to note that Gérard Genette's definitions of textual discourses in *Figures III* (Paris: Seuil, 1972) are not workable in the case of the Egyptian tale. None of his four categories based on the relationship of voice to subject works; neither the absent "hétérodiégétique," nor the present "homodiégétique," nor the first degree "extra-diégétique," nor the second degree "intra-diégétique" narrators can be applied.

20. The concept of women's time to which I refer here is found in an article by Julia Kristeva, translated by Alice Jardine and Harry Blake in *Signs* 7, no. 1 (Autumn 1981): 5–35. It originally appeared as "Le Temps des femmes," *34/44: Cahiers de recherche de sciences des textes et documents*, 5 (Winter 1979). She proposes a concept of "monumental time" that is less a chronology than a signifying space. Kristeva sees in the dichotomy man/woman an opposition between two rival entities which belongs to metaphysics. She notes that feminism is in the process of becoming a religion, a challenge to identity, not because it effaces differences, but because it de-dramatizes what she calls the "flight to the death," i.e., it seeks other means of regulating difference than the insupportable situation of tension. She concludes that these esthetic practices are a modern reply to the eternal question of morality.

21. For a critique of the "marriage plot" and "heroinism," refer to Brownstein. For explorations into the character of the heroine in fiction and autobiography, see Patricia Meyer Spacks, *The Female Imagination* (New York: Alfred A. Knopf, 1975), and *Imagining a Self*. For works on the female as hero, see Lee R. Edwards, *Psyche As Hero: Female Heroism and Fictional Form*

(Middletown, Conn.: Wesleyan University Press, 1984), and Grace Stewart, *A New Mythos: The Novel of the Artist as Heroine, 1877–1977* (St. Alban's, Vt.: Eden Press Women's Publications, 1979). This quest is examined by Elaine Showalter in *A Literature of Their Own: British Novelists from Brontë to Lessing* (Princeton: Princeton University Press, 1977). She categorizes it as the third of a three-part construction of major phases in the development of women writers, which I summarize as: (1) imitation and internalization of standards of traditional roles; (2) protest and advocacy of minority rights, demands for autonomy; and (3) self-discovery, turning inward, freedom from dependency and search for identity. The first is feminine, the second feminist, and the third female.

22. Refer to Wayne C. Booth, *The Rhetoric of Fiction* (Chicago: University of Chicago Press, 1961).

23. Judith Fetterley was the first to quote this term and to suggest that critics give voice to a different reality. See *The Resisting Reader: A Feminist Approach to American Fiction* (Bloomington: Indiana University Press, 1978).

24. Refer to Michel Serres.

25. This quote is from the first chapter. See Homer, *The Odyssey: The Story of Odysseus,* trans. W. H. D. Rouse (New York: Mentor Books, 1949), 18.

26. John J. Winkler, in *Constraints of Desire: The Anthropology of Sex and Gender in Ancient Greece* (New York: Columbia University Press, 1988), suggests that "the ambiguities of Penelope's situation and the double bind placed on Greek women generally are captured not only in what the poet represents but on a second level—by the author's own cunning in deliberately avoiding too close a look at what Penelope might be thinking and scheming." This suggestion results from a perspective of authorial intent which I do not share. It seems impossible to ascertain why Homer did not write about Penelope. All the reader can testify to is that Homer did not say much about her. The present study attempts to demonstrate the function of Penelope in the ongoing story. The explanation of the original source of the essence/existence dichotomy is found in note 28 below.

27. A reference is made to this similarity in Serres's work.

28. I refer here to Plato's *chora* as conceptualized by Kristeva in her chapter on "sémiotique et symbolique" in *La Révolution du langage poétique*. She proposes that this *chora* is a space-receptacle symbolic of a nursing mother. In psychoanalytic terms, its function in the semiotic order is pre-oedipal: "le corps de la mère est ce pas-encore-un que le sujet conscient et désirant imaginera comme un 'réceptacle'." Kristeva gives this *chora* a semiotic function (23–27); yet, as she states, it can only occur in the symbolic.

29. I am using concepts of cyclical and linear time defined by Mircea Eliade in *The Myth of the Eternal Return: Cosmos and History,* trans. Willard R. Trask 1954 (New York: Bollinger Foundation. Princeton: Princeton University Press, 1974). Cyclical time is associated with archaic societies which renegerate themselves through periodical rituals, thereby refusing to accept

themselves as historical beings; linear time is situated by Eliade at the beginning of recorded history, the advent of Christ, and it progresses toward the future.

Notes to Chapter 2

1. For thorough information on this correspondence, refer to Charlotte Charrier's monumental dissertation: *Héloïse dans l'histoire et dans la légende* (Paris: Librairie Ancienne Honoré Champion, 1933), 644.

2. On the question of authenticity, Charrier finds that some of the passages are too objectionable to have been written by a woman, although she points out that they were revised by Abelard. This problem is also addressed and left unsolved in *Beyond Their Sex: Learned Women of the European Past,* ed. Patricia H. Labalme (New York: New York University Press, 1980).

3. Paul Zumthor makes the point that "individual experience, even on the level of the deep intention of the text, is transcended" in the Middle Ages because authors refer to themselves in the third person as well as in the first person. He states that, although Abelard's *Historia calamitatum* and St. Augustine's *Confessions* are exceptions to that tradition, the latter falls somewhat within it since it ends with a commentary on Genesis. Certainly, Abelard, who wrote his story as an example for a friend—whose presence he inserts in the address of his letter—also adheres to this view of a commonality: all sinners sharing the same experience. On the other hand, one could argue that Abelard sets himself apart as an individual by including this letter in the manuscript containing his personal correspondence. See "Autobiography in the Middle Ages?" in *Genre* 6 (March 1973): 29–48.

4. Two major works will be discussed later: Peggy Kamuf's study, *Fictions of Feminine Desire: Disclosures of Heloïse* (Lincoln: University of Nebraska Press, 1982), and feminist reading, *Plus jamais l'amour éternel: Héloïse sans Abélard* (Québec: Nouvelle Optique, 1981).

5. For this background information, I am grateful to Georges Duby's work in *Medieval Marriage: Two Models from Twelfth-Century France,* trans. Elborg Forster (Baltimore: Johns Hopkins University Press, 1978), 137.

6. Joseph Barry remarks in his study of couples that the text of the correspondence dates back to the dawn of the twelfth century, when Paris had not yet been touched by the southern concept of "amour courtois." Refer to *A la Française: le couple à travers l'histoire,* trans. C. Blanchet and L. Lassen (Paris: Seuil, 1985). The references in the letters to love poems dedicated to Heloïse, however, contradict Barry's theory.

7. Kamuf's study minutely and specifically illustrates Heloïse's skills and the strength of her arguments. Her letters "attempt to dodge the immobilizing terms that Abelard has placed on their experience. . . . This deconstruction of stable meaning is the activity which threatens the edifice Abelard has built and in which he has enclosed, along with Heloïse, his unruly past" (44).

159

8. See *Discourses of Desire: Gender, Genre, and Epistolary Fictions* (Ithaca: Cornell University Press, 1986), 66.

9. All parenthetical citations to the correspondence refer to M. Gréard's French translation from the Latin, *Lettres complètes d'Abélard et d'Héloïse*, traduction nouvelle (Paris: Garnier frères, 1970), 114. Hereafter, pages and translations are mine and are given in parentheses in the text. Because Gréard's is the translation used throughout the centuries in France, I will preserve the original.

10. Many works have now been published on the condition of early European women. Refer in particular to Frances Gies and Joseph Gies, *Women in the Middle Ages* (New York: Thomas Y. Crowell, 1978). Also, see Régine Pernoud, *La Femme au temps des cathédrales* (Paris: Stock, 1980).

11. The shift from Eve to Mary and Adam to Christ is explicated in Leif Grane, *Peter Abelard: Philosophy and Christianity in the Middle Ages*, trans. Frederick and Christine Crowly (New York: Harcourt, Brace & World, 1964). Angela M. Lucas notes that not only does Mary replace Eve, but Christ replaces Adam; see *Women in the Middle Ages: Religion, Marriage and Letters* (New York: St. Martin's Press, 1983).

12. Julia Kristeva traces the image of the *dame* back to the Virgin Mary in "Un nouveau type intellectuel: le dissident" et "Héréthique de l'amour," *Tel Quel* 74 (Hiver 1977): 3–8 and 30–49.

13. Grane, 40.

14. Abelard followed St. Paul's line, permitting "no woman to teach or to have authority over men, and ordering her to keep silent" (Lucas, 6). In her unorthodox analysis of the correspondence, Brisson speaks of the head of men "en position dominante, tenue haute, érigée comme le phallus. . . . Il [l'homme] peut se placer à la tête des autres, comme le mari est, saint Paul le dit expressément, la tête de la femme" (in the dominating position, [the head] held high, as erect as the phallus. . . . He [man] can place himself at the head of others, as the husband is, Saint Paul said so expressly, the head of the woman/wife) (122).

15. Saint Augustine, *Confessions*, 2 vols., trans. Pierre Labriolle (Paris: Societé d'Editions "Les belles lettres," 1947), 12.

16. Charrier (172–73) writes that only one text contained in the manuscript is documented; only the funeral oration can definitely be attributed to Heloïse.

17. Reference is made here to Kristeva's study of maternity in *Pouvoirs de l'horreur* (124). In this work, she writes that the fusion to women (the maternal) occurs in the *impropre*, a "lieu impropre de la fusion . . . une puissance indifférenciée" (124). In French, "impropre" signifies both not proper and unclean. Kristeva's theory that the maternal is associated in men's artistic expressions with impurity and impropriety is based on her recognition of the maternal in their works as a desirable yet horrifying space of "undifferentiated power." In other words, the maternal is a space where dominance could not occur.

18. Terence Hawkes, *Structuralism and Semiotics* (Berkeley: University of California Press, 1977), 21.
19. See Catherine Belsley, "Constructing the Subject: Deconstructing the Text," *Feminist Criticism and Social Change: Sex Class and Race in Literature and Culture*, eds. J. Newton and D. Rosenfelt (New York: Methuen, 1985), 54.
20. Monique A. Piettre emphasizes this aspect of the sacred woman in her study of women throughout the ages. The cult of the *dame* infiltrated Christian devotion to the virgin. Mary became the *Notre-Dame* to whom most of the cathedrals of France were dedicated. See *La condition féminine à travers les âges* (Paris: Editions France-Empire, 1974), 170.
21. Meg Bogin concludes, after her examination of the topic of love in the writings of women troubadours of the Middle Ages, that their language was more straightforward than men's. Women troubadours were less frequently given to word play than men. In fact, they rejected symbolic love. See *The Women Troubadours* (New York: Paddington Press, 1976).
22. Working on the metalanguage of universal symbols, Durand states that men are obsessed with construction. Even the symbol itself is a mental "reconstruction" of a "constructed" object. Following this line of thinking about construction as an archetypical physical and mental activity, Durand proposes that men build places to represent what they do not have, and that *sacred* places reproduce that which they do not possess, i.e., the uterus. See Durand, 88–92.
23. Refer to Susan Rubin Suleiman, *Subversive Intent: Gender, Politics, and the Avant-Garde* (Cambridge: Harvard University Press, 1990), 133. Her mention that in the Arthurian legends the Holy Grail "becomes a pagan symbol originally associated with the goddess of love" (172) validates my own contention of the ineffability of women's sexuality in canonized texts.

Notes to Chapter 3

1. Refer to Antoinette Bourignon, *La Vie de Damlle Antionette Bourignon, écrite par elle-méme*, ed. Pierre Poiret (Amsterdam: J. Riewerts & Pierre Arents, Librairies, rue de la Bourse, 1682), 143. All translations hereafter will be mine.
2. All quotes are from Jeanne Marie (Bouvier de La Motte) Guyon, *Autobiography of Madame Guyon*, trans. Thomas Taylor Allen, 2 vols. (London: Kegan Paul, Trench, Trubner & Co., 1897), I, 7.
3. See *Jeanne Guyon* (Paris: Flammarion, 1978), 84.
4. Marie-Florine Bruneau, in "The Writing of History as Fiction and Ideology: The Case of Madame Guyon," *Feminist Issues*, 5, no. 1 (Spring 1985): 27–38, notes about Guyon: "She is dangerous also because her teaching finds disciples. Wherever she goes, she is listened to, to the great dismay of ecclesiastical officials" (35).

5. Jane Chance, in *Woman as Hero in Old English Literature* (Syracuse, N.Y.: Syracuse University Press, 1986), finds that Anglo-Saxon women whose role called for passivity and peace-making patterned their behavior on the Virgin Mary. Antithetical to this chaste and pious archetype was Eve, who personified evil female concupiscence.

6. It was the essential proof against the accusations of witchery leveled at her. She claimed to be guided by God and, as only a virgin could be worthy of God's visit, if her prosecutors could prove that she was not a virgin, her extraordinary courage and skill in battle would have been attributed to the devil. She must be a witch. Most of the narratives in the records of her trial are testimonies from medical experts who were consulted and who examined her to ascertain that she was a virgin. These comments are based on documents from archives quoted in Régine Pernoud, *Jeanne d'Arc par elle-même et par ses témoins* (Paris: Seuil, 1962).

7. For more information and a feminist approach to the movement, see Jeannette Geffriaud Rosso, *Etudes sur la féminité aux XVIIe et XVIIIe Siècles* (Pisa: Libreria Goliardica, 1984).

8. I refer here to Tzvetan Todorov's structural study of genres, which brings him to the problem of truth and belief. In the fantastic, one suspends belief; see *Les Genres du discours* (Paris: Seuil, 1978).

9. See Benjamin Sahler, ed., *Madame Guyon et Fénelon: la correspondance secrète* (Paris: Dervy Livres, 1982), 238. All translations from the French are mine.

10. See *Histoires d'amour* (Paris: Ed. Denoël, 1983), 387. Kristeva views the trial of love as a hymn to a narcissistic power which puts into question the referential and communicative power of language.

11. Bruneau, in "La vie de Madame Guyon: frigidité et masochisme en tant que dispositifs politiques," *French Forum* (May 1983), 101–107, speaks of Guyon's entrance into the political field to gain approval. It seems more likely that she was trying to escape power games than to participate in them. Her brand of mysticism was too radical to be "socialement valorisé" (102).

12. Ibid., "A l'intérieur du pouvoir" (105).

13. Frances Mossiker, *Madame de Sévigné: A Life and Letters* (New York: Alfred A. Knopf, 1983), 11.

14. See *Réalité vecue et art épistolaire: Madame de Sévigné et la lettre d'amour* (Paris: Bordas, 1970), 113.

15. Refer to Alicia Suskin Ostriker, *Stealing the Language: The Emergence of Women's Poetry in America* (Boston: Beacon Press, 1986), 198. She writes of the challenge women present to literature by speaking of themselves as mothers and by defying generic categories: "The appropriation of the creativity-procreativity metaphor by women is a conscious challenge to traditional poetics and beyond that to traditional metaphysics, for the gynocentric vision is not that the Logos condescends to incarnate itself, but that Flesh becomes Word. . . . Women writers tend to defy genre categories by blur-

ring distinctions between the private writing of the diary and the public writing of fiction'' (199).

16. Madame de Sévigné (1626–1696), Marie de Rabutin Chantal, *Correspondance* (Paris: Gallimard, 1972), I, 216, 315.

17. Ellen L. Bassuk demonstrates the import of the rest cure as substitute for sexual intercourse in ''The Rest Cure: Repetition or Resolution of Victorian Women's Conflicts?'', *The Female Body in Western Culture: Contemporary Perspectives,* ed. Susan Rubin Suleiman (Cambridge: Harvard University Press, 1986), 139–51.

18. For an elaboration of the psychological aspect of the symbiosis between mother and daughter in Sévigné's letters, see Elizabeth C. Goldsmith, ''Giving Weight to Words: Madame de Sévigné's Letters to Her Daughter,'' *The Female Autograph,* eds. D. C. Stanton and J. P. Plottel (New York: New York Literary Forum, 1984), 107–18.

19. Controlling women's text of the body is discussed in several writings. Refer to the following articles in *The Poetics of Gender,* ed. Nancy K. Miller (New York: Columbia University Press, 1986). For problems of editing and authors, see Mary Ann Caws, ''The Conception of Engendering: The Erotics of Editing,'' 42–62. She calls the liberty men take in editing women's texts the right of a seigneur. Certainly, one would say that the confessor abrogates himself this right over the text of the memorialist, as the word ''seigneur'' refers not only to the nobility, but to the lord Jesus whom he represents. Also, Nancy K. Miller, in ''Arachnologies: The Woman, The Text and the Critic,'' 270–97, points out that it is the woman who leaves her text open who is the master. She theorizes that the reader's being in relation to a void threatens *his* mastery.

Notes to Chapter 4

1. All quotations will refer to *Les Confessions* (Paris: Garnier Frères, 1964) and to the number of the letter in the French edition of *Julie ou la Nouvelle Héloïse* (Paris: Garnier-Flammarion, 1967).

2. A few recent studies provide valuable information. Gita May has written on Rousseau in her works on Staël and Sand. Refer to *De Jean-Jacques Rousseau à Madame Roland: Essai sur la sensibilité préromantique et révolutionnaire* (Genève: Librairie Droz, 1964); also, her article comparing Rousseau's autobiographical work to George Sand's, ''Des *Confessions à Histoire de ma vie* et l'ombre de Rousseau,'' *Présence de George Sand* 8 (1980): 40–47. For her more recent evaluation and vindication of Rousseau, see ''Rousseau's 'Antifeminism' Reconsidered,'' *French Women and the Age of Enlightenment,* ed. Samia I. Spencer (Bloomington: Indiana University Press, 1984), 309–17. For another recent article re-validating the positive impact of Rousseau's heroine on women writers of the next century, refer to Madelyn Gutwirth's ''Woman as Mediatrix: From Jean-Jacques Rousseau to Ger-

maine de Staël," *Woman as Mediatrix: Essays on Nineteenth-Century European Women Writers,* Contributions in Women's Studies, 73 (Westport, Conn.: Greenwood Press, 1987): 13–29.

3. A work by John C. O'Neil also distinguishes these two meanings of the verb "to see" in Rousseau. O'Neil also finds a breaking down of barriers—the process called "intersubjectivity" in the present study—between subject and object in the promenades: "He [Rousseau] hesitates to subscribe to any fixed pattern of thinking and momentarily diminishes the existing barriers between subject and object." Refer to *Seeing and Observing; Rousseau's Rhetoric of Perception,* Stanford French and Italian Studies (Saratoga, Calif.: Anma Libri & Co., 1985), 4.

4. Georges Poulet writes of Rousseau's associating thought to promenades as living a metaphor. Rousseau resembles a man who walks alone in the dark, one who has difficulty, but who wishes to walk with assurance in life. See *Etudes sur le temps humain,* 3 vols. (Paris: Plon, 1949), III.

5. René Démoris makes an interesting comment about memoirs and the sex of the writer. About woman, he writes: "Si elle devient auteur, le roman peut devenir plus vrai, mais ce surplus de vérité se paie, comme le constate Bayle, par une chute en moralité." (If she becomes an author, novel becomes more true, but this surplus of truth is paid, as Bayle observes, by a moral laxness.) He pursues this thought: " . . . assumant une fonction virile dans une société en évolution, [la femme] est ⌐⌐⌐ ⌐⌐⌐ ⌐⌐⌐ ⌐⌐⌐ en cause les cadres traditionnels d'explication qui sont d'origine masculine" (assuming a virile function in a society in evolution, woman is in a good situation to question traditional interpretations of masculine origin). He then casts doubts on the authenticity of women's works, stating that Mme de la Guette's memoirs are of doubtful authenticity. Later, however, he assures the reader that Rousseau's memoirs are true. (En passant, we must note that all critics agree that *Les Confessions* are not memoirs but autobiographical writings.) The important point here is that Démoris inadvertently supports a feminist thesis; Rousseau's situating himself in the female position vis-à-vis writing permits him to revolutionize models of heroism. See *Le roman à la première personne: du classicisme aux Lumières* (Paris: Librairie Armand Colin, 1975), 264.

6. See Susan Bordo.

7. Refer to Kristeva's "pheno-text" and "geno-text" in *La Révolution du language poétique.*

8. François Van Laere's study of the phenomenology (a conscience which apprehends itself) of Rousseau's epistolary novel leads him to the conclusion that three modalities of time condense into one eternal, unified, psychological present. See *Une Lecture du temps dans* La Nouvelle Héloïse (Neuchatel, Switzerland: Editions de la Baconnière, 1968).

9. How prevalent the subject of male and female differences is in Rousseau's work is proven in a number of studies, among them a book where Joel

Schwartz takes a mild view of dominance in sexual intercourse: "Human beings like to rule one another; there is nothing necessarily wrong with this (though there is much about absolutely unchecked rule that is dangerous) and there is much that may be positive about it." See *The Sexual Politics of Jean-Jacques Rousseau* (Chicago: University of Chicago Press, 1984), 143.

10. See Zumthor.

11. See Gaston Bachelard, *La poétique de l'espace* 1957 (Paris: Presses universitaires de France, 1974).

12. How the superiority of Rousseau's hero is symbolized in spatial terms is the subject of a study by Lloyd Bishop, *The Romantic Hero and His Heirs in French Literature* (New York: Peter Lang, 1984).

13. I owe this theory of an affirmation of positive negative space to Kern's study, *The Culture of Time and Space*. He sees a shift in the European apprehension of time during the eighteenth century: "The philosophers of the Enlightenment looked to antiquity for values they had lost in their struggle with Christianity" (63).

14. This is in reference to the theories developed by Gilligan in her study of men's and women's stories about the self. See *In a Different Voice*.

15. Jean Guehenno, in his biography of Rousseau, *Jean-Jacques*, 2 vols. (Paris: Gallimard, 1962), provides several proofs of the autobiographical nature of the epistolary novel.

16. I am referring here to Eliade's proposal that the Middle Ages were dominated by these two conceptions of time. See *The Eternal Return* (144–45).

17. Literature often reiterates the trope of lame men and distortion of language. Victor Hugo, for instance, puts Quasimodo's speech into question.

18. In *Writing the Truth* (Berkeley: University of California Press, 1987), he suggests that Rousseau writes in a "self-directed discourse whose implications seemingly concern only the writing subject" (182).

19. Charrier notes that Rousseau is "severe" toward Abelard and "pities" Heloïse (476).

20. Nina Auerbach, in her study *Woman and the Demon: The Life of a Victorian Myth* (Cambridge : Harvard University Press, 1982), addresses the subject of Rousseau's influence on women's writings in relation to a characteristic of the Medusa female archetype in "perpetual metamorphosis" (238).

21. We are struck by the convoluted way Rousseau poses as a feminist. In Lettre XXVII (215), his Julie scolds St. Preux for forgetting to mention "les soins domestiques et l'éducation des enfants" in his letter about the role of women. The author adds his own personal feminist note here to praise St. Preux for forgetting that women should above all be concerned with domestic and motherly chores. He addresses his male readers: "Eh! que deviendraient le monde et l'Etat, auteurs illustres, brillants académiciens, que devriendriez-vous tous, si les femmes allaient quitter le gouvernement de la littérature et des affaires, pour prendre celui de leur ménage? [Note de Rousseau]" (215). (Eh! what would become of the world and the state, illustrious

authors and brilliant academicians, what would you all become, if women
were to leave the rule of literature and commerce to take up the rule of
their household?)
22. Durand recognizes this. Also, in "Rousseau and the Text as Self," *Narcissism and the Text; Studies in Literature and the Psychology of the Self*, eds.
Lynne Layton and Barbara Ann Schapiro (New York: New York University
Press, 1986), 78–96, Susan Grayson addresses the question of narcissism.
She argues that Rousseau's narcissistic preoccupations acknowledge a split
self, and she names two identities: "Rousseau the writer, the fallen self of
civilization; and Jean-Jacques the man, the idealized self of Nature" (81).
These two selves are reflected in water, "natural mirrors" which "unlike the
brittle and unforgiving glass of civilization flatter him. If inaccurate, these
mirrors are no more so than those of Culture, which claim reflection but are
distorted" (86). My own work is based on Kristeva's idea that narcissism is
a basic archaic drive preceding identity. It is a motive for revolutionary action. In Rousseau's novel, St. Preux's narcissism consists of the attempts to
overcome one's limits and, as Kristeva theorizes in *Histoires d'amour*, its ultimate expression is found in the transports of love where defenses break down.
23. See *The Heroine's Text: Readings in the French and English Novel: 1722–1782* (New York: Columbia University Press, 1980), 115.
24. In "Emphasis Added: Plots and Plausibilities in Women's Fiction," *PMLA*
(1981), 36–48, Nancy K. Miller finds a different ethic in a recent reading of
the significance of the *aveu* to the intertext of women.
25. Elaine Showalter, in *A Literature of Their Own*, makes the interesting comment that all utopian ideals "lack zest and energy" (263).
26. The "impossible elsewhere" theory is put forth in Kristeva's study of Bellini
and motherhood. She demonstrates the lasting power of the cult of the
mother from its origin in the Middle Ages to its full exploitation in artistic
representations of the Renaissance. Using Bellini's works as an example, she
argues that, through the mother's body, a sort of subject is established at the
point where mother and speech split apart and that, consequently, the mother
is a *place* of splitting and, therefore, master of a pre-linguistic, social symbolic contract made by the human group. See *Desire in Language: A Semiotic Approach to Literature and Art*, trans. Thomas Gora, Alice Jardine, and
Leon S. Roudiez, ed. Leon S. Roudiez (New York: Columbia University
Press, 1980).
27. George Sand's works (particularly her early novels) praising the maternal
function show evidence of Rousseau's influence; not so much in her narratives of the mother-child relation, where her own ideology prevails, but in
her narratives of the impotence of women in the love relationship.
28. See *Violence and the Sacred*, trans. Patrick Gregory (1972; Baltimore: Johns
Hopkins University Press, 1977), 75.
29. Kristeva states that love is a hymn to the power of narcissism: "in the transports of love the limits of *'propre'* [proper and self in French] identity are

lost." In this work, she proposes to demonstrate that the discourse of love problematizes language: "Do we speak of the same thing when we speak of love?" (*Histoires d'amour*, 10).

30. In *Honey-Mad Women: Emancipatory Strategies in Women's Writings* (New York: Columbia University Press, 1988), 149–76, a study of dialogues as emancipatory strategies, Patricia Yaeger quotes Wollstonecraft's objections to Rousseau's statement that a woman's duty is to be agreeable to her master. She also quotes her remark that it is his "sensibility that led him to degrade woman by making her the slave of love" (1973). In this dialogue between Wollstonecraft and Rousseau, Yaeger compares him to the first seducer, Satan, because he "lures women away from the sweet light of reason" (172).

31. This is best observed in Annie Leclerc's *Parole de femme* (Paris: Grasset, 1974). Her phenomenological approach leads her to theorize that social inequities originate in men's sensory apprehension of the world. She suggests that their partiality to the visual leads to artificial distinctions, such as those between subject and object, and that this overdependence on the visual favors processes of separation, leading eventually to the division of humans into the social groups which form the hierarchies of patriarchal hegemony. Her approach, and the conclusion to which it inclines her, are not too foreign to Rousseau's own. The divergences and convergences of Rousseau's and Leclerc's ideas may be summarized as follows: both categorize the degree of ability to enjoy the senses according to gender; both suggest that women are more *sensible* than men; but Leclerc differs from Rousseau when she states that men favor the visual and women are more gifted for the enjoyment of the tactual. Rousseau never makes such a statement. The chief characteristic linking his writings to those of feminists is that both breach problems of identity through gender-linked sensory apprehensions and share a deep ethical commitment to social inequities. For less provocative theories, see Leclerc's subsequent publication, *Hommes et Femmes* (Paris: Grasset, 1985).

32. Grayson's psychological analysis of Rousseau's narcissism also addresses the island and supports my own thesis. The island, she writes, "serves the contact-shunning side of his personality." Rousseau becomes isolated "not through disinterest but through too intense a need for others, hypersensitivity to rejection, and fear of self-annihilation or loss of self-integrity in union with others. Jean-Jacques, the eighteenth-century apologist of Nature against culture, avoids risk in choosing a union with the forces of Nature" (86).

33. I refer here to Eugene Minkowski's work in *Lived Time: Phenomenological and Psychopathological Studies*, trans. Nancy Metzel (Evanston, Ill.: Northwestern University Press, 1970).

34. See *Oeuvres autobiographiques*, ed. Georges Lubin, 2 vols. (Paris: Gallimard, 1970–71), 1, 466. So much has been written about George Sand and her female heroes that it is impossible to list all of it here, but in an article on *mal du siècle* and the Romantic hero (*"Cherchez la Femme:* Male Malady

and Narrative Politics in the French Romantic Novel," *PMLA* 104, no. 2 [1989]: 141–51), Margaret Waller points out the secondary status given her in our canonized journals. Waller concludes her study with a mention that George Sand's *Lélia* "depicts a true sex-role reversal in which the *mal du siècle* hero is a woman" (149). She suggests that a man who is like a woman (the Romantic hero) is not the equivalent of a woman who is like a man, and this is a valuable contribution to studies of the Romantic hero; but comparing male and female paradigms of heroism in works written by men and in works written by women is an enterprise which is just beginning, and one is surprised that studies applying Waller's theory to a woman's novel, Sand's, remain to be published in journals with wide distributions.

Notes to Chapter 5

1. One of the first of such studies centers on the doubles. In "De J. Sand à George Sand: *Rose et Blanche* de Sand et Sandeau et leur descendance," *NCFS* 44 (1976): 169–82, Tatiana Greene analyzes the theme of the double in Sand's first novel published in collaboration with Jules Sandeau.
2. André Maurois, who titled his biography of Sand *Lélia ou la vie de George Sand* (Paris: Hachette, 1952), simplified the double theme of sexual and artistic impotence to one of carnal impotence: "*Lélia* n'était qu'un long aveu d'impuissance charnelle" (165).
3. Critics have noticed similarities in the works of Sand and Balzac. The most extensive study is Janis Glasgow's *Une esthétique de comparaison: Balzac et George Sand: La Femme abandonnée et Metella* (Paris: Nizet, 1978). Another notable one is Nancy E. Rogers's comparison of the *raconteur* styles of Balzac and Sand in "George Sand and Honoré de Balzac: Stylistic Similarities," *George Sand Papers: Conference Proceedings, 1978*, ed. Natalie Datlof et al. (New York: AMS Press, 1982), 130–43.
4. Marguerite Duras and Xavière Gauthier, *Les Parleuses* (Paris: Minuit, 1974), 38.
5. A version of this study entitled "The Metonymy of Women's Relationship to Narratives in *Ahura's Tale* and in Sand's *Les Couperies*" was given at the Seventh International George Sand Conference, Hofstra University, Hempstead, N.Y., 17 October 1986.
6. These essays were published posthumously in *Oeuvres autobiographiques*.
7. The autobiographical nature of *Les Couperies* is verifiable in Lubin's notes; he recognizes Sand's friends of 1830 in all the characters.
8. A close reading of the gender of narrative voices in a number of Sand's first works, entitled "Ecrire au féminin," was delivered at a conference at the Université de Tours, 12 June 1981, and published in *Friends of George Sand Newsletter* 4, no. 2 (1981), 26–28.
9. I refer to my study of the novel retracing a considerable number of indirect addresses to men as "nous" (we) by the narrator of this first novel to include

himself as one of their sex—even though the author is a woman. See "The Problem of Language in Sand's *Indiana*," *West Virginia George Sand Conference Papers*, ed. A. E. Singer (Morgantown: Department of Foreign Languages, West Virginia University, 1981), 22–27.

10. Sand's first published work, *Rose et Blanche*, was written in collaboration with Jules Sandeau.

11. All references to this novel will be to the P. Salomon edition (Paris: Garnier Frères, 1962), 117.

12. Salomon added a note to this passage in the novel, explaining how Sand's friend, Latouche, used to recommend that she avoid making "pastiches" of Balzac (*Indiana*, 288).

13. A version of this entitled "*Lélia:* From Romantic Tropes to Individual Ethic," was given at the Session on George Sand, Modern Language Association Convention, New York, 30 December 1984.

14. In "Female Fetishism: The Case of George Sand," *The Female Body in Western Culture*, ed. Susan Rubin Suleiman (Cambridge: Harvard University Press, 1986): 363–72, Naomi Schor finds that Sand's breakdown of "firm boundaries between characters subverts the fiction of individuation that is the bedrock of conventional realism" (369) and that this is nowhere more evident than in *Lélia*. I agree with her statement, and I would add that these "fictions" of individuation can be retraced to a period many centuries before the advent of realism. As I demonstrated in my opening chapter, they originated in ancient Greece.

15. Showalter finds that in British utopian novels written between 1880 and 1900, the theme of self-exploration is tainted with self-hatred. To escape from a confrontation with the female body in a world polarized by sex, the female hero withdraws into silence. See *A Literature of Their Own*.

16. In French literature, an early example of the tradition of autobiography in fiction is Hélisenne de Crenne's *Les Angoysses douloureuses qui procèdent d'Amours*, annotated by Paule Demats (Paris: Les Belles Lettres-Annales de l'université de Nantes, 1968). Barbara Johnson develops a sound theoretical foundation for the study of women's autobiographical fiction in a review of Dorothy Dinnerstein's, Nancy Friday's, and Mary Shelley's works, "My Monster/Myself," *Diacritics* 12 (Summer 1982), 2–10. Again, the self is seen as monstrous "since the very notion of a self, the very shape of human life stories, has always, from St. Augustine to Freud, been modeled on the man." The problem as stated in the present study is that, as Johnson words it, women have to "resist the pressure of masculine autobiography . . . " in order "to describe a difficulty in conforming to a female ideal which is largely a fantasy of the masculine, not the feminine, imagination" (10).

17. The P. Reboul edition of the novel is annotated with remarks about the author's life, some of them derogatory. This edition, which contains both the 1833 and 1839 versions, will be used throughout this chapter. See George Sand, *Lélia* (Paris: Garnier, 1960).

18. She writes in her autobiography: "Quelques-uns diront que je suis Lélia, mais d'autres pourraient se souvenir que je fus jadis Sténio. . . . Je puis être Trenmor aussi. Magnus, c'est mon enfance, Sténio ma jeunesse, Lélia est mon âge mur; Trenmor sera ma vieillesse, peut-être. Tous ces types ont été en moi" (*Oeuvres autobiographiques*, 2, 614–15).

19. *Correspondance*, ed. George Lubin, 24 vols. (Paris; Garnier, 1964–1990), 3, 93.

20. Sara Ruddick speaks of colluding with destructive practices as a response to a world where one's own values do not count. See "Maternal Thinking," *Feminist Studies* 6, no. 2 (1980): 342–67.

21. In "Le Corps féminin dans *Lélia*," *Revue d'histoire littéraire de la France* 76 (1976): 634–47, Béatrice Didier studies the feminine body in the novel. She finds no indications of a physical presence, with the exception of one hand.

22. Barbara A. Schapiro, in *The Romantic Mother: Narcissistic Patterns in Romantic Poetry* (Baltimore: Johns Hopkins University Press, 1983), discusses the maternal aspect of the Medusa archetype, which was as popular in France as in England at the time. Her conclusions that the English Romantics show more disturbances in object relations than their Neoclassical predecessors and that the relationship with the maternal Medusa occupies a central position in the imagery of every Romantic poet do not apply to French Romantics. Although they share a fascination with the Medusa archetype, for them she represents the anti-muse. Sand responded angrily to this Muse's refusal to help the poet create by turning her Lélia into a Medusa who is the *woman* writer herself. In a parody of the archetype, she confuses and frightens Magnus the priest.

23. In "*Lélia* and Feminism," *Yale French Studies* 62 (1981): 45–66, Eileen Boyd Sivert writes: "Lelia appears in some ways to be trapped in transition between the place of the traditional woman and that of the modern." I concur with this idea that Lélia's position is transitory, as I find the novel's spatio-temporal narratives disorienting. Furthermore, Sivert's proposal that Lélia's logic "leaves openings which seem to be invitations to escape from a language that is not Lélia's own" (47) does not contradict my own view that Sand deliberately distorts the narratives of traditional novels.

24. In *The Female Imagination*, Patricia Meyer Spacks's investigation of the emotions guiding the writings of women leads her to the conclusion that anger is the most prevalent expression of feeling, as "one encounters it everywhere in women writing about their own condition" (30).

25. For a comprehensive study of the reception of *Lélia* in George Sand's time, see Isabelle Naginski, "*Lélia*: Novel of the Invisible," *George Sand Studies* 6, nos. 1–2 (1984–85): 46–53.

26. In her correspondence Sand shows a keen interest in the St. Simonian school of thought. The mission of the St. Simonians' "Femme-Messie" was sex-linked; she was a "Femme-Mère," a civilizing influence. Yet this model

conformed with the Roman Catholic Virgin Mary archetype, who was celibate although she was a mother. The priest and the priestess lived separate lives. Refer to Maria Teresa Bulciolu, *L'école saint-simonienne et la femme* (Pisa: Goliardica, 1980).

27. Several writings on the subject of the metaphor of writer as prostitute support this theory. See *Sex, Politics, and Science in the Nineteenth-Century Novel.*

28. In *Passions Elémentaires* (Paris: Minuit, 1982), Luce Irigaray writes that love is affection or desire of the self "soi-même" (51) and, in an elegy on touch, that desire ends not when its object is seen but touched "dans l'invisible" (54).

Notes to Chapter 6

1. In fact, Sand uses the format to subvert all three traditional approaches to the study of fairy tales: cultural, psychoanalytical, and structuralist. The first approach may be seen in Marc Soriano's *Les contes de Perrault: culture savante et traditions populaires* (Paris: Gallimard, 1968). The second, in Bruno Bettelheim's *La psychanalyse des contes de fées,* trans. Theo Carlier (Paris: Robert Laffont, 1976). The third, in Vladimir Propp's *Morphologie du conte poétique,* trans. C. Kahn. 1965 (Paris, Seuil, 1970).

2. Carla L. Peterson writes that Germaine de Staël's Corinne's "oralizing" of written literature represents an attempt to "feminize" masculine literature by infusing the male text with "female quality," but I see a reverse of this formula as Sand, a woman writer, feminizes her male hero. Refer to *The Determined Reader: Gender in the Novel from Napoleon to Victoria* (New Brunswick, N.J.: Rutgers University Press, 1986), 48.

3. All quotes refer to *Consuelo: La Comtesse de Rudolstadt,* 3 vols. (Paris: Editions Garnier Frères, 1959), I, 41, 53.

4. It is mentioned in the first note of the Léon Cellier-Léon Guichard edition that Sand sent the first installment with a note precising: *"Consuelo, conte"* (*Consuelo,* I, 4).

5. See *Les Confessions,* 373. Sand also quotes Rousseau as her source when she wants to prove that the *"choristes"* (*Consuelo,* I, 12–13) of Porpora's school were prepared not to earn a living, but for marriage or convent.

6. Through fiction, Sand informed her readers of the extreme images of patriarchal plots which kill creativity in women writers, those of monster and angel; these images are analyzed by Sandra Gilbert and Susan Gubar in *The Mad-Woman in the Attic: The Woman Writer and the Nineteenth-Century Imagination.* (New Haven: Yale University Press, 1979), 17.

7. This is the basis of the codal system used by Roland Barthes in his analysis of Balzac's work; see *S/Z* (Paris: Seuil, 1970).

8. The conclusion of my own readings of Sand's works demonstrates that she portrayed women in more complimentary terms than the writers studied in Grace Stewart's *A New Mythos* (177).

9. See *A Literature of Their Own*, 103.
10. See Stanton's "Androgynography: Is the Subject Different?" (*The Female Autograph*, 5–22), 15.
11. In "Rousseau's 'Antifeminism' Reconsidered." Gita May compares the three autobiographers in terms of Rousseau's feminism.
12. In a letter to Sainte-Beuve, she writes: "Mon ami, donnez-moi conseil. J'ai envie de faire un roman sur un prétendu fils de Jean-Jacques Rousseau, perdu à l'hospice et perdu dans la foule, ignorant, cherchant, pressentant, et ne retrouvant pas son père, ayant ses idées, ses défauts, ses croyances, son génie enfin, mais sans la soupape du talent, et traversant avec tout cela la révolution." See Georges Lubin, "George Sand et 'Le fils de Jean-Jacques'," *Présence de George Sand* no. 8 (May 1980), 4–6.
13. All quotes refer to George Sand, *Oeuvres autobiographiques* (I, 13). Hereafter all translations will be mine.
14. In the essay entitled *Du Repentir*, Montaigne writes: "Je peins le passage." Refer to the *Ouevres Complètes*, eds. Robert Barral and Pierre Michel (Paris: Seuil, 1967), 327.
15. In "Two Interviews with Julia Kristeva," by Elaine Hoffman Baruch (*Partisan Review* 51, no. 1 [120–32]), Kristeva explains that self is not a French idea. "It is an idea belonging originally to Anglo-Saxon psychoanalysis, and it doesn't fare well in French psychoanalytic literature" (120).
16. I am referring to his study of ritual and myth, *Violence and the Sacred*. Girard states that the loss of difference "strips men of individual characteristics, strips them of identities. Language itself is put in jeopardy" (51). He does not pursue the subject of non-difference in sex, but speaks of the mixing of blood: "Incestuous propagation leads to formless duplications, sinister repetitions, a dark mixture of unnamable things. In short, the incestuous creature exposes the community to the same danger as do twins" (75).
17. See Julia Kristeva, "Women's Time."
18. See her study linking the formation of language to the mother, *Desire in Language*.
19. Sand's indoor adventure in a convent has been well analyzed by Ellen Moers in *Literary Women: The Great Writers*.

Notes to Chapter 7

1. Here is the quote in its entirety: "Le sentiment de l'hystérique d'avoir un 'discours futile, discours vain' (le féminisme en a fait une idéologie militante en déclarant le discours 'phallocrate' et en s'insurgeant contre lui)" (*Histoires d'amour*, 391).
2. See "My Memory Hyperbole," *The Female Autograph*, 276.
3. All quotes are from Hélène Cixous, Madeleine Gagnon, and Annie Leclerc, *La venue à l'écriture* (Paris: Union Générale d'Editions, 10/18, 1977), 52.
4. In *Illa* (Paris: des Femmes, 1980), 208.

5. In *L'arc* 61 (1975): 39–54. "Parce qu'elle [woman] est *donneuse*" (50).

6. In her *Subversive Intent*, Suleiman writes that Cixous represents a fantasy which "is not afraid to recognize in him- or herself the presence of both sexes, not afraid to open her- or himself up to the presence of the other, to the circulation of multiple drives and desires." She also concludes, as I do, that Cixous "called, instead, for a kind of writing that would . . . escape from the repressiveness of linear logic and teleological 'storytelling' . . . " (127–28).

7. *La Jeune née* (Paris: Union Générale d'Editions, 1975), 153.

8. I agree with another of Suleiman's statements, that "Annie Leclerc, Chantal Chawaf, and Julia Kristeva . . . opted for the expansive lyric mode when writing as mothers," and that "although lyric can be full of invention, it does not offer much possibility for humor or parody." I would make it clear, however, that Cixous should not be implied in this group. Suleiman does not clearly imply her, yet she makes this remark in a segment about her. Cixous's puns are powerful *and* humorous.

9. *Des Chinoises* (Paris: des Femmes, 1974).

10. "Two Interviews with Julia Kristeva." During this interview, Kristeva's discussion of abjection is elucidated. It is, she remarks, "something that disgusts you. . . . It is an external menace from which one wants to distance oneself, but of which one has the impression that it may menace us from the inside. The relation to abjection is finally rooted in the combat which every human being carries with the mother. For in order to become autonomous, it is necessary that one cut the instinctual dyad of the mother and the child and that one become something other" (124).

11. See "Difference on Trial: A Critique of the Maternal Metaphor in Cixous, Irigaray, and Kristeva," *The Poetics of Gender* (157–82). For another comparative reading of these writers, see Ann Rosalind Jones, "Inscribing Femininity: French Theories of the Feminine," *Making a Difference: French Literary Criticism*, ed. G. Greene et al. (London: Methuen, 1985). In this work, Jones examines the forms that feminist critique takes: the semiotic in Kristeva; the *difference* in Irigaray; the unimagined unconscious of motherhood in Cixous; and the rejection of *difference* in Wittig.

12. Refer to "True Confessions: Cixous and Foucault on Sexuality and Power," *The Thinking Muse: Feminism and French Philosophy*, ed. Allen Jeffner (Bloomington: Indiana University Press, 1989), 142.

13. See "Female Temporality and the Future of Feminism," *Abjection, Melancholia, and Love*, eds. John Fletcher and Andrew Benjamin (New York: Routledge, 1990), 68.

14. Refer to *Julia Kristeva* (New York: Routledge, 1990), 210.

WORKS CONSULTED

Abel, Elizabeth, Marianne Hirsch, and Elizabeth Langland, eds. *The Voyage in Fictions of Female Development.* Hanover, N.H.: University Press of New England, 1983.

Abelard, Pierre. *Lettres complètes d'Abélard et d'Héloïse.* Edited and Translated by M. Gréard. Paris: Garnier frères, 1970.

Alboury, Pierre. *Mythes et Mythologies dans la littérature française.* Paris: Armand Colin, 1969.

Amad, Gladys. *Le mythe des amazones dans la mosaïque antique.* Beyrouth: Dar el—Machreq, 1975.

Auerbach, Nina. *Woman and the Demon: The Life of a Victorian Myth.* Cambridge: Harvard University Press, 1982.

Saint Augustine. *Confessions.* Translated by Pierre Labriolle. 2 vols. Paris: Société d'Editions "Les belles lettres," 1947.

Bachelard, Gaston. *La Poétique de l'espace.* 1957. Paris: Presses universitaires de France, 1974.

Barry, Joseph. *A la Française: le couple à travers l'histoire.* Translated by C. Blanchet and L. Lassen. Paris: Seuil, 1985.

Barthes, Roland. *S/Z.* Paris: Seuil, 1970.

Bassuk, Ellen L. "The Rest Cure: Repetition or Resolution of Citorian Women's Conflicts?" In Suleiman, *The Female Body,* 139–51.

Beaujour, Michel. *Miroirs d'encre: Rhétorique de l'autoportrait.* Paris: Seuil, 1980.

Beauvoir, Simone de. *The Second Sex.* Translated by H. M. Parshley, New York: Knopf, 1957.

Belsley, Catherine. "Constructing the Subject: Deconstructing the Text." In *Feminist Criticism and Social Change: Sex, Class and Race in Literature and Culture,* edited by J. Newton and D. Rosenfelt. New York: Methuen, 1985.

Bettelheim, Bruno. *La psychanalyse des contes de fées.* Translated by Theo Carlier. Paris: Robert Laffont, 1976.

Bishop, Lloyd. *The Romantic Hero and His Heirs in French Literature.* New York: Peter Lang, 1984.

175

Bogin, Meg. *The Women Troubadours*. New York: Paddington Press, 1976.

Booth, Wayne C. *The Rhetoric of Fiction*. Chicago: University of Chicago Press, 1961.

Bordo, Susan. "The Cartesian Masculinization of Thought." *Signs* 2, no. 3 (1986): 439–56.

Bourignon, Antoinette. *La vie de Dam^{lle} Antoinette Bourignon, écrite par elle-même*. Edited by Pierre Poiret. Amsterdam: J. Riewerts & Pierre Arents, Librairies, 1682.

Brisson, Marcelle. *Plus jamais l'amour éternel: Héloïse sans Abélard*. Québec: Nouvelle Optique, 1981.

Brownstein, Rachel M. *Becoming a Heroine: Reading About Women in Novels*. New York: The Viking Press, 1982.

Bruneau, Marie-Florine. "*La vie* de Madame Guyon: Frigidité et masochisme en tant que dispositifs politiques." *French Forum* (May 1983): 101–7.

────── . "The Writing of History as Fiction and Ideology: The Case of Madame Guyon." *Feminist Issues* 5, no. 1 (Spring 1985): 27–38.

Bruss, Elizabeth W. *Autobiographical Acts: The Changing Situation of a Literary Genre*. Baltimore: Johns Hopkins University Press, 1976.

Bulciolu, Maria Theresa. *L'école saint-simonienne et la femme*. Pisa: Goliardica, 1980.

Bulfinch, Thomas. *The Age of Fable or Beauties of Mythology*. New York: Tudor Publishing Co., 1935.

Caws, Mary Ann. "The Conception of Engendering: The Erotics of Editing." In Miller, *The Poetics of Gender*, 42–62.

Chance, Jane. *Woman as Hero in Old English Literature*. Syracuse N.Y.: Syracuse University Press, 1986.

Chanter, Tina. "Female Temporality and the Future of Feminism." In *Abjection, Melancholia, and Love: The Work of Julia Kristeva*, edited by John Fletcher and Andrew Benjamin. New York: Routledge, 1990.

Charrier, Charlotte. *Héloïse dans l'histoire et dans la légende*. Paris: Librairie Ancienne Honoré Champion, 1933.

Cixous, Hélène. *Illa*. Paris: des Femmes, 1980.

────── . *La jeune née*. Paris: Union Générale d'Editions, 1975.

────── . "Le rire de la Méduse." *L'arc* 61 (1975): 39–54.

────── , ed. *La venue à l'écriture*. Paris: Union Générale d'Editions, 1977.

Crenne, Hélisenne [de]. *Les angoysses douloureuses qui procèdent d'Amours*. Commented by Paule Demats. Paris: Belles Lettres-Annales de l'université de Nantes, 1968.

Demoris, René. *Le roman à la première personne: du classicisme aux lumières*. Paris: Librairie Armand Colin, 1975.

Didier, Béatrice. "Le corps féminin dans *Lélia*." *Revue d'histoire littéraire de la France* 76 (1976): 634–47.

────── . *Le journal intime*. Paris: Presses universitaires de France, 1976.

Diel, Paul. *Le symbolisme dans la mythologie grecque: étude psychanalytique*. Paris: Payot, 1952.

Dubois, Page. *Sowing the Body: Psychoanalysis and Ancient Representations of Women*. Chicago: University of Chicago Press, 1988.

Duby, Georges. *Medieval Marriage: Two Models from Twelfth-Century France*. Translated by Elborg Forster. Baltimore: Johns Hopkins University Press, 1978.

Duchesne, Roger. *Réalite vécue et art épistolaire: Madame de Sévigné et la lettre d'amour*. Paris: Bordas, 1970.

Durand, Gilbert. *Figures mythiques et visages de l'oeuvre: de la mythocritique à la mythanalyse*. Paris: Berg International, 1979.

Duras, Marguerite, and Xavière Gauthier. *Les parleuses*. Paris: Minuit, 1974.

Edwards, Lee R. *Psyche as Hero: Female Heroism and Fictional Form*. Middletown, Conn.: Wesleyan University Press, 1984.

Eliade, Mircea. *The Myth of the Eternal Return: or, Cosmos and History*. Translated by Willard R. Trask. 1954. New York: Bollingen Foundation. Princeton: Princeton University Press, 1974.

Erickson, Erik H. *Identity: Youth and Crisis*. New York: W. W. Norton, 1968.

Fetterley, Judith. *The Resisting Reader: A Feminist Approach to American Fiction*. Bloomington: Indiana University Press, 1978.

Flinders, Petrie W., ed. *Egyptian Tales: Second Series XVIII to XIX Dynasty*. New York: Frederick A. Stokes, 1896.

Friends of George Sand Newsletter. 4, no. 2 (1981).

Gallop, Jane. *The Daughter's Seduction: Feminism and Pyschoanalysis*. Ithaca, N.Y.: Cornell University Press, 1982.

────── . "*Quand nos lèvres s'écrivent:* Irigaray's Body Politic." *Romanic Review* 74, no. 1 (January 1983): 82–91.

Gardiner, Judith Kegan. "On Female Identity and Writing by Women." *Critical Inquiry* 8 (1981): 347–63.

Genette, Gérard. *Figures III*. Paris: Seuil, 1972.

Gies, Frances and Joseph Gies. *Women in the Middle Ages*. New York: Thomas Y. Crowell Co., 1978.

Gilbert, Sandra M., and Susan Gubar. *The Madwoman in the Attic: The Woman Writer and the Nineteenth-Century Imagination*. New Haven: Yale University Press, 1979.

────── . *No Man's Land: The Place of the Woman Writer in the Twentieth Century*. Vol. 1. New Haven: Yale University Press, 1988.

Gilligan, Carol. *In a Different Voice: Psychological Theory and Women's Development*. Cambridge: Harvard University Press, 1982.

Girard, René. *Violence and the Sacred*. Translated by Patrick Gregory. Baltimore: Johns Hopkins University Press, 1977.

Glasgow, Janis. *Une esthétique de comparaison: Balzac et George Sand:* La femme abandonnée *et* Metalla. Paris: Nizet, 1978.

Goldsmith, Elizabeth C. "Giving Weight to Word: Madame de Sévigné's Letters to Her Daughter." In Stanton, 107–18.

Grane, Leif. *Peter Abelard: Philosophy and Christianity in the Middle Ages*. Translated by Frederick and Christine Crowly. New York: Harcourt, Brace & World, 1964.

Graves, Robert. *The White Goddess: A Historical Grammar of Poetic Myth.* 1948. New York: Farrar, Straus and Giroux, 1966.

Grayson, Susan. "Rousseau and the Text as Self." In *Narcissism and the Text: Studies in Literature and the Psychology of the Self,* edited by Lynne Layton and Barbara Ann Schapiro. New York: New York University Press, 1986.

Greene, Tatiana. "De J. Sand à GS: *Rose et Blanche* de Sand et Saneau et leur descendance." *NCFS* 4 (1976): 169–82.

Guehenno, Jean. *Jean-Jacques.* 2 vols. Paris: Gallimard, 1962.

Gusdorf, George. *La découverte de soi.* Paris: Presses universitaires de France, 1948.

Gutwirth, Madelyn. "Woman as Mediatrix: From Jean-Jacques Rousseau to Germaine de Staël." In *Woman as Mediatrix: Essays on Nineteenth-Century European Women Writers,* edited by Ariel H. Goldberger. Contributions in Women's Studies 73. Westport Conn.: Greenwood Press, 1987, 13–29.

Guyon, Jeanne Marie (Bouvier de La Motte). *Autobiography of Madame Guyon.* Translated by Thomas Taylor Allen. 2 vols. London: Kegan Paul, Trench, Trubner & Co., Ltd.

———. *Madame Guyon et Fénelon: la correspondance secrète.* Edited by Benjamin Sahler. Paris: Dervy Livres, 1982.

Hawkes, Terence. *Structuralism and Semiotics.* Berkeley: University of California Press, 1977.

Heilbrun, Carolyn G. *Toward a Recognition of Androgyny.* New York: Alfred A. Knopf, 1973.

Homer. *The Odyssey.* Translated by W. H. D. Rouse. New York: Mentor Books, 1949.

Irigaray, Luce. *Passions élémentaires.* Paris: Minuit, 1982.

———. *Speculum de l'autre femme.* Paris: Minuit, 1974.

Jardine, Alice A. *Gynesis: Configurations of Woman and Modernity.* Ithaca: Cornell University Press, 1985.

———. "Opaque Texts and Transparent Contexts: The Political Difference of Julia Kristeva." In Miller, 96–116.

Johnson, Barbara. *The Critical Difference: Essays in the Contemporary Rhetoric of Reading.* Baltimore: Johns Hopkins University Press, 1980.

———. "My Monster/My Self." *Diacritics* 12 (Summer 1982): 2–10.

———. *A World of Difference.* Baltimore: Johns Hopkins University Press, 1987.

Jones, Ann R. "Inscribing French Theories of the Feminine." In *Making a Difference: Feminist Literary Criticism,* edited by G. Greene et al. London: Methuen, 1985.

Kamuf, Peggy. *Fictions of Feminine Desire: Disclosures of Heloïse.* University of Nebraska Press, 1982.

Kauffman, Linda S. *Discourses of Desire: Gender, Genre, and Epistolary Fictions.* Ithaca: Cornell University Press, 1986.

Kavanagh, Thomas M. *Writing the Truth.* Berkeley: University of California Press, 1987.

Keller, Evelyn Fox. *Reflections on Gender and Science.* New Haven: Yale University Press, 1985.

Kern, Stephen. *The Culture of Time and Space: 1880–1918*. Cambridge: Harvard University Press, 1983.

Kofman, Sarah. *L'énigme de la femme: la femme dans les textes de Freud*. 1980. Paris: Editions Galilée, 1983.

Kristeva, Julia. *Des Chinoises*. Paris: des Femmes, 1974.

———. *Desire in Language: A Semiotic Approach to Literature and Art*. Translated by Thomas Gora, Alice Jardine, and Leon S. Roudiez. Edited by Leon S. Roudiez. New York: Columbia University Press, 1980.

———. "Héréthique de l'amour." *Tel Quel* 74 (Hiver 1977): 30–49.

———. *Histoires d'amour*. Paris: Denoel, 1983.

———. "My Memory Hyperbole." In Stanton, 261–76.

———. *Pouvoirs de l'horreur*. Paris: Seuil, 1980.

———. *Recherches pour une sémanalyse*. Paris: Seuil, 1969.

———. *La Révolution du langage poétique: l'avant-garde à la fin du XIXe siècle, Lautréamont et Mallarmé*. Paris: Seuil, 1974.

———. *Semiotikè: recherches pour une sémalanyse*. Paris: Seuil 1968. Reprint 1978. Paris: Seuil (Tel Quel).

———. *Semiotike*. Reprint. 1978. Paris: Seuil (Tel Quel).

———. *Soleil noir: depression et mélancholie*. Paris: Gallimard, 1987.

———. "Le Texte clos." *Langages* 12 (1968): 103–25.

———. "Two Interviews with Julia Kristeva." *Partisan Review* 51, no. 1, 120–32.

———. "Women's Time." Translated by Alice Jardine and Harry Blake. *Signs* 7:1 (Autumn 1981): 15–35. "Le temps des femmes." *4/44: Cahiers de recherche de sciences des textes et documents* 5 (Winter 1979).

Labalme, Patricia H., ed. *Beyond Their Sex: Learned Women of the European Past*. New York: New York University Press, 1980.

Lacan, Jacques. *Ecrits I*. Paris: Seuil, 1966.

Layton, Lynne, and Barbara Ann Schapiro, eds. *Narcissism and the Text: Studies in Literature and the Psychology of Self*. New York: New York University Press, 1986.

Lechte, John. *Julia Kristeva*. New York: Routledge, 1990.

Leclerc, Annie. *Hommes et Femmes*. Paris: Grasset, 1985.

———. *Parole de femme*. Paris: Grasset, 1974.

Lejeune, Philippe. *Le pacte autobiographique*. Paris: Seuil, 1975.

Lubin, Georges. "George Sand et 'Le fils de Jean-Jacques'." *Présence de George Sand* 8 (May 1980): 4–6.

Lucas, Angela M. *Women in the Middle Ages: Religion, Marriage and Letters*. New York: St. Martin's Press, 1983.

MacCormack, Carol P., and Marilyn Strathern, eds. *Nature, Culture and Gender*. Cambridge: Cambridge University Press, 1980.

Mallet-Joris, Françoise. *Jeanne Guyon*. Paris: Flammarion, 1978.

Marks, Elaine, and Isabelle de Courtivron, eds. *New French Feminism: An Anthology*. Amherst: University of Massachussets Press, 1980.

Maurois, Andre. *Lélia ou la vie de George Sand*. Paris: Hachette, 1952.

May, Georges. *L'autobiographie*. Paris: Presses universitaires de France, 1979.

May, Gita. "Des *Confessions* à *Histoire de ma vie* et l'ombre de Rousseau." *Présence de George Sand* 8 (1980); 40–47.

───── . *De Jean-Jacques Rousseau à Madame Roland: Essai sur la sensibilité pré-romantique et révolutionnaire.* Genève: Droz, 1964.

───── . "Rousseau's Antifeminism Reconsidered." In *French Women and the Age of Enlightenment.* Edited by Samia I. Spencer. Bloomington: Indiana University Press, 1984, 309–17.

Miller, Nancy K. "Emphasis Added: Plots and Plausibilities in Women's Fiction." *PMLA* (1981): 36–48.

───── . *The Heroine's Text: Readings in the French and English Novel: 1722–1782.* New York: Columbia University Press, 1980.

───── . ed. *The Poetics of Gender.* New York: Columbia University Press, 1986.

───── . "Rereading as a Woman: The Body in Practice." In Suleiman, *Subversive Intent,* 354–62.

───── . *Subject to Change: Reading Feminist Writing.* New York: Columbia University Press, 1988.

Minkowski, Eugene. *Lived Time: Phenomenological and Psychopathological Studies.* Translated by Nancy Metzel. Evanston: Northwestern University Press, 1970.

Misch, George. *A History of Autobiography in Antiquity* Cambridge: Harvard University Press, 1951.

Moers, Ellen. *Literary Women: The Great Writers.* Garden City, N.Y.: Doubleday, 1976; Anchor, 1977.

Montaigne, Michel de. *Oeuvres complètes.* Edited by Robert Barral and Pierre Michel. Paris: Seuil, 1967.

Mossiker, Frances. *Madame de Sévigné: A Life and Letters.* New York: Alfred A. Knopf, 1983.

Naginski, Isabelle. *George Sand: Writing for Her Life.* New Brunswick, N.J.: Rutgers University Press, 1991.

───── . "*Lélia:* Novel of the Invisible." *George Sand Studies* 6, nos. 1–2 (1984–85): 46–53.

Olney, James. *Metaphors of the Self: The Meaning of Autobiography.* Princeton: Princeton University Press, 1972.

O'Neil, John C. *Seeing and Observing: Rousseau's Rhetoric of Perception.* Stanford French and Italian Series. Saratoga, Calif.: Anma Libri & Co., 1985.

Ostriker, Alicia Suskin. *Stealing the Language: The Emergence of Women's Poetry in America.* Boston: Beacon Press, 1986.

Pernoud, Régine. *Jeanne d'Arc par elle-même et par ses témoins.* Paris: Seuil, 1962.

───── . *La femme au temps des cathédrales.* Paris: Stock, 1980.

Peterson, Carla L. *The Determined Reader: Gender in the Novel from Napoleon to Victoria.* New Brunswick, N.J.: Rutgers University Press, 1986.

Piettre, Monique A. *La condition féminine à travers les âges.* Paris: Editions France Empire, 1974.

Pilling, John. *Autobiography and Imagination: Studies in Self-Scrutiny.* London: Routledge & Kegan, 1981.

Poulet, Georges. *Etudes sur le temps humain.* 3 vols. Paris: Plon, 1949.

Preminger, Alex. *Princeton Encyclopedia of Poetry and Poetics.* Princeton: Princeton University Press, 1965.

Propp, Vladimir. *Morphologie du conte poétique.* Translated by C. Kahn 1965. Paris: Seuil, 1970.

Rabine, Leslie W. *Reading the Romantic Heroine: Text, History, Ideology.* Ann Arbor: University of Michigan Press, 1985.

Register, Cheri. "Literary Criticism," *Signs* 6, no. 2 (Winter 1980): 268–82.

Reinach, A. "L'origine des Amazones." *Revue de l'histoire des religions.* Paris: Ernest Leroux, Editeurs, 1913.

Rogers, Nancy. "George Sand and Honoré de Balzac: Stylistic Similarities." *George Sand Papers: Conference Proceedings* 1978. Edited by Natalie Datlof et al. New York: AMS Press, 1982, 130–43.

Rosso, Jeannette Gefriaud. *Etudes sur la feminité aux XVIIe et XVIIIe Siècles.* Pisa: Libreria Goliardica, 1984.

Rousseau, Jean-Jacques. *Les Confessions.* Paris: Editions Garnier Frères, 1964.

――――. *Julie ou la Nouvelle Héloïse.* Paris: Garnier-Flammarion, 1967.

――――. *Oeuvres complètes.* 2 vols. Paris: Pléiade, 1959.

――――. *Les Rêveries du promeneur solitaire.* Edited by H. Roddier. Paris: Garnier, 1960.

Rousset, Jean. *Narcisse romancier: Essai sur la première personne dans le roman.* Paris: Librairie Corti, 1973.

Ruddick, Sara. "Maternal Thinking." *Feminist Studies* 6, no. 2 (1980): 342–67.

Sand, George. *Consuelo: La Comtesse de Rudolstadt.* 3 vols. Paris: Garnier, 1959.

――――. *Correspondance.* Edited by Georges Lubin. 24 vols. Paris: Garnier, 1964–90.

――――. *Indiana.* Paris: Garnier, 1962.

――――. *Lélia.* Paris: Garnier, 1960.

――――. *Oeuvres autobiographiques.* Edited by Georges Lubin. 2 vols. Paris: Gallimard, 1970–71.

Schapiro, Barbara A. *The Romantic Mother: Narcissistic Patterns in Romantic Poetry.* Baltimore: Johns Hopkins University Press, 1983.

Schor, Naomi. *Breaking the Chain: Women, Theory and French Realist Fiction.* New York: Columbia University Press, 1985.

――――. "Female Fetishism: The Case of George Sand." In Suleiman, *The Female Body.*

Schwartz, Joel. *The Sexual Politics of Jean-Jacques Rousseau.* Chicago: University of Chicago Press, 1984.

Schweickart, Patrocinio P. "Add Gender and Stir." *Reader: Essays in Reader-Oriented Theory, Criticism, and Pedagogy* 13 (Spring 1985): 1–9.

――――, ed. *Gender and Reading: Essays on Readers, Texts, and Contexts.* Baltimore: Johns Hopkins University Press, 1986.

Serres, Michel. *Hermes: Literature, Science, Philosophy.* Edited by J. V. Harari & D. E. Bell. Baltimore: Johns Hopkins University Press, 1982.

Sévigné, Madame de. (1626–1696) Marie de Rabutin Chantal. *Correspondance.* 2 vols. Paris: Gallimard, 1972.

Showalter, Elaine. *A Literature of Their Own: British Novelists from Brontë to Lessing.* Princeton: Princeton University Press, 1977.

Singer, A. E., ed. *West Virginia George Sand Conference Papers.* Morgantown: Department of Foreign Languages, West Virginia University, 1981.

Singer, June. *Androgyny: Towards a New Theory of Sexuality.* New York: Anchor Press/Doubleday, 1976.

Singer, Linda. "True Confessions: Cixous and Foucault on Sexuality and Power." In *The Thinking Muse: Feminism and French Philosophy,* edited by Allen Jeffner. Bloomington: Indiana University Press, 1989, 136–55.

Sivert, Eileen Boyd. *"Lélia* and Feminism." *Yale French Studies* 62 (1981): 45–66.

Soriano, Marc. *Les contes de Perrault: culture savante et traditions populaires.* Paris: Gallimard, 1968.

Spacks, Patricia Meyer. *The Female Imagination.* New York: Alfred A. Knopf, 1975.

——— . *Imagining a Self: Autobiography and Novel in Eighteenth-Century England.* Cambridge: Cambridge University Press, 1976.

Spengemann, William C. *The Forms of Autobiography: Episodes in the History of a Literary Genre.* New Haven: Yale University Press, 1980.

Spivak, Gayatri Chakravorty. "Feminist and Critical Theory." In *For Alma Mater: Theory and Practice in Feminist Scholarship,* edited by Paula A Treichler, et al. Urbana: University of Illinois Press, 1985, 119–43.

Stanton, Domna. "Difference on Trial: A Critique of the Maternal Metaphor in Cixous, Irigaray, and Kristeva." In Miller, *Poetics,* 157–82.

——— . and Jeanine Plottel, eds. *The Female Autograph.* New York: New York Literary Forum, 1984.

Stewart, Grace. *A New Mythos: The Novel of the Artist as Heroine, 1877–1977.* St. Alban's, Vt.: Eden Press Women's Publications, 1979.

Suleiman, Susan Rubin. *Subversive Intent: Gender, Politics, and the Avant-Garde.* Cambridge: Harvard University Press, 1990.

——— . ed. *The Female Body in Western Culture: Contemporary Perspectives.* Cambridge: Harvard University Press, 1986.

Taylor, Anne Robinson. *Male Novelists and Their Female Voices: Literary Masquerades.* Troy, N.Y.: Whitston Press, 1981.

Todorov, Tzvetan. *Les genres du discours.* Paris: Seuil, 1978.

Tripp, Edward. *Crowell's Handbook of Classic Mythology.* New York: Thomas Crowell, 1970.

Van Laere, François. *Une lecture du temps dans* La Nouvelle Héloïse. Neufchatel, Switzerland: Editions de la Baconnière, 1968.

Vetterling-Braggin, Mary, ed. *Sexist Language: A Modern Philosophical Analysis.* Totowa, N.J.: Rowan and Littlefield, 1981.

Villier, Charles. *Histoire des clubs de femmes et des légions 1793–1848–1871.* Paris: Librairie Plon, 1910.

Waller, Margaret, *"Cherchez la Femme:* Male Malady and Narrative Politics in the French Romantic Novel." *PMLA* 104, no. 2 (1989): 141–51.

Weintraub, Karl Joachim. *The Value of the Individual: Self and Circumstance in Autobiography.* Chicago: University of Chicago Press, 1978.

Winkler, John J. *Constraints of Desire: The Anthropology of Sex and Gender in Ancient Greece.* New York: Routledge, 1989.

Yaeger, Patricia. *Honey-Mad Women: Emancipatory Strategies in Women's Writings.* New York: Columbia University Press, 1988.

Yaezell, Ruth Bernard, ed. *Sex, Politics, and Science in the Nineteenth-Century Novel: Selected Papers from the English Institute, 1983–84.* New Series 10. Baltimore: Johns Hopkins University Press, 1986.

Zumthor, Paul. "Autobiography in the Middle Ages?" *Genre* 6 (March 1973): 29–48.

INDEX

Abelard, Peter, 19, 67, 70, 84, 85, 160n.14; Heloïse and, 14–15, 36–40, 43, 45–53, 72, 141, 159n.3, 160n.14; as hero, 48–49; on heroism, 46; Jean-Jacques Rousseau on, 86; *Lettre à un ami*, 11, 39–40, 80; sexual desire and, 49–50
Abjection, 145–46, 147, 173n.10
Achilles, 24
Age of Enlightenment, 37, 83
Ahura's Tale, 13–14, 16, 29–30, 30, 33, 67, 69, 78, 102, 116, 125, 133, 149; compared to *The Odyssey*, 30–31, 34–35; narrative voice in, 27–28, 157n.19
Alienation, 12, 33, 79; Narcissus and, 21–22
Amad, Gladys, 24
Amazonianism, 41, 42, 51, 76, 103, 143; in criticism, 95, 167nn. 30, 31
Amazons, 23, 25, 109, 111, 113; Greek heroes and, 12, 13, 15, 23–25, 51, 96, 156nn. 8, 10; as muse and the Medusa, 24–25
Androgyny, 107, 133
Angel-Monster dichotomy, 117, 118–19, 135–36, 171n.6
Archetypes, 12–13, 19, 71, 98–99, 121, 153n.9; Amazons and Greek heroes, 12, 13, 15, 23–25, 51, 96,

156nn. 8, 10; Echo and Narcissus, 12–13, 19–21, 25, 96–97, 143; in *Lélia*, 109; Medusa and Hermes, 12, 13, 26–27, 124, 148
Aristocracy, The: the Church and, 38–39, 63
Arouet, François-Marie, 83
Artistic creation: prostitution and, 16, 116, 118–19, 123–24, 133–35; sexuality and, 16, 109–12, 118–19, 125, 136
Athena, 31
Augustine, Saint, 48, 62, 84, 131; *Confessions*, 37, 45–46, 56, 80
Author, 30, 101; female, 115–16; narrator and, 124–25, 125, 126, 130–35, 141–43. *See also* Narration; Narrative voice
Autobiography, 12, 16–17, 56, 139, 140–43, 143–44, 143–47, 152n.8; Heloïse and, 40–43. See also *Ahura's Tale; Confessions* (Augustine); *Confessions, Les* (Rousseau); *Couperies, Les*
Automatic writing, 68, 69–70, 138, 148
Autonomy, 21–22, 42; quest for, 12–13, 16, 20, 21, 30, 35, 45, 129, 153n.10; quest for in *The Odyssey*, 31–33

185